D1524117

THE YORKTOWN CAMPAIGN

AND

THE SURRENDER OF CORNWALLIS

1781

BY

HENRY P. JOHNSTON

AUTHOR OF "THE CAMPAIGN OF 1776 AROUND NEW YORK AND BROOKLYN"
"OBSERVATIONS ON JUDGE JONES'S LOYALIST HISTORY OF THE AMERICAN REVOLUTION" ETC.

ILLUSTRATED

Entered according to Act of Congress, in the year 1881, by
Harper & Brothers,
In the office of the Librarian of Congress, at Washington.

Reprinted 1981 by Eastern National
1997 Printing

Eastern National provides quality educational products and
services to America's national parks and other public trusts.

Library of Congress Cataloging in Publication Data
Johnston, Henry Phelps, 1842-1923.
The Yorktown campaign and the surrender of Cornwallis,
1781.
Reprint. Originally published: New York: Harper &
Brothers, 1881.
Includes bibliographical references.
1. Yorktown (Va.)—Siege, 1781. 2. Southern States—
History—Revolution, 1775-1783. I. Title.
E241.Y6J7 1981   973.3'37   81-19573
ISBN: 0-915992-19-1 (pbk.)   AACR2

Cover: Detail from John Gauntlett's 1755 drawing of Yorktown
from the York River. The Mariners' Museum. Design by Paul
Bacon.

PREFACE.

IT is much to the credit of our people that they are not slow in appreciating an event or anniversary of really national significance. The Centenary of the Declaration of Independence was fittingly celebrated the country over, and the lesser episodes of the Revolution have in turn been remembered in the localities of their occurrence. This disposition to show a proper admiration and gratitude for the great things done by our ancestors, is clearly one not to be discouraged; and if the printer and sculptor succeed in keeping it alive from one generation to another, their work will be recognized as of peculiar value to the nation.

In the surrender of Cornwallis at Yorktown, a century back, we have the last of these interesting events—the crowning success which assured our Independence. How much we owe to it every one must be sensible. The fact that the General Government takes the lead in the observance of its centennial anniversary, is some indication of the importance to be attached to it. We are promised both a grand celebration and a grand monument on the Yorktown field, as a public and authoritative recognition of what the victory helped so greatly to secure for us.

The present work assumes to give an account of this final campaign of the Revolution in the light of the old and such new material as our historical collections offer. The quite recent publication of Washington's Manuscript Journal, covering the operations of 1781, would alone furnish a temptation to re-study that period. Its value can hardly be overrated. Considerable space is given to the movements of Cornwallis and Lafayette in Virginia, which had an important influence in shaping the closing events; and here a number of unpublished letters of Lafayette have served to establish uncertain points. We can now follow him from camp to camp in his many marches over that State. The co-operation of the

French, which was indispensable to success, is brought out more fully by the letters and journals of several French officers, which have also been lately translated and published. Scattered manuscript letters of American officers, returns of prisoners, and material captured at Yorktown, preserved in the Department of State at Washington, and plans of the siege by British, French, and American engineers who surveyed the works, have been consulted, in addition to considerable original material already in print. A list of the authorities on this period is inserted, with a number of documents, in the Appendix.

When, half a century or more ago, they were erecting that granite pile on Bunker Hill, some very practical people asked, " What good will a monument do ?" Edward Everett, rousing himself to one of his finest efforts, replete with classical illustration, silenced them by asking in return, " What good will anything do ?" and the monument went up. The preservation of their history, in some form or other, seems to be one of the first duties of a people; especially where the record is praiseworthy and inspiring, as in our own case, the neglect is unpardonable. There are few brighter chapters in American history than that which presents the success of the Revolution ; and at this particular time we may revive it, perhaps, with advantage, as tending, in a certain way, to strengthen the national good-feeling with which we enter upon the second century of our experience. We cannot but take a common pride in Yorktown.

New York City, 1881.

CONTENTS.

ILLUSTRATIONS AND MAPS.

THE YORKTOWN CAMPAIGN.

CHAPTER I.

SIGNIFICANCE OF THE EVENT.

THE surrender of Cornwallis at Yorktown, Virginia, on the 19th of October, 1781, marks the successful close of the American Revolution. True, peace had yet to come, and the final treaty was not to be ratified until two years later; but the decisive character of the event was speedily recognized by England's civil and military leaders, and by the spring of the year 1782 both parties had suspended, as if by common consent, all further aggressive operations. The independence of the United States may be said to have been then and there assured beyond question.

By the men of that time—the men of the Revolution—the intelligence of this signal victory was received with the deepest joy and gratitude. No incident of the struggle, the surrender of Burgoyne not excepted, aroused such universal and spontaneous enthusiasm. At Philadelphia, upon the arrival of the news, the Continental Congress proceeded in a body to church, joined in a special service of thanksgiving, and at a later session resolved to erect a marble column at Yorktown in commemoration of the triumph. It voted honors to the allied army and its chiefs, and recommended to the people the observance of a national fast. As the news spread through the towns and villages the inhabitants indulged in every variety of celebration. Bonfires, illuminations, salutes, processions, " ox-roasts," public meetings, addresses, and sermons were the order of the day. The completeness of the victory, its magnitude, its unexpectedness, in view of the slender prospect of such an event but a few weeks before, added zest to the general rejoicing; while back of this remained the more satisfying conviction that the success had sounded the death-knell of British domination in America, and that the late colonist and subject had at last made good his determination to live under a government of his own. With Yorktown men looked upon the Revolution as accomplished.

An event with such a result becomes a starting-point in our history. We are, in a certain sense, under the profoundest obligations to it. It announced to the world that the Declaration of Independence in 1776 was no manifesto of a groundless and unsuccessful rebellion, but the corner-stone of a new structure erected upon the ruins of England's colonial system on this continent. It introduced us, through the consequent peace, to the family of nations as one of their number. Practically our autonomy dates from it; and it is in this light, in appreciation of this boon, that the National Congress of to-day carries out the good intentions of the Congress of 1781, and erects the intended monument upon the field of the victory.

The Revolution, of course, was not achieved at Yorktown alone. All the previous events of the struggle must be associated with it. Yorktown is to be regarded, rather, as a representative and crowning victory—the end of a six years' contest, the last and most brilliant of a series of blows delivered in spite of a series of defeats sustained. Each contributed its part. Without Lexington and Quebec, and Saratoga and Germantown, and Valley Forge and Monmouth, and Cowpens and the other fields, both of victory and defeat, Yorktown, it need hardly be said, would have been long deferred, if it ever came. Upon that field we have the legitimate fruition of the faith, the courage, and the trials displayed and endured through all the tedious years of the war. If Bunker Hill represents a resolution made to resist Parliamentary aggression to the end, Yorktown represents that resolution kept. Yorktown represents both the struggle and the success of the Revolution.

And yet, while acknowledging that the victory, in this sense, secured the independence of the United States, do we give it its fullest and broadest significance? Here some interesting speculations are suggested. No doubt the attainment of independence—separate national life—where a people are ripe for it, is a grand result, every way worth commemorating. The globe is dotted over with memorials and battle-fields, reminding the race of earnest and noble efforts—some successful, some not—to throw off oppressive rule and secure self-rule. These struggles adorn history, making its brightest pages. But in our own case we may go farther. At this distance of time we may combine with this fact of independence certain distinctive and far-reaching effects following in its train, which already add to its dignity and grandeur. Taking in the entire range of such effects, both those developing and those possible, the future historian with a philosophic turn may put some old truths of to-day in a new form. Not dwelling so much upon the single circumstance of the rise of a separate nation here, he is likely to call attention to the more strictly ethnological fact that our Revolution permanently divided one of the dominant families of the human race. He will notice that as a result of Yorktown the Anglo-Saxon branch was bisected; that with the success of the Colonists it shot out into two careers, for one of which an entirely new field, an undeveloped continent, lay open. At a time when tendencies in Europe looked toward the closer unification of similar people, here he will find a disruption.

This question of the race and its subdivisions, now coming forward more prominently as a distinct study, must eventually directly concern ourselves. The questions inviting renewed investigation relate to the starting-point of the European families, their lines of earliest migration, the discovered relationship of their languages to the most ancient forms in Asia, the parting of one group from another, and the slow but observable continuation of the process of dispersion and commingling in modern times. There can be little doubt that the separation of the Anglo-Saxon family a century since is also destined to attract the attention of the future ethnologist, precisely as the Anglo-Saxon of to-day himself studies with peculiar interest those two Conquests of England which laid the foundation of the original branch. As the modern Englishman perhaps reflects with curiosity upon the fact that his ancestors, eight centuries back, may have been either native or Teuton or Norman, so, possibly, the Anglo-American of the Mississippi Valley or the Pacific Slope, eight centuries hence, may indulge in a similar curiosity respecting the origin of his ancestors, and wonder if they ever were Englishmen. That the common Anglo-Saxon civilization of the past has worked upon the whole benignly for mankind, is acknowledged; the Anglo-Saxon himself certainly believes and rejoices in it. May not a career even more progressive be expected of that element in it which has made this continent its home, and which, while continually drawing and learning from the old, is now developing here under its own new and favorable conditions? Whatever great things are the outcome, we must date them, in a certain measure, from Yorktown.

Putting the matter in more practical shape—what has been the effect of the Revolution of 1776 thus far upon these two groups of the same family, the English and Americans? The answer must have a sort of test character; and from the latter it comes without hesitation. It has been our habit to claim very marked and salutary effects upon ourselves, the tendency being to assume too much, perhaps. The doubter, in fact, will modify the claim with a pointed question or two. What, for instance, would, in all likelihood, have been the status both of this continent and Great Britain had there been no Revolution—no separation? If the England of to-day stands, as she claims, at the head of civilization, why should she not have held the same proud pre-eminence with her American possessions added? Are the United States so superior to Great Britain that the effects of the Revolution are observable at a glance? If not, what evident and solid good has the separation done either side? These are questions more readily asked than answered, for the answers must, in some degree, be speculative. But they may be met, and met with counter-questions. Is it certain that, but for our Revolution, the England of to-day would have been all that she is? Is it in the least probable that Colonial America would have stood where independent, autonomous America stands? Would universal interests have been as happily served?

It is enough, in this connection, to state these questions without discussing them. As for ourselves, no one can doubt that we have taken a long stride in advance of what we could have taken as an appendage, or even as a powerful arm, of the British Empire. It will hardly be claimed that we could have developed our individuality, or risen to our present acknowledged prominence, tied to Mother England's apron-strings. On the contrary, we have had here the rebound and exhilaration of a people suddenly freed from irksome ties, conscious of a destiny, building up a political system out of their own ideas of liberty and self-respect, opening up an immense territory for all who will come, disputing the sovereignty of the sea, and surprising the world with enterprises and benefits. From the germ of the Revolution the nation has blossomed into what Carlyle has so fitly described as the "American Saxondom."

How far England is better off by the separation is another point. Ever since Charles Dickens—the humor and accuracy of whose pictures is quite as much appreciated here as in England—put us in a somewhat ludicrous light before his countrymen (and, in truth, long before), a certain element among them have been slow to admit that we have had the slightest influence upon Great Britain's welfare. In some respects the separation would be regarded as an advantage to her. Speaking politically and historically, however, a considerable influence has passed from these shores to the other side. The struggle for rights and privileges between king and subject, culminating first in Magna Charta and again in their own Revolution, was continued in a more constitutional form in the reigns of the Georges, and received a fresh impetus at home by its success in the Colonies here. That much necessarily followed. It is not to be assumed that the successful revolt of three million Englishmen, on this side, against king, ministry, and parliament, had no effect upon the political situation in England herself; especially as the revolting subjects were among her freest and most enlightened subjects, who claimed that they were asserting their rights under the home constitution against the exercise of arbitrary power not authorized, as they felt, by that constitution. One result did follow upon the surrender of Cornwallis—a change of ministry. The throne had been defeated; public sentiment called for the close of the war and a new policy generally. Then there followed steadily all those schemes of parliamentary and other reforms which give the English subject to-day far more liberty and privilege than he enjoyed a century ago, and which, but for the American Revolution, he would not have obtained within as short a period. The English people, in fact, seem to the observer on this side about as closely wedded to the idea of self-government as the American. Is not the tendency there away from prerogative?

Whether universal world-interests would have been served as well had the separation never occurred, is another question by which to test the significance of Yorktown and the Revolution. Had there been no other interruption of her progress, the British Empire, with America as part of her dominion, would in all probability have risen to a power of overshadowing influence. At the time of the Revolution she monopolized the seas, and her trade and commerce were carried on upon the most exclusive principles. As her population and territory increased, as America contributed more and more to her wealth and land and naval strength, it may be seriously questioned whether she would have grown correspondingly lenient and liberal toward her rivals or neighbors. Would she have relaxed her grasp upon the world? Great empires seem to have followed out common policies: they overawe or absorb or repress surrounding people. This has been their record. Did Yorktown, then, break up an empire which threatened to become overwhelming? Necessarily we are led here into speculation, but it is within the proper range of inquiry to note what possible or probable results were, judging from the experience of history, averted by a given event. This conclusion, at least, may be confidently stated, that for Great Britain Yorktown proved to be what Marathon and Platæa were for Persia, what Blenheim was for France, what Waterloo and Sedan were for the two Napoleons—a levelling blow, curbing power, resenting aggression, adjusting the relation between rights and authority upon a nicer balance, and cutting out new ruts for the course of events. If in addition it has contributed in any degree to hasten what is called Progress and the welfare of humanity, and has assured a greater measure of peace throughout the globe than would otherwise have been the case, the event is to be regarded with the deepest interest.[1] Reviewing it from every stand-point, and we may recall those salient words of Webster spoken under the shadow of Bunker Hill, that the American Revolution was " the prodigy of modern times, at once the wonder and the blessing of the world."

Every incident of an event which has secured such happy results seems to be worthy of being recorded and remembered; and in the succeeding chapters it is proposed to give a history of what may be called the Yorktown Campaign. The British general who was finally compelled to surrender appears as the leading figure in the scene. His career will be noticed with some degree of fulness, and the second and third chapters are devoted to operations on his part that remotely or directly led to his overthrow. The remaining chapters include the immediate movements on both sides, culminating in the siege and capitulation.

---

[1] " At all events," says Mr. Freeman, the English historian, " the American Union has actually secured, for what is really a long period of time, a greater amount of combined peace and freedom than was ever before enjoyed by so large a portion of the earth's surface. There have been, and still are, vaster despotic empires, but never before has so large an inhabited territory remained for seventy years in the enjoyment at once of internal freedom and of exemption from the scourge of internal war." — *History of Federal Government from the Foundation of the Achaian League, etc.*, vol. i., p. 112.

CHAPTER II.

OPERATIONS LEADING TO YORKTOWN.—CORNWALLIS IN THE CAROLINAS.

IN its efforts to subdue the American rebellion the British Government followed out successively two grand schemes of operation, with intervals of inaction and apparent quandary. The first plan was to crush the head of the reptile; and, failing in this, the second was to cut its body in two. Either scheme might have done the work; neither succeeded. Great Britain miscalculated the vitality of the monster.

The contest opened in dead earnest at New York, in 1776. Seventeen hundred and seventy-five had been the year of uprising, of preparation, of Bunker Hill. Seventeen hundred and seventy-six brought the enemy fully aroused, when they defeated the untrained American force on Long Island, and, in September, captured New York City. A year later they took Philadelphia. That same fall Burgoyne marched down from the St. Lawrence to seize Albany and control the Hudson.

The strategy and policy of these movements were apparent. From the two cities the British intended to overawe the Central States of Pennsylvania and New York, and the effect of Burgoyne's success was expected to be the complete severance of the strong New England Colonies from the rest of the country. With British ships supreme upon the sea, and British armies holding the lines of communication inland, any effective military co-operation and transfer of supplies on the part of the North would have been difficult, if not wholly impossible. We might thus have found the head and front of the revolt, as the enemy regarded it, from Massachusetts to Pennsylvania reduced to a fatally disjointed and shattered condition within eighteen months after the capture of New York. This result, however, was not to be. Burgoyne was entrapped in the forest. New York and Philadelphia had not become centres of recovered territory. In less than a year Philadelphia was given up, for the sake of concentration, and by the close of 1778 the forces of Great Britain occupied nothing more than New York and its environs in the whole stretch of her recent possessions from the Potomac to the Penobscot.

2

Here was manifest failure; indeed, confession of failure. The Northern Colonies, as a point of attack, were still a unit. However inferior to
the enemy their troops may have been, both in numbers and discipline,
they could still co-operate. The men from Massachusetts, New York,
Pennsylvania, and Virginia still stood "shoulder to shoulder" under
Washington's command. Together they held West Point and the Highlands—the key of the entire situation—and subsisted upon supplies drawn
alike from the Eastern and Middle States. The original scheme of breaking up this united opposition had not worked; and in consequence the
enemy will be found developing, in the latter years of the war, another
plan for bringing the Colonists to terms.

Baffled at the North, but without abandoning it, the British leaders
next turned their attention to the conquest of the less populous South.
It was a change of tactics—a thrust at a more exposed and vulnerable
point. They proceeded upon the assumption that, if the Southern provinces should first be subdued and recovered in fact, the Northern could
thereafter be reduced by isolation and exhaustion. Matters would be
more simplified. Cut the rebellious Union in two and weaken its power,
was in effect the new policy of the home cabinet. The plan promised
well, especially as the enemy's naval supremacy enabled them to move
their troops to distant points with ease and comparative speed; and for a
time its execution was attended with success. Developing with circumstances, it did not necessarily imply inactivity at the North.

Lord Germaine, the King's war minister, who had become impatient
over the protracted struggle, appears to have been the author of this scheme.
The first step was to make a permanent conquest of Florida and Georgia,
and then of the Carolinas: operations to begin in the fall of 1778. "A
line of communication was to be established across South and North Carolina, and the planters on the sea-coast were to be reduced to the necessity
of abandoning, or being abandoned by, their slaves. Five thousand additional men were at a later date to be sent to Charleston; and, on the
landing of a small corps at Cape Fear, Germaine believed that 'large
numbers of the inhabitants would doubtless flock to the standard of the
king, whose government would be restored in North Carolina.' Then,
by proper diversions in Virginia and Maryland, he said, it might not be
too much to expect that all America to the south of the Susquehanna
would return to its allegiance." [1] Nothing but disappointment at the re-

---

[1] Germaine to Clinton (most secret), March 8th, 1778, as given in Bancroft, vol. x.,
p. 284. How earnestly the home government urged the Southern scheme, and how failure

sults of the war thus far could have prompted these new operations. Burgoyne had surrendered; France had made the cause of America her own by alliance; and the determination of the Northern Colonists had shown no sensible wavering under the successes of Sir William Howe in the capture of New York and Philadelphia. It was clearly a necessity to make a better record. There could have been no call for a Southern campaign were the Northern and Middle Colonies upon the point of submission, as their reduction would inevitably have been followed by that of the rest. After 1778, accordingly, we find activity in the South. On December 29th of that year Savannah was taken by the enemy, and in January following Augusta occupied. Major-general Benjamin Lincoln, of Massachusetts, was sent to oppose the enemy's further progress; but in 1780, in attempting to defend Charleston, disaster befell him. Sir Henry Clinton, the British commander-in-chief at New York, headed an expedition to South Carolina, besieged Lincoln, and obliged him to surrender, with two thousand Continentals and as many militia, on the 12th of May. Then, proceeding into the interior of the State, the enemy established themselves at the principal points to overawe the inhabitants and hold the territory. Their main force took up a position beyond the town of Camden. Clinton, after the surrender of Charleston, returned to New York.

The general now to figure conspicuously in the Southern operations, who had come from New York with Clinton, and to whom the latter had assigned the duty of securing and extending the conquests already made, was the Earl Charles Cornwallis, lieutenant-general in the British army, and second in command of the King's forces in America. He made his first appearance in the field at the Battle of Long Island, in 1776; then at the capture of New York; again at Trenton, where Washington blinded

---

would disappoint it, appears from the following from Lord Germaine to Clinton, under date of May 2d, 1781: "The reduction of the Southern provinces must give the death-wound to the rebellion, notwithstanding any assistance the French may be able to give it; and if that were the case, a general peace would soon follow, and this country be delivered from the most burdensome and extensive war it ever was engaged in. As so much, therefore, depends upon our successes in America, you cannot be surprised that the eyes of all the people of England are turned upon you, nor at the anxiety with which the King and all his servants wait for accounts of your movements. And as I am most immediately interested of any of them in your success, you will, I hope, excuse the earnestness and frequency of my exhortations to decision in council, and activity, vigor, and perseverance in execution of his Majesty's pleasure, which you are now fully informed of."—*Parliamentary Register*, 1782–'83.

LORD CORNWALLIS. [AFTER THE PAINTING BY COPLEY, R.A.]

him with camp-fires while he silently marched to his rear, out of harm's way, through Princeton; at Brandywine also, and Germantown, and finally at the South. Representing an old family in London, where he was born in 1738, he spent his school-days at Eton, entered the army at eighteen, was elected to Parliament, where he voted against the taxation of

America, and at the opening of the war joined in suppressing the Colonists. A man now in the prime of life, displaying superior military capacity, never lacking in resources—cold, severe, active—the confidence reposed in him by the army and the home government flattering in the extreme—and we have the leader who was to march destructively through the South, until he submitted at Yorktown to have his name forever associated with the very event he sought to prevent — the final victory which secured American Independence.

The instructions which Cornwallis received from Clinton, upon the latter's departure, were of a general character. He was expected, first of all, to see that Charleston was secure, and then add to the territory already overrun as opportunity offered and his judgment approved.[1] Clinton left him an ample force, and confided much to his discretion and abilities. An ambitious officer could not have found himself in a more gratifying position than Cornwallis then occupied, with the entire Southern field open to him for the exercise of his military talents. Nor was he slow in improving the opportunity, as we find him immediately laying out plans, in connection with Clinton, for the further reduction of the South. While there was a general understanding between the two as to the policy to be pursued, the details—the *when* and *how* of the operations—were left to Cornwallis. His first anxiety was to secure what he already had, namely, Charleston and a good part of South Carolina; and to do this he proposed to invade and obtain a foothold in North Carolina, while Clinton sent an expedition into the Chesapeake to co-operate with him to the extent of engaging the attention of Virginia, and threaten any Continental force that might seek to go southward from that State. North Carolina, in other words, was to be held as a barrier for the protection of the States below it. The conquest of Virginia did not then enter into the plan. It was as early as August 6th, 1780, that Cornwallis wrote to Clinton : " It may be doubted by some whether the invasion of North

---

[1] *From instructions to Lieutenant-general Earl Cornwallis, dated Head-quarters, Charleston, June 1st, 1780.*

" Upon my departure from hence you will be pleased to take command of the troops mentioned in the enclosed return, and of all other troops now here, or that may arrive in my absence. Your Lordship will make such changes in the position of them as you may judge most conducive to his Majesty's service, for the defence of this most important post and its dependencies. At the same time, it is by no means my intention to prevent your acting offensively, in case an opportunity should offer, consistent with the *security of this place*, which is always to be regarded as a *primary object*."—*Clinton's Answer.*

Carolina may be a prudent measure; but I am convinced it is a necessary one, and that if we do not attack that province, we must give up both South Carolina and Georgia, and retire within the walls of Charleston." The battle of Camden followed, upon the 15th of August, when Cornwallis met Gates and inflicted upon him the most complete defeat the Americans had suffered in the open field. After this important success the British general explained his projects to his chief a little more fully. On August 23d he wrote: "It is difficult to form a plan of operations, which must depend so much on circumstances. But it at present appears to me that I should endeavor to get as soon as possible to Hillsborough [N. C.], and there assemble and try to arrange the friends who are inclined to arm in our favor, and endeavor to form a very large magazine for the winter—of flour and meal from the country, and of rum, salt, etc., from Cross Creek, which I understand to be about eighty miles' carriage. But all this will depend on the operations which your Excellency may think proper to pursue in the Chesapeake, which appears to me, next to the security of New York, to be one of the most important objects of the war." Clinton approved of this, and on the 10th of October lent his co-operation by sending General Leslie, with a force of two thousand two hundred and six, rank and file, to the Chesapeake, with orders to establish a station at Portsmouth, on the Elizabeth River, and make a diversion in favor of Cornwallis, by going up toward Richmond. All further orders he was to receive direct from that general.

Cornwallis found a rough road to the realization of his plans. Camden had suddenly increased his reputation, and presented him to the South as the prospective master of her territory; but he was soon to discover that he could sustain himself only by the utmost exertions under the greatest difficulties. His new antagonist in the field, since the defeat of Gates, was General Nathaniel Greene, who proved himself his equal in all respects, except in the possession of a veteran army upon which he could depend. The story of Greene's noble efforts to thwart the designs of the enemy has been too often told to need repetition; it is with his dangerous opponent, who is to become the central figure at Yorktown, that we are more concerned in this connection. It is enough to say that Greene quickly put new life into the remnants of Gates's defeated force, and made his presence irksome to the British. The first check Cornwallis received occurred on the 8th of October, after he had advanced as far as Charlotte, in North Carolina. There he learned that Major Ferguson, one of his best partisan officers, had been killed, and his command destroyed, or taken, at King's Mountain, by backwoodsmen, under Williams, Shelby, Campbell, and other militia colonels. This defeat operated to such a degree in depressing the spirits of the Loyalists in that section of the country, and encouraging the friends of America, or Whigs, that Cornwallis determined to fall back to South Carolina again, where he took up a position at Wynnsborough, some twenty-five miles west of Camden.

The King's Mountain affair, however, had only postponed the occupation of North Carolina until re-enforcements could reach the British camp. Leslie was ordered down to Charleston from Portsmouth, and in January, 1781, he joined Cornwallis. To replace his force in the Chesapeake, Clinton, although he could " ill spare it," as he wrote, sent Arnold, December 11th, with another expedition, to Portsmouth, under the same directions that Leslie lay, to co-operate with the army under Cornwallis.[1] The original design was to be prosecuted, and opinions were expressed also as to carrying the war beyond into Virginia. Thus Clinton, writing to Cornwallis, November 6th, says: " If my wishes are fulfilled they are that you may establish a post at Hillsborough, feed it from Cross Creek [Fayetteville], and be able to keep that of Portsmouth. A few troops will do it, and carry on desultory expeditions in Chesapeake, till more solid operations can take place, of which I fear there is no prospect without we are considerably re-enforced. . . . Operations in Chesapeake are but of two sorts: solid operations with a fighting army, to call forth our friends and support them; or a post, such as Portsmouth, carrying on desultory expeditions, stopping up in a great measure the Chesapeake, and, by commanding James River, prevent the enemy from forming any considerable depots upon it, or moving in any force to the southward of it." These opinions bear upon subsequent operations in Virginia.

Re-enforced by Leslie, Cornwallis once more, in January, 1781, set out for North Carolina. His force, on the 15th of that month, numbered, all told, about three thousand four hundred, officers and men; by the returns, three thousand two hundred and twenty-four were rank and file. Greene,

---

[1] *Clinton to Cornwallis, New York, December 13th,* 1780.

" Wishing, however, to give your Lordship's operations in North Carolina every assistance in my power, though I can ill spare it, I have sent another expedition into the Chesapeake, under the orders of Brigadier-general Arnold, Lieutenant-colonels Dundas and Simcoe. . . . As I have always said, I think your Lordship's movements to the southward most important, and, as I have ever done, so I will give them all the assistance I can."—*Clinton's Answer.*

who was watching the enemy from the banks of the Pedee, could muster scarcely fifteen hundred Continentals and six hundred militia. Could Cornwallis strike him and win another Camden, British interests might become securely rooted in all the South. But, just at the moment of his advance the second time, he met with a second disaster. Morgan, whom Greene had detached far to his right on the South Carolina border, won, on the 17th of January, the brilliant victory at Cowpens over Tarleton, Cornwallis's dashing cavalry leader, by which the enemy suffered a loss, in casualties and prisoners, of very nearly eight hundred men. This was a crippling blow—quite enough to cause a cautious general to halt; but Cornwallis, understanding perfectly that another retreat, under the circumstances, would amount to an admission of fear and weakness on his part, and still further discourage loyalty where he had come to revive it, promptly determined to go on. His own words at this crisis are important: " My plan for the winter's campaign," he wrote to Germaine, " was to penetrate into North Carolina, leaving South Carolina. in security against any probable attack in my absence. Lord Rawdon with a considerable body of troops had charge of the defensive, and I proceeded about the middle of January upon the offensive operations. . . . I hoped by rapid marches to get between General Greene and Virginia, and by that means force him to fight without receiving any re-enforcement from that province; or, failing of that, to oblige him to quit North Carolina with precipitation, and thereby encourage our friends to make good their promises of a general rising to assist me in establishing his Majesty's government. The unfortunate affair of the 17th of January [Cowpens] was a very unexpected and severe blow; for, besides reputation, our loss did not fall short of six hundred men. However, being thoroughly sensible that defensive measures would be certain ruin to the affairs of Great Britain in the Southern Colonies, this event did not deter me from prosecuting the original plan."[1] So, despite Cowpens, Cornwallis, in the last days of January, put all his troops in light marching order, burnt his baggage, and pushed forward through drenching rains to overtake both Greene and Morgan, and occupy North Carolina.

This move is interesting, for it leads indirectly to Yorktown. No one could then have dreamed that Cornwallis at the Catawba, and Washington upon the Hudson, seven hundred miles apart, each looking at different objective points, would within eight months meet face to face midway down the coast and settle the issue. Cornwallis, certainly, did not dream

---

[1] " Cornwallis Correspondence," Ross, vol. i., p. 516.

of it, and yet it was he who set the events in motion that culminated in his overthrow. The Yorktown Campaign began with him, when he started out to crush Greene and reduce North Carolina to subjection. That was its first stage.

Into the details of these earlier movements it is not intended to enter here. Greene, too weak to meet the enemy, retreated rapidly. The enemy followed as rapidly. Night and day the chase was continued through North Carolina, until Greene skilfully saved himself at the Virginia line by putting the river Dan between his troops and their pursuers. Cornwallis, having thus accomplished one object of his invasion in driving Greene out of the State, anticipated the restoration of the King's authority within its lim-

GENERAL NATHANIEL GREENE.

its. But once more "a capital misfortune" under the disguise of a victory befell him, and again his expectations failed of realization. Greene, receiving re-enforcements, recrossed the Dan and offered the enemy battle at Guilford Court House, on the 15th of March. Cornwallis gladly seized the opportunity, in the hope of breaking up Greene's force and opening the way into Virginia, which would be his next object, and the well-known battle at Guilford followed. It was an obstinate contest, resulting in the retreat of the American troops. But it was not a *Camden* defeat for them. In this fact lay very material consequences. So great a loss had the British sustained, both in officers and men, that their nominal advantages could not be pursued. On the contrary, their victory had entailed upon them the positive effects of a defeat. It proved too costly—too great a drain upon their effective strength to permit them even to remain where they were. Cornwallis, indeed, established himself at Hillsborough, as contemplated in his plan, raised the royal standard, and issued proclamations calling upon the King's true subjects to assert themselves, and offering them protection. But hardly had he assumed this attitude of a conqueror and deliverer before we find him obliged to retire from the heart of the State to the coast, for the avowed purpose of recruiting and refitting his exhausted and sadly diminished force. Hillsborough he exchanged for Wilmington, at the seaboard, which he reached on the 7th of April, and the defeated Greene was left practically master of the situation, with South Carolina open to his advance. The move to Wilmington was a clear admission that, for the time being, the scheme of reducing North Carolina had failed.

At Wilmington, now, the Southern invasion develops a new phase: we reach the second and vital step that led Cornwallis to Yorktown.

As the march into North Carolina contemplated no such result as a retirement to the seaboard, and as the reduction of that State had been declared indispensable for the security of all below it, it lay with Cornwallis either to re-enforce himself, were that possible, from Charleston and return to Hillsborough, or fall back once more to his base in South Carolina. This was the alternative, if the original scheme was to be adhered to. But at Wilmington, under the altered condition of things, Cornwallis changed his plan, and, abandoning the Carolinas for the present, decided to move directly into Virginia, unite with Phillips and Arnold, and there renew operations with the Chesapeake as his base. What these operations would be he did not then know himself.

The success of the entire Southern scheme hinged upon this move to Virginia, and its merits have been discussed both by the principal actors in the scenes, and by subsequent military and historical writers. Some important points were involved. Why did not Cornwallis retire from North to South Carolina after Guilford Court House? Why not even after reaching Wilmington? Why did he march to Virginia? Why, at all events, without the previous approval of his commander-in-chief? The change was a radical one, and the responsibility proportionately great. For all these questions, however, Cornwallis had apparently satisfactory replies, and in his final answer to Clinton, in the controversy which arose between them after the war, he makes a ready and pointed defence. Speaking of his move to Virginia, he says: " I came to this resolution principally for the following reasons: I could not remain at Wilmington, lest General Greene should succeed against Lord Rawdon [who was left in command in South Carolina], and, by returning to North Carolina, have it in his power to cut off every means of saving my small corps, except that disgraceful one of an embarkation, with the loss of the cavalry and every horse in the army. From the shortness of Lord Rawdon's stock of provisions and the great distance from Wilmington to Camden, it appeared impossible that any direct move of mine could afford him the least prospect of relief. In the attempt, in case of a misfortune to him, the safety of my own corps might have been endangered ; or, if he extricated himself, the force in South Carolina, when assembled, was, in my opinion, sufficient to secure what was valuable to us, and capable of

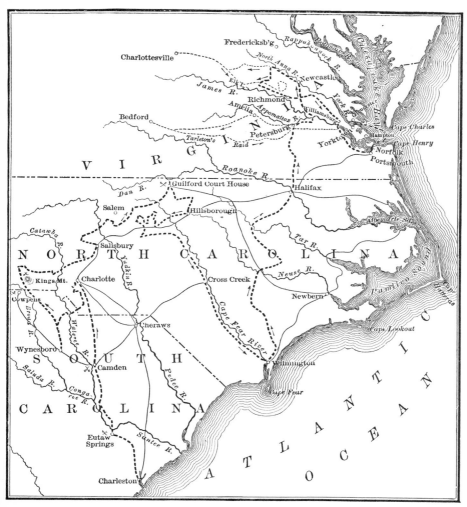

MAP SHOWING THE ROUTE AND OPERATIONS OF CORNWALLIS IN THE SOUTH. [FROM FADEN'S MAP, LONDON, 1787.]

defence in that province. I was likewise influenced by having just received an account from Charleston of the arrival of a frigate with despatches from the commander-in-chief, the substance of which, then transmitted to me, was that General Phillips had been detached to the Chesapeake and put under my orders, which induced me to hope that solid operations might be adopted in that quarter; and I was finally persuaded that, until Virginia was reduced, we could not hold the more southern provinces, and that after its reduction they would fall without much difficulty."

Assuming thus the entire responsibility, and conscious that he would have at least the approval of the home ministry, with whom he was a favorite, Cornwallis marched from Wilmington on the 25th of April, and on the 20th of May arrived at Petersburg, Virginia, where a junction was effected with the force under General Phillips. Phillips himself had unfortunately fallen a victim to a fever a few days before.

Sir Henry Clinton never approved of this move, pronouncing it contrary to the spirit of his instructions, which required Cornwallis to hold and secure South Carolina. By entering Virginia he was abandoning it. " Had you intimated the probability of your intention," wrote Clinton to Cornwallis, in May, "I should certainly have endeavored to have stopped you, as I did then as well as now consider such a move likely to be dangerous to our interests in the southern colonies." And thirteen years later, when Clinton was answering the criticisms of the historian Stedman, he again insisted that " Cornwallis had been ordered and had promised, in case of failure in North Carolina, to fall back on South Carolina and secure it." The two generals continued the controversy with some acrimony, but Cornwallis had the moral support of the home government, and the commander-in-chief actually found himself obliged to accommodate his own future plans to this movement of his subordinate.

CHAPTER III.

CORNWALLIS AND LAFAYETTE IN VIRGINIA.

INTERESTING scenes, preliminary to the grand result, now open in Virginia.

Cornwallis had at last reached the State whose control, from its central position, he believed would be followed by the control of all America. Precisely how this coveted result was to be brought about in the case of the States to the northward does not appear. As to the reduction of Virginia, however, his Lordship had some definite ideas. He would have had Clinton abandon New York, if necessary, concentrate all available forces in the Chesapeake, and, moving up the large navigable rivers, occupy the territory, compel the submission of the inhabitants, and establish the royal authority. The scheme contemplated a previous decisive victory over any American army brought to the defence of the State. It presupposed, also, the existence of a considerable Tory element in the population, which, however, did not exist in Virginia. The State could have been held only by sheer conquest, in which case it could scarcely have become a satisfactory central base of operations. Any temporary advantage gained there would doubtless have been offset by the moral effect of the abandonment of the Northern field. That step in the eyes both of America and Europe would have meant failure in the strong Colonies, instead of a change of base. Clinton, the commander-in-chief, seems to have thoroughly appreciated this when he declined to entertain Cornwallis's suggestion. Indeed, Clinton, although charged sometimes with indecision and incompetency, understood the American situation quite as clearly as Cornwallis or the home government; and in asking for a re-enforcement of ten thousand men and the assurance of a continued naval supremacy for the operations of 1781, he but represented, like a faithful head, the true necessities of the case. England's force in America that year was inadequate for her purposes.

That the reduction of Virginia would have been followed by the apparent submission of the States below is possible. A Continental force might have found it difficult to subsist and replenish losses, cut off from Virginia and the resources of the States above.[1] Both sides certainly regarded the field as a most important one, and the events transpiring there were closely and anxiously watched.

When Cornwallis entered the State he found for his antagonist the youthful Lafayette—a name America delights to honor. His services in the Revolution are a familiar record; but above these stands the unalloyed motive, the noble spirit, that brought him here. In 1776, then nineteen years of age, he was stationed on duty at Metz as an officer in the French army; and it was there that he first understood the merits of the American struggle. "It happened at this time," says President Sparks, "that the Duke of Gloucester, brother to the King of England, was at Metz, and a dinner was given to him by the commandant of that place. Several officers were invited, and among others Lafayette. Despatches had just been received by the duke from England, and he made their contents the topic of conversation; they related to American affairs—the recent declaration of independence, the resistance of the Colonists, and the strong measures adopted by the ministry to crush the rebellion. The details were new to Lafayette; he listened with eagerness to the conversation, and prolonged it by asking questions of the duke. His curiosity was deeply excited by what he heard, and the idea of a people fighting for liberty had a strong influence upon his imagination. The cause seemed to him just and noble from the representations of the duke himself, and before he left the table the thought came into his head that he would go to America, and offer his services to a people who were struggling for freedom and independence. From that hour he could think of nothing but this chivalrous enterprise."

As a youth of noble birth and large fortune, and "allied to one of the first families of the court," his intention to engage in the American contest became known to the French government, and his departure was prohibited. But, after failing in one attempt, he succeeded in quitting France in the disguise of a courier, and, with De Kalb and other foreign officers, sailed for this country from the Spanish port of Passage, in April, 1777. After a seven-weeks' voyage he reached Georgetown, South Carolina, on June 15th, and Charleston on the 19th, where he procured horses

---

[1] In 1780 and 1781 equipments, clothing, and ammunition for the Southern troops could be obtained only from Philadelphia and the scanty depots from which Washington's army in the Highlands was supplied.

for himself and companions to proceed to Philadelphia. Riding nearly nine hundred miles, he reached the city in the course of a month, and sought admission to the American army.

Congress at first denied Lafayette's application, as coming from one of the increasing number of foreigners who expected commissions; but he immediately represented that he wished to offer himself simply as a volunteer without pay, when that body, appreciating his devotion and enthusiasm in their cause, resolved on the 31st of July that "his services be accepted, and that in consideration of his zeal, illustrious family and connections, he have the rank and commission of major-general in the Army of the United States." Washington, marching soon after through Philadelphia to oppose the enemy coming up from the head of the Chesapeake, met Lafayette for the first time at that city, complimented

THE MARQUIS DE LAFAYETTE. [FROM THE ENGRAVING PUBLISHED BY HIS FAMILY.]

him upon "his zeal and his sacrifices," and invited him to make his home at his own head-quarters. The young marquis gladly accepted the flattering invitation, and three weeks later we find him writing to his wife as follows, in regard to the commander-in-chief: "This excellent man, whose talents and virtues I admired, and whom I have learned to revere as I know him better, has now become my intimate friend; his affectionate interest in me instantly won my heart. I am established in his house, and we live together like two attached brothers, with mutual confidence and cordiality. This friendship renders me as happy as I can possibly be in this country." [1]

---

[1] "At every period of life, and above all, in his youth, Lafayette displayed a cold and

The beautiful statue of Lafayette, at the lower end of Union Square, in New York City, represents him in buoyant attitude, offering his services to America. The most valuable services he rendered in the field were those rendered here in Virginia. At Brandywine, his first engagement, in 1777, he fought bravely as a volunteer, and received a wound. He shared the hardships of the army at Valley Forge; figured at Monmouth and in Rhode Island in 1778; returned to France in 1779, where his influence was exerted in obtaining the first French re-enforcements for America under Rochambeau; and in 1780, coming again to the United States, he was placed at the head of Washington's select body of troops, known as the corps of Light Infantry. Finally, early in 1781 he appears in Virginia to be constantly active in an independent command until the investment of Yorktown.

What took this now popular and trusted officer to the southward was the attention paid by the enemy to the Chesapeake. Clinton, as we have seen, had sent thither the three expeditions under Leslie, Arnold, and Phillips. The two latter alone operated up the James as far as Richmond. Arnold sailed from New York on the 16th of December, 1780, and on the 3d of January anchored off Jamestown Island. Two days later he entered and plundered Richmond, and on the 7th withdrew to take up a fortified position at Portsmouth. His movements were carefully watched by Washington, who, upon hearing of his whereabouts, organized a land and naval expedition to check the traitor's inroads, and, if possible, effect his capture. Major-general Baron Steuben was then in Virginia, with Generals Muhlenberg, Weedon, Nelson, and others; but their forces being untrained militia, the commander-in-chief considered it necessary to send to their assistance a body of Continentals from his own army. The detachment was composed of twelve hundred of his best soldiers— Light Infantry—and the command he gave to Lafayette. He also persuaded Rochambeau to despatch the small French fleet from Newport, then under Monsieur Destouches, with a few troops, to blockade Arnold by sea, while Lafayette should compel his surrender with the land-forces.

But this expedition failed of its object. The English fleet, under Arbuthnot, intercepted the French ships near the entrance to the Chesa-

grave exterior, which sometimes gave to his demeanor an air of timidity and embarrassment which did not really belong to him. His reserved manners and his silent disposition presented a singular contrast to the petulance, the levity, and the ostentatious loquacity of persons of his own age; but, under this exterior, to all appearances so phlegmatic, he concealed the most active mind, the most determined character, and the most enthusiastic spirit."—*Memoirs of Count Ségur*, vol. i., p. 106.

peake, where, on March 16th, a naval action occurred, with eight sail of the line on a side, in which each admiral claimed the victory. As Destouches, however, could not co-operate with Lafayette and returned to Newport, the material advantage remained with the British. Lafayette had in the mean time marched with all speed to the head of the Chesapeake and embarked for Annapolis. Leaving his troops there to proceed down the bay in French frigates which he supposed Destouches could send up, he set out in advance with some officers in an open boat, made his way to Williamsburg, on the Virginia peninsula, and then on the 19th across the James to Suffolk, where General Muhlenberg was guarding the roads leading out of Portsmouth. A reconnoissance was made toward the latter place preparatory to a close investment of Arnold's position, when word came of the naval failure, and Lafayette returned to Annapolis, in order to rejoin Washington's army, as required by his chief.

At the head of the Elk, however, on his march northward, Lafayette received new and important instructions from the commander-in-chief, dated April 6th. It had been ascertained that Clinton had despatched General Phillips—that excellent officer who had surrendered with Burgoyne—with another expedition to take command in the Chesapeake, whose force combined with Arnold's would number something over three thousand men. As this indicated an intention on the part of the enemy to prosecute operations in Virginia on a larger scale than heretofore, either in conjunction with Cornwallis or separately, it was the unanimous opinion of Washington and his general officers that Lafayette, instead of returning north, should immediately turn his detachment southward again, and place himself under the orders of General Greene, who needed every possible assistance. Lafayette accordingly faced about and marched to Baltimore, where he borrowed two thousand pounds from the merchants with which to buy linen, shoes, and hats for his soldiers, who had marched from the North in winter clothing. The ladies of the city gave a ball in honor of the patriotic young French general, and offered to make up the shirts and blouses for his soldiers. To the troops themselves, it seems, nearly all of whom had been detached from the New England regiments, the prospect of service in the distant South was extremely repugnant, and some desertions occurred. After hanging one deserter and dismissing another, Lafayette issued an order announcing that the detachment was setting out on an arduous and dangerous campaign, in which a superior enemy was to be met and fought under difficulties of every sort, and that the general, on his part, was determined to encounter them; but that if any of the soldiers were inclined to abandon him they need not fear the crime

3

and danger of desertion, as every one who should apply to head-quarters for a pass to join their corps in the North could obtain it immediately. From that hour, as Lafayette states in his " Memoirs," " all desertions ceased," and not one of his men would leave him. The corps was composed of three veteran light infantry battalions, under Colonel Vose, of Massachusetts; Lieutenant-colonel Gimat, a French officer, late aid to Lafayette; and Lieutenant-colonel Barber, of New Jersey; and its conduct during the campaign won the praise and confidence of its leader.

Expecting that Phillips and Arnold would speedily occupy the line of the James and secure Richmond, Lafayette, starting from Baltimore on the 19th of April, hastened to reach that place before them. Leaving his tents and artillery to follow, he impressed wagons and horses, and making forced marches by way of Alexandria, Fredericksburg, and Bowling Green, arrived at Richmond on the evening of the 29th, a few hours in advance of the enemy.[1] Phillips made his appearance opposite the town on the following morning. Surprised at Lafayette's celerity, he fell down the river again about as far as Jamestown Island; but receiving word from Cornwallis, on the 7th of May, that he proposed to march into Virginia and unite with Phillips at Petersburg, the latter returned to that place on the 10th. Lafayette endeavored to prevent or delay

---

[1] Steuben, who with militia was not strong enough to oppose Phillips, sent his aid, Captain North, to Lafayette to represent the situation. North found the marquis at Bowling Green, who replied to the baron as follows:

"Bowling Green Tavern, April 27th, 1781.

"DEAR BARON,—. . . I feel for you, my dear sir, and easily imagine that, with your inferiority, you cannot make such a resistance as you would wish. From what Captain North says, I am inclined to believe that by this time you are at Chesterfield Court House.

"Richmond must be now the object for both parties—your point of retreat at the Court House is the more judicious, as it enables us to form a junction. As long as we can keep the ferry at Richmond, we might look at that place. But the falls being a natural protection to our boats, I think every boat that can be collected in the river ought to rendezvous at the lowest crossing-place above the falls. . . . This detachment will be at Richmond or Westham the day after to-morrow, if the rain don't prevent it—the artillery and every other apparatus is far behind. As soon as I arrive at Richmond I will write to you more particularly. But as far as I may judge for the present (taking it for granted that you are now at the Court House), the point above the falls must be considered by us as the most proper point to cross the river, and I heartily wish you may not be dislodged from the Court House before the detachment arrives. . . .

" Very affectionately, and with great regard, I have the honor to be, dear Baron,
" Your most obedient servant,
" LAFAYETTE."
[From the " Gates MS. Papers," N. Y. Hist. Soc.]

the junction of these forces by occupying Petersburg first, but did not succeed, and on the 20th, as already stated, the junction was effected.

Lafayette, who was at Richmond when Cornwallis reached Petersburg, being now within Greene's department, had received orders from that general to halt and take command of all troops in Virginia, and defend the State.[1] To this one object, from this time forth, he directed his entire attention; and his first anxiety was to make himself stronger. The nucleus of his force was his own detachment from the Northern army. Brigadier-generals Muhlenberg and Weedon, Virginia Continental officers, and Generals Nelson, Stevens, and Lawson, State brigadiers, were then, or recently had been, in different parts of the field with small and fluctuating bodies of militia; while Major-general Steuben, who had come south with Greene, was endeavoring to organize regiments for the Virginia line from recruits enlisted for eighteen months. In addition, what was to prove a most important acquisition, General Wayne was daily expected to report with the Pennsylvania line to Lafayette, and serve with him until further orders from Greene. But all these troops, could they have been united in time, would still have been unable, from the inexperience of a large proportion of them, to resist the progress of the enemy; and Lafayette applied in every direction for more men and supplies. He .wrote to Jefferson, the retiring governor, later to Nelson, the new governor, to Morgan at Winchester, to Weedon at Fredericksburg, and to others, to exert themselves in the emergency. The famous Morgan, who was at home recruiting his health after Cowpens, was especially urged to lend his help. " Our regular force," wrote Lafayette to him from Richmond, May 21st, " is near one thousand ; our militia are not very strong upon the returns, and much weaker in the field. We have not a hundred riflemen, and are in the greatest need of arms. The Pennsylvanians were long ago to join us, and their march has been deferred from day to day; no official account of them, nor of a battalion of Maryland recruits. Under these circumstances, my dear sir, I do very much want your assistance, and beg leave to request it, both as a lover of public welfare and as a private friend of

---

[1] "The moment I got intelligence that Lord Cornwallis was moving northerly, I gave orders for the marquis to halt and take the command of Virginia, and to halt the Pennsylvania line and all the Virginia drafts."—*Greene to Jefferson.* GREENE'S *Greene,* vol. iii., p. 556.

In a letter to Steuben from Wilton, a few miles below Richmond, May 17th, 1781, Lafayette writes: "General Greene directs that my detachment be stationed in Virginia, where I am to take command of the troops. What necessity had obliged me to do was at the same time consistent with the arrangements of the general."—*Gates MS.*

yours. I ever had a great esteem for riflemen, and have done my best to see them much employed in our armies. But in this little corps they are particularly wanting. Your in-

fluence can do more than orders from the. Executive. Permit me, therefore, my dear sir, entirely to depend on your exertions." And to this he added that his own presence in camp would alone be a "very great re-enforcement."[1] The Virginia House of Delegates and Governor Jefferson seconded this appeal to Morgan. But Morgan was delayed in taking the field by a Tory insurrection in Hampshire County, to the north-west; and the planting season—the common excuse, in the spring, throughout all the Colonies—kept the militia from

GENERAL DANIEL MORGAN.

coming forward.in any considerable numbers. Arms also, as Lafayette represents, were wanting, while the lack of good swords and proper equipments was the main reason why the little army contained so few cavalry, who were needed even more than riflemen. The enemy mounted their troopers on the best horses Virginia could afford; but Lafayette could bring to his aid neither troopers nor horses. Among small re-enforcements to this branch of the service that he received soon after the campaign opened was a volunteer company of fifty or sixty spirited young men, who mounted and armed themselves at their own expense, under Lieutenant-colonel John Mercer, of Fredericksburg—an excellent officer, who had resigned his commission when General Charles Lee, whose aide he had been at Monmouth, was dismissed for his conduct in that engagement. Three or four weeks later another company—the Baltimore Troop of Light Dragoons, under Captain Nicholas R. Moore, composed also of "men of fortune"—arrived from Maryland, and won Lafayette's respect for making "great sacrifices to serve their country."[2]

---

[1] Graham's " Life of General Morgan," p. 376.

[2] " The richest young men of Virginia and Maryland had come to join him as volunteer dragoons; and, from their intelligence as well as from the superiority of their horses, they had been of essential service to him."—*Lafayette's Memoirs*, vol. i., p. 263; *Lee's Memoirs*, vol. ii., p. 197 ; *Lafayette to Morgan, Graham*, p. 389.

Not very promising was the outlook, and, in outlining his intentions to the commander-in-chief, the marquis was obliged to admit that nothing more than a weak defensive could be attempted. The first impulse of his temper was to risk something; but, reflecting how certainly the State would be involved in ruin by the defeat of his command, he became "extremely cautious." "Were I to fight a battle," he wrote to Washington, May 24th, "I should be cut to pieces, the militia dispersed, and the arms lost. Were I to decline fighting, the country would think itself given up. I am therefore determined to skirmish, but not to engage too far, and particularly to take care against their immense and excellent body of horse, whom the militia fear as they would so many wild beasts." This plan he followed to the end, and by it saved himself, his army, and the State. Learning on the 27th that the enemy had crossed the James below, he evacuated Richmond, already abandoned by nearly all its residents, and headed toward Fredericksburg, to keep open his communications with Wayne and the North. Against the four thousand five hundred regulars under Cornwallis he could present a force of but two thousand militia, the corps of one thousand Light Infantry, and forty dragoons—the remnant of Armand's Legion. "I am not strong enough," he wrote, "even to get beaten."

So a new situation had rapidly developed: Virginia the theatre of active operations — Lafayette facing Cornwallis — a meagre, incomplete American force opposed to the British veterans of Camden and Guilford Court House, united with the strong detachments brought down by Arnold and Phillips. All eyes were now fixed upon this field, watching the development of the enemy's designs.

But, while the progress of Cornwallis was at first alarming, it is to be observed that his operations were intended to be only partial or preliminary. He had now reached a point where he could not act as independently as before, and must subordinate his movements to those of his commander-in-chief. It was out of his power alone to conquer Virginia. He therefore proposed to accomplish, in the first instance, a secondary object, and this he distinctly expressed to Clinton, on May 26th, as follows: "I shall now proceed to dislodge Lafayette from Richmond, and with my light troops to destroy any magazines or stores in the neighborhood which may have been collected either for his use or for General Greene's army. From thence I purpose to move to the Neck at Williamsburg, which is represented as healthy, and where some subsistence may be procured, and keep myself unengaged from operations which might interfere with your plan for the campaign, until I have the satisfaction of hearing from you." This purpose is to be borne in mind in following out his present movements.

Cornwallis moved forward from Petersburg on the 24th. "The boy cannot escape me," he is reported to have written, in an intercepted letter, in referring to Lafayette; and he sought to make good the assertion.[1] He crossed the James from Mead's to Westover, twenty-five miles below Richmond, occupying nearly three days in the movement. The horses swum over, a distance of two miles. It was "an easy entrance," says Tarleton, "into a fertile quarter of Virginia." On the 27th they encamped near White Oak Swamp. Simcoe and his dragoons, patrolling in front, imposed upon and took "several gentlemen" who were watching the motions of the British. On the 28th they were at Bottoms' Bridge, on the Chickahominy. The evening before, Lafayette had encamped on the same stream at Winston's Bridge, twenty miles west of them, and eight miles north of Richmond. He was not to be caught in the town.[2] On the 29th they had reached Newcastle, on the Pamunky,

---

[1] The histories of this campaign, from Gordon down, introduce this phrase. Bancroft, however, calls attention to the fact that Clinton used the expression to Germaine, "Lafayette, I think, cannot escape him," and that the former must have been manufactured from the latter; but it seems that Captain Welles, of the Light Infantry, states, as early as June 16th, 1781, that it was understood in camp that Cornwallis had called Lafayette "an aspiring boy."—*MS. Letter.*

[2] In his summary of this campaign ("Memoirs," vol. i., p. 452) Lafayette says: "The great disproportion of the American corps, the impossibility of commanding the navigable rivers, and the necessity of keeping the important side of James River, do not allow any opposition" to Cornwallis, who on the 24th–27th "crosses to Westover; . . . our troops at Winston's Bridge; a rapid march of the two corps, the enemy's to engage an action, the Americans to avoid it, and retain the heights of the country with the communication of Philadelphia, which is equally necessary to our army and to the existence of that of Carolina."

The following letter from Lafayette to Steuben, dated Richmond, May 26th, 1781, is also of interest in this connection: ". . . Lord Cornwallis arrived at Petersboro' the 20th inst., with the Twenty-third, Thirty-third, and Seventy-first British, a Hessian regiment, Tarleton's Legion, Hamilton's corps, two hundred Tories, some Light Infantry and Guards. They moved, the 24th, to Maycox, sending their boats from City Point to that place, where they crossed over about one thousand men, and employed themselves yesterday in getting over the remainder to Westover, where they remained quiet yesterday evening. Our baggage and stores were sent off yesterday by the route of Brook's Bridge; and should the enemy's movements be rapid toward Richmond, I must trust to you for giving directions relative to the removing of the stores and the secur-

and on the 30th Hanover Court House, where they found some French twenty-four-pounders, which were spiked or thrown into the river. At Page's, the present Hanovertown, and Aylett's warehouses a large quantity of tobacco was destroyed. Cornwallis then pushed on to the North Anna, encamping in the vicinity of Hanover Junction on the 1st of June, and threw forward Tarleton and Simcoe to ascertain Lafayette's position.

But Lafayette had retreated rapidly, and could not be overtaken by the British. From Winston's Bridge he turned, on the 28th, to the left, and marched to Dandridge's, where Goldmine Creek runs into the South Anna. This put him some twenty-five miles west of the enemy, and at a point where he could look to Fredericksburg, or to Wayne, at the upper Potomac, or to Steuben, who had taken position with his Virginia recruits at Point of Forks, west of Richmond, where the Fluvanna unites with the James. While at Goldmine Creek he wrote as follows to Steuben, May 29th: "Lord Cornwallis has sent people to examine the fords of the James River—he did since intend to turn our left flank—these schemes he seems to have abandoned, and is on his way to Fredericksburg. I am apprehensive an expedition will go by water up Powtomack, as General Leslie is said to have gone down to Portsmouth. We march on a parallel line with the enemy, keeping the upper part of the country, and disposed to turn back in case this movement is only a feint. I wish all our stores may be collected at the Court House [Albemarle]. The enemy's cavalry increase every day. The gentlemen do not please to take their horses out of the way, and the impressing warrants are so contracted that we cannot get one, while the enemy sweep everything that is in their way and many miles around. I request you will urge the Assembly to have us furnished with horses; if they do not, it is impossible we can defend this country." [1]

Observing, on the 30th, that Cornwallis intended to prevent his junction with Wayne, Lafayette pushed directly north, crossing the North Anna probably at Anderson's Bridge, and on June 2d was at Mattapony Church, in Spottsylvania County, a few miles north-east of Mount Pleasant. Weedon, at Fredericksburg, had reported that all valuable stores had been removed from that place and Falmouth, and the marquis had

---

ing the remainder of the boats at Tuckahoe. I have detained De Contun with twelve of Armand's corps, which I could not possibly do without; the remainder of them you will order as you please. There are fifty men of White's dragoons at Staunton, which I wish most earnestly to have mounted and equipped. Our want of cavalry is most sensibly felt. Most of the militia horse are gone, and the times of the remainder will be out next week."—*Gates MS.*   [1] Gates MS. papers.

then no other object than to reach Wayne. On the 3d his head-quarters were at Corbin's Bridge, on the Po, where he wrote to Morgan to move the Burgoyne prisoners from the Shenandoah Valley into Maryland as soon as possible, as Cornwallis might attempt their rescue; and then, on the 4th, continuing his march through Spottsylvania and the edge of the memorable " Wilderness," he crossed the Rapidan at the well-known Ely's Ford, twenty miles above Fredericksburg. Here Lafayette's troops felt secure from pursuit, especially as heavy rains soon rendered the ford impassable. Here, also, Wayne was heard from, marching down from Frederick to the Potomac.[1]

Meanwhile Cornwallis halted at the North Anna. The " celerity " of Lafayette's march on the retreat put an engagement out of the question. Once Tarleton came up with him at the Mattapony, and made the Light Infantry " stand to arms," but he was twenty miles in advance of the main army, and no fighting took place. His principal trophy was a " rebel " mail he captured, including a letter from Lafayette to Jefferson, which could have afforded the enemy but little consolation. It was a prophetic declaration that the British success in Virginia, which resembled the French invasion and possession of Hanover, in the Seven Years' War, was likely to end in similar failure, " if the government and country would exert themselves at the present juncture." It only remained now for Cornwallis to turn his attention to the destruction of stores, and from the North Anna, accordingly, we find him diverting his course. His own report to Clinton best expresses the object of his subsequent movements.

---

[1] The route from Richmond is described as follows by a militia officer: " I joined the marquis's army the night they left Richmond, and encamped with the army at Winston's Plantation, I believe in the County of Hanover. The next day to Scotch Town, thence to Dandridge's, in the said county, where the army halted a day or two. The route from thence was in the direction of Fredericksburg. After marching about two days, halted at Corbin's Bridges, in the County of Spottsylvania, where the army lay two nights and one day. The route from thence was to Culpepper County, near the Rackoon Ford, where we halted until Wayne's brigade joined."—BURK's *Virginia*, vol. iv., p. 507, note.

That Lafayette crossed the Rapidan at Ely's Ford appears from a letter dated from that point June 4th. From " Matoponi Church," June 3d, he wrote this note to Steuben: " I have to inform you that an express, with despatches from his Excellency Governor Jefferson to me, has fallen into Tarleton's hands. I am fearful there was some despatches from you accompanied them, containing some plans and information of our stores. I wish you to inform me as soon as you can. I wish the expresses to be directed to come by the route of Orange Court House—they should always pursue a safe route, even if they are detained some time longer."—*Gates MS.*

LIEUTENANT-COLONEL TARLETON, BRITISH LEGION. [FROM THE PAINTING BY SIR JOSHUA REYNOLDS IN THE GOVERNOR'S MANSION, RICHMOND, VA.]

"After passing James River at Westover," he writes, "I moved to Hanover Court House, and crossed South Anna. The Marquis de la Fayette marched to his left, keeping above at the distance of about twenty miles. By pushing my light troops over the North Anna, I alarmed the enemy for Fredericksburgh, and for the junction with General Wayne, who was then marching through Maryland. From what I could learn of the present state of Hunter's iron manufactory [at Falmouth, opposite Fredericksburg], it did not appear of so much importance as the stores on the other side of the country, and it was impossible to prevent the junction between the marquis and Wayne: I therefore took advantage of the marquis's passing the Rhappahannock and detached Lieutenant-colonels Simcoe and Tarleton to disturb the Assembly, then sitting at Charlotteville, and to destroy the stores there, at Old Albemarle Court House, and the Point of Fork; moving with the infantry to the mouth of Byrd Creek, near the Point of Fork, to receive these detachments."

These expeditions were the alarming incidents of Cornwallis's invasion. They startled the inhabitants east of the mountains into a realization of their insecurity. Their depressing effect was of more consequence than the material damage inflicted; but even this, as the result of Lafayette's energy and happy manœuvres, was not to be of long duration. The raid to Charlottesville was conducted by Tarleton; that to the Point of Fork, west of Richmond, where the James is formed by two branches, by Simcoe.

At Charlottesville the Virginia Legislature had convened to concert measures for the better defence of the State. Its dispersion was an object, and in addition powder and a few arms had been stored there. Tarleton met with some success in his enterprise. Taking one hundred and eighty dragoons and seventy mounted infantry, he proceeded west to Louisa Court House, made a forced march to Charlottesville, and nearly surprised the entire Assembly, on Monday, June 4th, seizing some of its members, and all but capturing Jefferson, the governor. He also destroyed the stores. Simcoe, with one hundred cavalry and three hundred infantry, succeeded, on his part, in compelling Steuben to retreat rapidly from the Point of Fork, on the 5th, and destroyed arms and supplies. Both raiders then joined Cornwallis at Elk Hill, a few miles below Point of Fork, which he reached, with the main army, on the 7th.[1]

---

[1] Simcoe and Tarleton make much of these raids, but their descriptions are colored. With the former's account in his "Journal" read Kapp's "Life of Steuben." Tarleton states that he took a General Scott prisoner at Charlottesville, which proves to be an

Lafayette, who from Ely's Ford had moved along the northern bank of the Rapidan to Raccoon Ford above, was distressed to hear of these incursions, but had wisely decided to wait for the Pennsylvania line before placing himself in front of the enemy. He tells us in his "Memoirs" that he had made "all his calculations so as to be able to effect a junction with that corps, without being prevented from covering the military magazines of the Southern States, which were at the foot of the mountains on the heights of the Fluvanna." But the Pennsylvanians were delayed, and he was "thus obliged to make a choice."

The delay in the arrival of Wayne and his corps was to be referred mainly to those common and vexing causes which had embarrassed American operations from the beginning of the war—lack of supplies, quartermaster's stores especially, and unsatisfied pay-rolls.[1] This officer had been ordered southward in February, but could not leave until May.

---

error—the Continental General Scott not then being in the State, and no other by that name serving in Virginia. Colonel John Smith wrote from Winchester, June 18th (MS. letter), that "no money was taken by Tarleton, nor did our Types fall into his hands." Perhaps the best American account of Tarleton's doings is that in Burk's "History of Virginia," vol. iv. Tarleton certainly rode very rapidly, and would probably have caught more than three or four members of the Legislature, but for Captain John Jouett, a resident on the route, who, like Paul Revere, at Boston, suspecting the object of the enemy, mounted a swift horse and reached Charlottesville first, giving the alarm in time. (See records of Virginia Assembly, June 12th, 1781, for a resolution to present Jouett an "elegant sword and pair of pistols," for apprising that body of its danger.)

As to Governor Jefferson, Burk says that he was entertaining the Speaker and other members of the Assembly when news came of Tarleton's approach. The Speaker immediately convened and then adjourned the Legislature to Staunton. Captain McLeod, of Tarleton's Legion, took the direct route to Jefferson's house by the Secretary's Ford. The party, says Burk, "were already ascending the winding road that leads from that point to the summit of the hill called Monticello, on which stands Mr. Jefferson's house, when Lieutenant Hudson, who had fortunately descried this rapid advance, gave the family a further and last alarm. A carriage had already been provided, and in this Mrs. Jefferson and her children were safely conveyed to Colonel Carter's house, on the neighboring mountain. Mr. Jefferson himself, directing his riding-horse, which a blacksmith was then shoeing at a distant shop, to be, with all possible speed, led to a gate opening on the road to Colonel Carter's plantation, walked to that gate by a foot-path, which considerably shortened the route, and, finding his injunction obeyed, was enabled soon to rejoin his family. In less than ten minutes after his leaving the house it was entered by McLeod."—*History of Virginia*, vol. iv., p. 502.

[1] Colonel Grayson, of Virginia, wrote from Philadelphia, April 17th, 1781: "The Marquis la Fayette is on his march to the southward—Wayne, with a thousand men, can't move a peg at present for the want of cash; if we get him off in ten days from this, it is as much as I expect."—*Am. Hist. Record*, vol. ii., p. 87.

His force, composed of the greater part of the Pennsylvania line, as re-organized since its mutiny in January, consisted of three regiments—in all, a thousand men—commanded by the brave and experienced colonels, Richard Butler, Walter Stewart, and Richard Humpton. Nine officers and ninety men, with six field-pieces, from Proctor's Fourth Continental Artillery, completed the detachment. Nor, when all was in readiness, were the men to leave in the best of humor. They had recently been paid off in the current notes without their depreciated value added, and dissatisfaction at once ran high. Certain leaders went so far as to mani-fest the old dangerous spirit of insubordination, which called for and received prompt and effective treatment. A drum-head court-martial was held in camp, and seven of their number tried and executed.[1] This disturbance quelled, the troops left York, Pennsylvania, on the morning of May 26th, and on the 30th were at Frederick, Maryland. There, in reply to urgent letters to push on to Virginia, Wayne wrote as follows to Lafayette: "I well know the necessity of an immediate junction, and beg leave to assure you that our anxiety for that event is equal to your wishes; may it be speedy and propitious. I wish our numbers were something more; however, we must endeavor to stem this torrent; and if we have it not in our power to command success, I trust, my dear Marquis, that we shall produce a conviction to the world that we de-serve it."

Crossing the Potomac the following day, the 31st, at Noland's Ferry, the command passed through Leesburg on June 4th, and that night en-camped at Cook's Mills, on Goose Creek. There, on the 5th, the sick and the heavy baggage were left, and the march resumed eighteen miles to the Red House, in the vicinity of Thoroughfare Gap. Rains and heavy roads prevented rapid progress. On the 7th the men halted to "refresh and furbish up," and not till the 9th did they reach Raccoon Ford, at the Rapidan, by way of Norman's Ford, on the Rappahannock. At last, on the 10th, they fell into the same road with and joined La-fayette's force about a dozen miles south of the crossing.[2] Wayne, rid-ing in advance of his troops, appears to have reached the marquis's head-quarters on the 7th.

This important junction effected—a re-enforcement of a thousand good soldiers under a gallant leader—Lafayette lost no time in march-

---

[1] Wayne's papers, published in Philadelphia *Casket*, 1829; "Journal" of Lieutenant Denny, Penn. Hist. Soc. Publications.

[2] Feltman's "Journal," Penn. Hist. Soc. Publications.

ing toward his powerful antagonist. His increase of force had not rendered him the less cautious; but there were magazines still within the enemy's reach, and to protect these he proposed to strain every nerve. Indeed, as Lafayette feared, Cornwallis had already organized an expedition to destroy them, which Tarleton, as usual, was to lead. With the Seventy-sixth Highlanders attached to his Legion as mounted infantry, this eager raider was directed to march to Albemarle Old Court House, upon the north bank of the James or Fluvanna River, some distance above the Point of Fork, destroy the stores collected there; move upon Steuben below, employ "every means" to break up his force; and, proceeding as far as the Dan, intercept any detachments marching up from the southward. "I likewise recommend it to you," ran the orders of Cornwallis, "to destroy all the enemy's stores and tobacco between James River and the Dan; and if there should be a quantity of provisions or corn collected at a private house, I would have you destroy it, even although there should be no proof of its being intended for the public service, leaving enough for the support of the family; as there is the greatest reason to apprehend that such provisions will be ultimately appropriated by the enemy to the use of General Greene's army, which, from the present state of the Carolinas, must depend on this province for its supplies."[1] The success of this expedition, which was to move on the morning of the 10th, would have caused the Americans serious embarrassment; but, unexpectedly, on the eve of its start Cornwallis countermanded his order, and Tarleton remained in camp. In explanation of this, the latter officer states in his "Campaigns" that intelligence had been received that the stores at Albemarle Court House had been removed, and that Steuben was too distant to reach. There can be little doubt, however, that the true reason which influenced Cornwallis to hold Tarleton back was, the more important information that Lafayette, re-enforced by Wayne, was marching down from the Rapidan, and in forty-eight hours might be in close proximity to the British. An opportunity would thus be offered to strike at the marquis, in which case Tarleton's presence would be necessary. This explanation is supported by the facts that Cornwallis, who had proposed to countermarch to Richmond on the 10th, did not move until the 15th, and that in the mean time Tarleton was kept busy watching and reporting the movements of the Americans.

From the Rapidan, Lafayette had, in fact, marched with all speed

---

[1] Tarleton's "Campaigns," p. 354.

toward the enemy. There was no delay after Wayne joined him. The troops all moved straight on, the same day, the 10th, as far as the North Anna. Crossing that stream at Brock's Bridge, twelve miles east of the present Gordonsville, they traversed Louisa County southward, and encamped on the 11th near Boswell's Tavern, at the South Anna.[1] From this point it was necessary to advance cautiously, for it will be observed that, to reach the main road from the enemy to Charlottesville and Staunton, whither the Albemarle stores had been removed, but where they were still exposed to a raid, he must present his flank to an attack by the British van. That road, known as the Three Notches Road, he must reach at some point, to protect the stores to the west; but to proceed directly from Boswell's in the usual way would have been somewhat hazardous. Fortunately, an old road, little known and long unused, ran through the woods in the same direction, and of this Lafayette promptly availed himself. Repairing it during the night of the 11th, the troops on the following morning took up their march along this route. Hardly more than a foot-path they found it, rough and narrow, overgrown with thickets, through which the artillery was dragged with difficulty; but they were completely concealed from the enemy's patrols, and when at evening they encamped in "an impregnable position" behind Mechunck Creek, thirteen miles east of Charlottesville, near "one Allegree's," they were gratified to know that they had placed themselves directly between Cornwallis and the magazines which he had hoped to destroy.[2]

At this point Lafayette felt a sensible relief, and on the morning

---

[1] At the present Munford's Bridge.

[2] This march appears to have put the enemy a day behind in their information and movements. Simcoe moved at midnight of the 13th upon Bird's Ordinary, on the Three Notches Road, only to find that the marquis was twenty-four hours in advance of and fifteen miles beyond him.

The militia officer quoted *ante* says further, in regard to the march: "The route from thence [Raccoon Ford] was in by-roads in direction of the Rivanna River, through Orange, the upper end of Louisa and Fluvanna Counties. Near Boswell's Tavern the army halted one night, and the next day was marched along a new road to Mechunck Creek, which road goes by the name of the Marquis's Road to this day. The army halted a day or two at this place, and the route from thence was generally in the course most direct to Williamsburg."—BURK's *Virginia*, vol. iv., p. 507, note.

The command halted on the night of the 10th, after a hard march, at Brock's Bridge, where one of Lafayette's letters is dated. For the next two days the diary of Captain McLellan, of the Pennsylvania line, runs: "June 11th.—Marched at 5, and halted at South Anna Creek [Boswell's, present Munford Bridge], being ten miles. June 12th.—Marched at 7, and halted at Machunk."—*Penn. Archives*, N. S., vol. xi.

after his arrival wrote to Steuben as follows: "Mechunk Creek, Allegre's, 13th June. . . . Our junction with the Pennsylvanians is formed, and we have again got between the enemy and our stores. Nothing has been lost but what was left on the Point, and the few articles that, notwithstanding your and my directions, it had been thought proper to send to Charlottesville. I have ordered the stores to be removed higher up, and am now in a better situation to defend them. I request, my dear sir, you will immediately return this way, and, with the Continentals and militia under your command, hasten to form a junction with us. . . . Should the enemy cross James River, what I do not believe, and none of them has yet attempted, it must be with a view to reconquer Carolina. In this case you would be in the way, and I would request every obstruction to be given them, as I shall myself follow them as expeditiously as possible. But, on the contrary, should they make the conquest of this State their main object, our united force is not too much to resist them. In case you had received some different directions from the General [Greene], my dispositions will, of course, be suspended and go for nothing."[1]

It had now been three weeks since the opening of the campaign in Virginia. The immediate and obvious results were almost wholly in favor of the enemy. They had gone where they pleased, and destroyed much public and private property. There had been no fighting, for there was no force which dared to meet them. Lafayette had played his part well in keeping out of harm's way, but not until later was he to command confidence and be fully appreciated. Attention was turned upon Cornwallis as the present scourge. Leading men in the State had become thoroughly alarmed, and discussed the situation with fear and suspense. Virginia, indeed, was quite unprepared for an invasion so sudden as this. Long security, occasionally disturbed on her western frontier or at the seaboard, had thrown her off her guard in the matter of an effective home defence. The centres of operation being north and south of her, less dread of danger had been felt within her borders, especially in the interior, and she was now called upon to suffer, in part, the consequences of unreadiness. All this was well understood by her public men. Among others, and perhaps more than any other, Richard Henry Lee was aroused to the critical state of affairs, and he sought the means of salvation. He saw no help except through the interposition of Congress, and the presence of Washington himself in Virginia. His letters

---

[1] Gates MS.

to delegates from his own and other States were urgent in the matter. To Lovell, member from Massachusetts, he wrote: "I love liberty, and wish that the whole human race enjoyed it; and I have a peculiar affection for that of the eastern part of the Union. Let me entreat you, therefore, sir, and your worthy associates from the East, not to slumber a moment over our present actual state. Decision, despatch, and much wisdom are indispensably necessary, or I verily believe we shall be lost to ourselves and you. I do not write under any influences of vain apprehensions, but from the cool, considerate dictates of judgment founded upon good materials. A very great majority of the people of this country are Whigs, and very determined to maintain their independence; and, being so, how they came into their present state of thraldom is beside my present purpose to inquire. Like good physicians, the Congress will consider that the inordinancy of the symptoms must be subdued, before application can with safety be made to the cause." Then, as to the remedy, Lee continued: "Let General Washington be immediately sent to Virginia with two or three thousand good troops. Let Congress, as the head of the Federal Union in this crisis, direct that, until the Legislature can convene and a governor be appointed, the general be possessed of dictatorial powers, and that it be strongly recommended to the Assembly, when convened, to continue those powers for six, eight, or ten months, as the case may be. . . . You may be assured, sir, that if this is quickly done, and arms and ammunition forwarded, the enemy's possessions in the South will be very few, and the prospects they may propose to themselves from a truce thus rendered abortive."[1] To Washington Lee wrote quite as urgently, pressing him to come to Virginia. So, too, did Jefferson, who thought that if the commander-in-chief lent his "personal aid" to the State, the difficulty would then be "how to keep men out of the field." John Cadwalader, of Maryland, was of the same opinion. He felt that the British were playing a deep game, the success of which might involve America in ruin. Writing to Washington from Annapolis, June 5th, he says: "That the enemy intend to make the Southern States the scene of action, the ensuing campaign, is past a doubt; and the consequences are easily foreseen, unless considerable re-enforcements very soon arrive either from France or the Northern army. . . . The possession of these States must be of the last importance to the enemy; because in these they possess the tobacco, rice, indigo, and naval stores, which to them, perhaps, are more valuable than all the other States together. These, too, are separated by a great natural line from the other States; and it appears to me more than probable, considering all circumstances, that Great Britain finds it impracticable to possess themselves of all America, and is now preparing to conquer these States, in hopes that the powers of Europe, by their interposition, will secure them to her."

THOMAS JEFFERSON. [FROM THE ORIGINAL PORTRAIT BY GILBERT STUART.]

Then, with Lee and Jefferson, he added his wish, as well as "the wish of every person he had conversed with," that Washington would immediately take the command in Virginia.

Deeply as the commander-in-chief was moved by these appeals, he could only return a negative answer. It will be seen that he had just entered upon a definite plan of operations in the North, which he hoped would relieve the pressure upon the South, and its alteration could not be entertained. There was the further consideration that Washington was the only American officer who had the power to command the French auxiliaries, who were about to join him for an active campaign. But one other general, next to the chief, could by his presence and movements have allayed the alarm in Virginia more speedily than Lafayette; and this was Greene. Much, however, as he wished to come to the State, he felt that he must stay in South Carolina, where the enemy had lately been re-enforced. "I feel for the sufferings of Virginia," he wrote to Jefferson, June 27th, "and, if I had been supported here in time, I should have been there before this with a great part of our cavalry. But, though I have not had it in my power to join the army, I hope your Legislature are convinced that I have left nothing unattempted in my power to afford you all possible protection." "The importance of cavalry," he continues, "and the consequences that might follow the want of it, your Excellency will do me the justice to say I early and earnestly endeavored to impress upon your Legislature, and they must blame themselves if they experience any extraordinary calamities. You would have been in a tolerable situation had your cavalry been sufficiently augmented, and the last re-enforcement from New York had not arrived. This gave the enemy such a decided superiority that there appears nothing left but to avoid a misfortune until re-enforcements can be got from the northward. I have the highest opinion of the marquis's abilities and zeal, and flatter myself that nothing will be left unattempted to give all the protection to the State that his force will admit. Your militia are numerous and formidable, and I hope, if General Morgan is out with them, they will be useful." [1]

So neither Washington nor Greene, at the two extremes of the field, could go to the threatened centre in Virginia, and Lafayette was left to continue its defence as best he could. Events proved that the confidence reposed in him by his superiors was not misplaced. "What a herculean task we have," wrote Greene to him, "to contend with a formidable enemy with a handful of men!" But the marquis was equal to it. His shoulders seemed to broaden under the accumulating responsibilities; and when the campaign closed with Yorktown, neither friends nor enemies were slow to recognize how greatly his services had contributed to the event.

But to return to the field. Lafayette had at least accomplished two things: he had become stronger by retreating, and upon his reappearance

---

[1] Greene's "Greene," vol. iii., appendix.

before the enemy had, for the time being, stopped Tarleton's threatened raid. Interest, accordingly, centred on the enemy's next move. It remained to be seen whether Cornwallis would persist in his attempt upon the stores in spite of Lafayette—whether he would advance upon and engage him while Tarleton struck out upon his expedition, as originally proposed, or whether he would turn back toward the coast. One thing is certain, that Lafayette, although further re-enforced at the Mechunk, according to previous appointment, by six hundred mountain riflemen from Augusta and adjacent counties, under General Campbell, of King's Mountain fame, had still no intention of risking a battle; and, had the enemy moved upon him, he would doubtless have retreated along the line of his stores and communications either toward Greene below or to the northward.

All doubt upon these points was solved on the 15th, when Cornwallis broke camp at Elk Hill and faced eastward toward Richmond. Here, finally, was a retrograde march by the enemy—a favorable turn, apparently, for affairs in Virginia. The Americans, troops and people alike, regarded it with relief and satisfaction, and naturally construed the movement into an admission, on the part of Cornwallis, that he had been disappointed in failing to destroy all the magazines, and in not finding a loyal element ready to support the King's authority when established. The growing proportions of Lafayette's force were also supposed to have moderated his inclination to continue his invasion; and Lafayette himself took this view in part. But, of course, Cornwallis had not changed his tactics either from fear or compulsion. Although not having destroyed as much as he had hoped, he was still master of the situation, and could move at will in any direction. He had carried out his first intentions, and was turning back to the waters of the Chesapeake, to await instructions and arrange further plans with his commander-in-chief at New York.

As the enemy marched back Lafayette followed, hanging upon their rear — a new sensation for his command. He had not, as sometimes stated, assumed the offensive. His force was still weak in quality compared with the British regulars, and he could do little more than watch and skirmish. Marching rapidly, Cornwallis entered Richmond on the 16th. Lafayette, moving from the Mechunk on the 14th, along the line of the South Anna, kept off a distance of about twenty miles. What with the heat and not over-abundant supplies, it was a wearing time for his men. The entry in Lieutenant Feltman's journal for the 15th runs: "A great scarcity of water, and a very fatiguing march. . . . Refreshed ourselves in an orchard with Colonel Robinson." Captain Roger Welles, of the Connecticut Light Infantry, acknowledging a letter from his father, wrote on the 16th: "It found me very destitute of summer clothes and almost every other necessary requisite to render life tolerable in this uninhabited world. We frequently march whole days without seeing anything like a house except a log hut or two."[1] On the other hand, as to personal experiences in the enemy's camp, Captain Samuel Graham, of the Seventy-sixth Regulars, writes, in his "Memoirs:" "Our encampments were always chosen on the banks of a stream, and were extremely picturesque, as we had no tents, and were obliged to construct wigwams of fresh boughs to keep off the rays of the sun during the day. At night the blazing fires which we made of the fence-rails illuminated the surrounding scenery, which, in this part of America, is of the most magnificent description. There was but one wish in the army, which was to come up with the marquis. At parting with my friends in the evening, it was always 'Prœlium pugnatum est!'"[2]

On the 17th Lafayette's camp was once more at Dandridge's, on the South Anna, in Hanover County, north-west of Richmond, with detachments and patrols well thrown out toward the enemy. One of these parties, four hundred strong, under Muhlenberg, tempted Tarleton, who was posted at Meadow Bridge, on the Chickahominy, and on the 18th he made a forced march to surprise it. Hearing of this, Lafayette at once despatched Wayne with the Pennsylvanians and Light Infantry to intercept him. Both failed. Tarleton missed Muhlenberg, who retreated in time; Wayne, after a night march of thirteen miles, missed Tarleton, who had also turned back. On the 19th another re-enforcement reached the marquis in the shape of General Steuben, with about four hundred and fifty Virginia eighteen-months men, increasing the American force to two thousand Continentals and three thousand two hundred militia and riflemen. Steuben himself, afflicted with the gout and overcome by incessant exertion and fatigue, soon retired to the vicinity of Charlottesville to recuperate.

From Richmond Cornwallis resumed his march coastward on the 20th. Lafayette, who changed his camp every day, continued to follow, his advance entering the town twenty hours after the enemy left.[3] It was not

---

[1] MS. letter.

[2] "Memoirs of General Graham." Privately printed. Edinburgh.

[3] From Lafayette's position at Mechunk's Creek, in the vicinity of the present Boyd's Tavern, the route lay along the right bank of the South Anna. On June 15th, the day after leaving Mechunk, the marquis was probably near Boswell's. There he wrote

quite a month since he had quitted it to keep out of his Lordship's way. But by no means were the tables turned as yet. Lafayette was far from pursuing his late pursuer. However ignorant he might be of the true cause of the enemy's retreat, he well understood that at any moment it might be turned into an advance and chase again, and that it behooved him to be studiously wary in following. He kept to his rule of retaining "a posture of defence," manœuvring only, and above all avoiding a general engagement. At the same time he watched the enemy's rear, and sought opportunities to strike at it;[1] and in a day or two the opportunity came. Once, on the 23d, Cornwallis stopped, and was on the point of making a sudden countermarch to attack Lafayette, who had ventured

---

again to Steuben, who had retreated toward North Carolina after Simcoe's raid, to join him as soon as possible: "Lord Cornwallis is retiring to Richmond, and we are following him. . . . I will be, the day after to-morrow, at Col. Dandridge's, twenty-two miles from Richmond. I understand it is twenty-five miles from Carter's Ferry. Should you be able to join us by the 17th or 18th it will make me very happy."— *Gates MS.*

On the next day Lieutenant-colonel Barber wrote to his wife as follows: "On Pomonkie River, forty miles from Richmond, June 16th, 1781 [the South Anna was then also called the Pamunkey]. . . . We as yet have had no action with the enemy. They have made a third tack, and are now at Richmond. Their behavior wears the appearance of a retreat. Since my last we are re-enforced very considerably—Wayne has come with three battalions. We now begin to imagine ourselves a match for the enemy, and unless they receive re-enforcements they must undoubtedly retire to Portsmouth. From the most accurate intelligence the enemy are about 4000 strong, and we expect within three or four days to have that number of militia."—*MS. Letter.*

On the 18th Lafayette was at Allen's Creek, and at night at Goldmine Creek again, where he wrote to Steuben: "Col. Dandridge's house, twenty-three miles from Richmond, 18th June, 1781. . . . The enemy are at Richmond and its vicinity. We are upon ground in this neighborhood where we shall remain for your junction, which I request may be made to-morrow as early as possible." For the 21st and 22d Lieutenant Feltman's record is this: "June 21st.—Arrived at Col. Simm's Mills. Marched at 12 o'clock A.M., eight miles, and lay at Burrill's Ornery, destitute of every necessary of life. 22d.—This day we passed through Richmond in twenty hours after the enemy had evacuated it—a number of houses being destroyed by the enemy. They also destroyed a great quantity of tobacco, which they threw into the streets and set fire to it."

[1] The Wayne Papers show that Lafayette wished to attack, if he could do so safely, as, for instance, the following note:

"Head-quarters, 21st June, 1781.

"MY DEAR SIR,—By the time you receive this you must have accounts from the enemy. Should they be near us, this would be the good time for the night attack; but I am afraid we shall not have the opportunity. Whatever road the enemy take, you will please to proceed in that route, and, if opportunity offers, to attack them. You will do for the best.   Yours,   LAFAYETTE.

"GEN'L WAYNE."

nearer to him than usual. The alarm reached Wayne's camp, and the troops eagerly formed for action and stood to their arms for several hours. Cornwallis, however, kept on to Williamsburg; the American advance to Bottoms' Bridge, and on the 25th to New Kent Court House.

Lafayette's army at this date was composed of about forty-five hundred men, divided as follows: The New England Light Infantry, eight hundred effectives, under Muhlenberg, and Wayne's Pennsylvanians, seven hundred and fifty, were the Continental veterans — equal to the best in the English army. The three Virginia militia brigades were commanded by Generals Stevens, six hundred and fifty men; Lawson, seven hundred and fifty; and Campbell, with his seven hundred and eighty riflemen. The Virginia Continental regiment of eighteen-months men, commanded just now by Colonel Christian Febiger, an excellent officer, but generally by Lieutenant-colonel Thomas Gaskins, numbered four hundred and twenty-five. The artillery—detachments from the Second and Fourth Continental Regiments—was two hundred strong, with eight or ten guns. The regular cavalry was represented by only sixty indifferent horsemen, to whom are to be added about as many volunteer dragoons.[1] It was Lafayette's policy to scatter this force on different roads, to convey the impression of large numbers. It never encamped in line, and was so handled that concentration could be rapidly effected. Spies were thus likely to be deceived, and deserters could not give full information. Select detachments of Continentals and riflemen generally formed the advance, led by good officers, such as a small legion of the cavalry and a few infantry, commanded by Major William McPherson, of Pennsylvania, in whose abilities Lafayette had much confidence. Majors Richard Call and John Willis, two experienced officers of the Virginia line—the former of the Third Continental Cavalry—also commanded parties of one hundred or more good riflemen each; while Lieutenant-colonel John Mercer, already referred to, was constantly reconnoitring with his volunteer troop. Major Galvan, a French officer, of Vose's Massachusetts Light Infantry, had an "advanced guard" from his own corps. Organized in this way, and always on the move, marching as often by night as by day, Lafayette followed the British down the peninsula.

On the 26th occurred the first skirmish of the campaign; not a great affair—but it indicated a growing confidence on Lafayette's part,

---

[1] These figures are given by Colonel Febiger in a letter of July 3d, 1781.—*Bland Papers.*

and a natural wish not to let the enemy reach their shipping without a brush. On the day before, Simcoe's Rangers had been collecting cattle and burning stores above Williamsburg, where Cornwallis had halted. Wayne, with Lafayette's approval, despatched most of the advanced parties, under Colonel Richard Butler, one of the heroes of Stony Point, to intercept him on his return. Butler, with McPherson, Call, and Willis, marched from the American outposts all night of the 25th, but would still have failed to overtake Simcoe, had not McPherson, at sunrise, mounted fifty of the Light Infantry behind as many dragoons and pushed hard after him. Simcoe, meanwhile, had gone into camp six miles above Williamsburg, near Spencer's Ordinary, when McPherson dashed in upon his pickets. A trumpeter gave the alarm, and a brief hand-to-hand cavalry skirmish took place. McPherson was unhorsed, but escaped, and his dragoons scattered and retreated, under cover of the riflemen, who were coming up. The latter soon became engaged with the Rangers, and a desultory fire was kept up. Wayne, who had followed Butler with the Pennsylvania line, apprehending the situation, pushed Major Hamilton forward with several companies to support the cavalry and riflemen. Simcoe regarded the American attack as a serious one, and sent word to Cornwallis without delay, who immediately moved the whole army forward to his aid; but no further fighting occurred. The loss on each side was about thirty.[1]

For the week to come there was no material change in the situation. Cornwallis had halted. His future movements could not be divined. Lafayette still hovered in his vicinity, shifting his camp almost daily. The record for the 3d of July in Feltman's diary is brief but expressive: "Manœuvres retrograde and many; the troops almost worn out; very hot weather." On that date the position of the troops was as follows: General Campbell, with the riflemen, in front, near Bird's Ordinary, sixteen miles from Williamsburg; Febiger's Virginia detachment four miles in his rear; Wayne and Muhlenberg one mile and a half farther back; and in their rear the militia and artillery.[2] Febiger states that the army had not been encamped so closely as this for nearly three weeks. On the 4th the troops celebrated "Independence" in true camp style, parading and firing salutes. Notwithstanding their constant and fatiguing duty,

---

[1] See return of American loss in Appendix. Simcoe describes this skirmish minutely, leaving the impression that it was a considerable engagement, won by his generalship.

[2] Colonel Febiger to Colonel Bland, July 3d, 1781.—*Bland Papers.*

NOTE

Lafayette leaves Richmond, May 27.
   ,,   ,, returns, following
     Cornwallis, June 21.
   ,,   ,, passes through from
     Malvern Hill, Aug. 1-2.

LAFAYETTE -----
CORNWALLIS ....

Albemarle Old C.H.

Willis R.

James or Fluvanna River

Charlottesville June 13

Rivanna River

Mechunk Cr.

V

Point of Fork

CORNWALLIS June 7-14

I

James River

June 14

Wayne joins June 10

Racoon Ford

Rapidan R.

Norman's Ford

Wayne June 8

Elg's Ford June 4

Rappahannock R.

Three Notched Road

Boswell's June 11

Tarleton's Raid June 11

South Anna R.

Brock's Br. June 10

Corbin's Br. June 3

Mattapony Church June 2

Wilderness

Spotsylvania C.H.

Fredericksburg

R

Jack's Br.

Dandridge June 16

Allen's

North Anna R.

Anderson's Br. May 31

N

I

Rappahannock River

R.

May 29-31

Ground Br. June 4

Hanover C.H.

Cub Creek

Ely's Ford June 1

Bowling Green

RICHMOND Aug. 14th

LAFAYETTE May 27

Page May 28

Winston's Br. May 28.

Meadow Br.

White Oak Swamp May 27

New Castle May 29

Aylett's

Pamunkey R.

A

LAFAYETTE May 24

CORNWALLIS May 24

Petersburg

Appomatox R.

Westover

Malvern Hill July 6-10

Bottoms Br. May 23

New Kent C.H.

Chickahominy R.

Mattapony River

Rappahannock

River

Aug. 4-6

Aug. 10-13

Spencer's Ord. June 26.

Green Spring July 6.

Williamsburg Sept. 7

YORKTOWN

Gloucester

YORK RIVER

JAMES R.

being subject to alarms and calls to march at all hours, day and night, they seem to have been in good spirits, under the conviction that they had at last put Cornwallis upon his guard and saved the State. An interesting letter from camp, written on the 4th, indicates satisfaction with results thus far. "Lord Cornwallis," says the writer, "is now in Williamsburg. His single tour to Virginia has cost the King more money, by the loss of forts, men, cannon, stores, magazines, and supposed Carolina territory, than it would have cost the whole nobility of England to have made the tour of the world. His Lordship had a most fatiguing march to the Point of Fork and back again. The marquis was to him what Fabius was to Hannibal. Before Wayne made his junction he never lost sight of his Lordship; and when the junction was formed, by the single manœuvre of opening a march through the wood which intersected his Lordship, preserved the stores at Old Albermarle Court House, which the enemy had principally in view. As yet the war between the marquis and his Lordship has been a war of posts and marches. The King of Prussia and the Emperor carried on a war much in the same manner. It is a question, however, whether this will have a like conclusion, as theirs was closed without a battle. The vanguard of this army is within twelve miles of Williamsburg. His Lordship does not seem quite satisfied with its neighborhood. There is in it, also, men who have given him reason to fear them—General Campbell, who took a little army from him at King's Mountain, and General Morgan, who took another at the Cowpens."[1]

Events now hastened Cornwallis to his fate at Yorktown. His leisurely withdrawal from the heart of the State indicated some settled purpose on his part of which the Americans were ignorant. It is to be repeated that he was not forced to retreat to Williamsburg. Then why had he gone there? What would be his next move? Lafayette could only wait and see. Cornwallis hoped that from Williamsburg, or some point on the Chesapeake, he would be able, by the consent and co-operation of Clinton at New York, to renew the Virginia Campaign as soon as the heated season was over. He had entered the State for the one purpose of eventually subjugating it; he favored "solid operations" there. Clinton agreed with him, but claimed that the force was not to be had for so extensive an undertaking. Cornwallis, we have seen, suggested the abandonment of New York, if necessary, while Clinton could not assent. But the question of future operations in Virginia soon ceased to

[1] Letter from "A Gentleman in Lafayette's Army," in Baltimore paper, July, 1781.

be a primary matter with the British commander-in-chief, as we shall presently find that Washington was now threatening him, and he felt obliged to send to Cornwallis for a portion of the troops previously sent to the Chesapeake. The latter promptly obeyed, and, to embark the troops, determined to retire to Portsmouth by crossing the James River at Jamestown Island.

Lafayette's opportunity now seemed to be at hand. Might he not inflict upon Cornwallis a damaging stroke while he was crossing the James? As a successful dash could be turned to good account at that juncture in still further cheering the spirits of his own troops, and putting a brighter face upon the situation in Virginia, the marquis proposed to make the attempt; and what followed is known in Revolutionary annals as the action or affair of "Green Spring." Lafayette failed to accomplish what he hoped might be possible, but, on the contrary, suffered a repulse, which has been variously criticised; and, in noticing the affair, the point is material how far he departed on this occasion from his policy of acting on the safe defensive, and committed himself to the chance of a disastrous defeat.

BATTLE OF GREEN SPRING.

The collision occurred on the 6th. Lafayette's movements on that and the previous day seem to have been conducted with his usual caution and vigilance. Learning through Mercer that the enemy had left Williamsburg, and were at the bank of the James, and fathoming their intention, he broke up his camp on the 5th, and marched to Bird's Tavern with all the troops.[1] The Continentals and advance parties kept on to Chickahominy Church, or Norrell's Mills, eight miles from Jamestown, where they lay on their arms all night.[2] On the following morning "corroborating advices" arrived, to the effect that the enemy were engaged in crossing, and that only the rear guard remained on the Jamestown side. Lafayette, thereupon, determined to despatch Wayne with five hundred men to "come up" with it. Wayne took Colonel Stewart's Pennsylvania battalion, with Mercer's, McPherson's, Galvan's, Call's, and Willis's small parties, and marched to the Green Spring Farm, within half a mile of the British outposts. At this point conflicting intelligence was received. Mercer, on one hand, ascertained through a negro that

---

[1] On the 5th Lafayette was encamped below New Kent Court House. Bird's Tavern was sixteen miles from Williamsburg, on the road to the Court House. Green Spring Farm lies a few miles west of Williamsburg.

[2] Lafayette's Letters. Feltman's "Journal."

both Cornwallis and Tarleton were still on the north side of the river, while others reported the frequent passage of boats to the opposite bank. Under these circumstances Lafayette, who had joined Wayne and the advance, decided, not far from one o'clock in the afternoon, to send for the remaining Pennsylvanians and all the Light Infantry, left six miles back at Norrell's Mills, to be nearer Wayne, in case he encountered the enemy in considerable force. Upon receiving the order, the troops at the Mills marched promptly and very rapidly to Green Spring. The militia, who are commonly represented as also having marched to the same spot, remained at Bird's Tavern, at least twelve miles in the rear, and took no part in the movements of the day.

The Green Spring Farm, whose mansion had been the residence of Sir William Berkeley, an early Governor of Virginia, fell off, along its south-eastern edge, into low, marshy ground, some four hundred yards wide, across which ran a narrow causeway and road which intersected the main road from Williamsburg to Jamestown. By following the latter road a mile or more from the marsh the camp of the enemy would be reached, pitched compactly behind woods on the bank of the river opposite the north end of Jamestown Island. The enemy were still there. Cornwallis had shrewdly conjectured that Lafayette would take the occasion to attack his rear, and when he learned of his approach he did everything to confirm his antagonist in the belief that at that time, the afternoon of the 6th, only his rear remained to cross. Simcoe's Rangers and the baggage alone had passed over. If Lafayette approached near enough, the main body of the British army was ready to fall upon him.

Pending the arrival of the troops from Norrell's Mills, Wayne spent most of the afternoon skirmishing with the enemy. The patrols of Tarleton's Legion, which covered their front, were driven back over the morass, and the infantry pickets attacked in the woods on the other side. This continued between three and five o'clock. Wayne's entire advance crossed the morass, gaining ground steadily as the riflemen, under Majors Call and Willis, supported by Mercer, Galvan, and McPherson, with a few dragoons and light infantry, kept up an effective fire in front. Stewart's Pennsylvania battalion acted as a reserve. The striking feature of this preliminary skirmishing was the art practised by Cornwallis in attempting to draw Wayne and Lafayette to destruction. The falling back of Tarleton's outposts was intended to convey the impression that nothing but the rear-guard of the British remained on this side of the James, and that it was in no condition to resist beyond the bank of the river under cover of the shipping. In the woods the infantry pickets made a stand, to confirm the impression that they were finally forced to fight, whereas, in reality, Cornwallis had ordered them to hold their position, in order to conceal the main army from view, lying in open ground immediately behind. Some sharp work seems to have been done here. The riflemen, says Lafayette, "threw down" successively three officers commanding the enemy's picket; and Captain Graham, of the Seventy-sixth Foot, confirms this in his "Memoirs," as follows: "The picket-guard of Colonel Dundas's brigade, consisting of men of the Seventy-sixth Regiment, commanded by Lieutenant Balneaves, an officer of the Eightieth Regiment, was ordered to resist as long as possible, which they did for a length of time. The lieutenant was killed; and Lieutenant Alston, of the same regiment, having taken the command, was severely wounded; and after him Ensign Wemyss, of the Seventy-sixth, was also wounded, when the picket received orders to retire." It will be noticed that in his General Orders, and in his letter to General Greene of July 8th, Lafayette compliments the riflemen on the gallantry and skill displayed by them on this occasion.

About five o'clock in the afternoon, accordingly, we find Wayne and his detachment of five hundred men engaged within a short distance of Cornwallis and all his army, Simcoe's Rangers excepted. Wayne, of course, did not dream that his position was so hazardous. On the other hand, Cornwallis was uncertain what force supported the American riflemen; and while he could readily have crushed Wayne at four o'clock, he postponed an advance until he was assured that there was something in his front worth striking at.

Meanwhile, shortly before five o'clock, the Light Infantry and the two remaining Pennsylvania battalions, Butler's and Humpton's, with some artillery, arrived at the Green Spring Farm, "by a most rapid move," from Norrell's Mills. Lafayette now had with him at the front all his veteran Continentals, who, though a match for any equal force of the enemy, were quite unequal to the force Cornwallis could just then draw up scarce a mile in advance.• Had the former been firmly convinced that the greater part of the British army had actually crossed the river, and accepted the resistance of the picket line in front of the riflemen as proof of the fact, we should doubtless have seen him marching his united body of Continentals immediately upon the enemy, and taking advantage of the remaining daylight to deliver his meditated blow. But, instead of this, he sent forward to Wayne, across the morass, only the Pennsylvanians and Gimat's battalion of light infantry, under Major Wyllys, of Connecticut. The two other battalions of infantry, Vose's and Barber's, he formed in line as a reserve at Green Spring. This indicated caution. It appears, indeed, that Lafayette had graver doubts in regard to the weakness of the enemy than either Wayne or any other officer in his army who had the means of judging. The very obstinacy of their picket line in covering their position excited his suspicion. To satisfy himself as far as possible by personal observation, he left his command for a short time, and, riding to a tongue of land at the river's bank, discovered that the enemy had made a parade of the few troops who had crossed over " in such a manner as to appear numerous." At once he returned " with all possible haste," with the purpose of declining a general action. By quietly and rapidly withdrawing Wayne to Green Spring from the front, where the riflemen were still engaged as a cover, he could have made good his retreat during the night, in case Cornwallis should attempt to pursue and force an engagement.

It was at this interesting moment, during the brief absence of Lafayette, that the serious action of the day was precipitated. While the reports of the affair fail to agree exactly as to the opening incidents, its general features are satisfactorily described. Cornwallis, writing to Clinton, says: " Nothing, however, appeared near us but riflemen and militia till near sunset, when a body of Continentals, with artillery, began to form in the front of our camp. I then put the troops under arms, and ordered the army to advance in two lines. The attack was begun by the first line with great spirit. There being nothing but militia opposed to the light infantry, the action was soon over on the right. But Lieutenant-colonel Dundas's brigade, consisting of the Forty-third, Seventy-sixth, and Eightieth Regiments, which formed the left wing, meeting the Pennsylvania line, and a detachment of the Marquis de la Fayette's Continentals, with two six-pounders, a smart action ensued for some minutes, when the enemy gave way, and abandoned their cannon. The cavalry were perfectly ready to pursue ; but the darkness of the evening prevented my being able to make use of them." The facts are here presented with substantial accuracy, but the true merits of the action do not appear. Comparing Lafayette's and Wayne's reports, we find that the enemy's success is qualified by the admirable conduct of the American troops engaged. It was an action in which the latter found themselves suddenly attacked by the entire British army, and yet skilfully avoided disaster.

It is not clear from Wayne's report what particular movement on his part finally induced Cornwallis, after the two hours' picket firing, to advance his main body. " At three o'clock," he states, " the riflemen, supported by a few regulars, began and kept up a galling fire upon the enemy, which continued until five in the evening, when the British began to move forward in columns. The marquis, anxious to view them near, had proceeded rather far upon their left. It was, therefore, thought proper to order Major Galvan, at the head of the advanced guard, to meet and attack their front; who, after a spirited though unequal contest, retired upon our left." This Major Galvan, introduced as beginning the engagement proper, led a small detachment of fifty or sixty Light Infantry, and with them supported the riflemen in the skirmishing of the afternoon. In Lafayette's report the major and his party figure more prominently. According to the marquis, Galvan was directed by Wayne, while the former was making observations at the river bank, to attempt the capture of a piece of artillery which the enemy had placed in an exposed position. Galvan at the skirmish line made the attempt in a dashing manner; whereupon, says Lafayette, "the whole British army came out and advanced to the thin wood occupied by General Wayne." This was the beginning of the real work of the day, and in twenty minutes it was over.

Cornwallis, assured, either by Galvan's demonstration or by previous actual observation, that Lafayette's Continentals were now in his front, moved his troops forward in two lines.[1] The light infantry, under Lieutenant-colonel Yorke, formed the right of the front line, and Lieutenant-colonel Dundas's brigade, composed of the Forty-third, Seventy-sixth, and Eightieth Regiments, the left. The Guards, Twenty-third, Thirty-third, and Hessians, with Tarleton's Legion, which fell back through intervals made by the infantry, formed the second line. Upon the other side, Wayne was also preparing for an advance with the re-enforcements which had just reached him. Making Stewart's battalion his centre, he placed the two other Pennsylvania battalions upon its right and left, while Gimat's light infantry, composed mainly of Connecticut companies, under Major Wyllys, continued the line to the right. Two field-pieces, under Captain Duffy and Captain-lieutenant Crossley, of Pennsylvania, and a third under Captain Joseph Savage, of Massachusetts, were the only artillery at hand. Hardly nine hundred men could Wayne count in his line at this critical moment; hardly, too, had he formed it when the riflemen were found retreating rapidly upon his left, followed soon after by Galvan's "advanced guard" retiring before the British advance. It would appear, also, that Wyllys and his light infantry on the right had been advanced, but were obliged to fall back into line again. Wayne

---

[1] Tarleton states that the British army advanced "upon the first cannon-shot from the enemy."

then perceived that he was confronted by the entire force of the enemy, whose line overlapped and endangered his flanks. Instant decision was necessary as to the proper move to make. A sudden retreat might end in panic. To await the shock of the approaching enemy would be ruinous. It was "a choice of difficulties," says Wayne; and under such

GENERAL ANTHONY WAYNE. [TRUMBULL.]

circumstances his choice was never uncertain. With the instinct of a leader and the courage of a lion, he determined to become the assailant —to advance and charge. Could the British be surprised and checked in the first instance, a final retreat would be effected with greater safety. The movement was successful, though costly. Wayne's line hastened forward, under a fire of musketry and grape-shot, to within seventy yards of the enemy, when both combatants came to a stand, and for fifteen minutes a sharp and well-contested action occurred. Dundas's brigade, immediately opposed to Wayne, was encouraged by Cornwallis in person; and Lafayette, who returned from the river to give the order for retreat, exposed himself at the front, when he saw that Wayne had become engaged. A horse led by his side was shot, while nearly every field-officer was dismounted. The exchange of fire continued brisk and destructive. All the horses of Duffy's and Crossley's guns were killed or disabled, and Crossley himself, with six or seven other Pennsylvania officers, was wounded, while men were falling rapidly. Wayne was making a brave fight against heavy numbers, but it could only be of short duration. The right of the enemy's line, having nothing but the re-treating riflemen and advance parties before it, threatened to envelop the Americans; and, the pressure on their front increasing, they abandoned the field and retreated rapidly through the woods and across the morass to Green Spring, where they were re-formed under cover of Vose's and Barber's light infantry, drawn up as a reserve at that place. The lateness of the hour prevented the enemy's horse from pursuing.[1]

Lafayette remained at Green Spring several hours, and then fell back before daylight to Chickahominy Church. Lawson's riflemen were placed in advance, and on the 7th the dispositions were such that retreat before the enemy, had they been disposed to follow up their advantage, could have been effected without further loss. The casualties

---

[1] Captain Davis and Lieutenant Feltman, of the Pennsylvania line, describe this action briefly in nearly similar terms. The former's account, as printed in the *Village Record*, Westchester, Penn., is as follows: "Marched at 5 o'clock A.M. for Jamestown, where the enemy at this time lay in force. When the army had advanced within five miles of this town, the First Pennsylvania Battalion was detached, with a number of riflemen, to Green Springs, which brought on a scattering fire that continued for three hours, when a body of light infantry came with the other two battalions of Pennsylvania troops. The line was displayed, and we advanced; by this time the enemy was meeting us, when a general action ensued. At the distance of one hundred yards we charged on their main body, under a heavy and incessant fire of grape and canister shot; at this instant we opened our musketry. Their right flanking our left, a retreat was found necessary; with the loss of two pieces of artillery, we retired to a church, where we lay this night."

Compare extracts from Captain Davis's papers, published in *Penn. Magazine of History*, 1881; also Lafayette's report to Greene, given in the "Additional Correspondence" of the American edition of Lafayette's "Memoirs," vol. i., p. 525. Wayne's report is in Sparks' "Correspondence of the Revolution."

on the 6th were considerable, amounting to four sergeants and twenty-four rank and file killed ; five captains, one captain - lieutenant, four lieutenants, seven sergeants and eighty-two rank and file wounded, in addition to a few riflemen whose number was not ascertained. Twelve were reported missing, making a total loss of about one hundred and forty-five.[1] Two of the guns, one of which had been captured at the Battle of Bennington, were left on the field. The enemy's loss was reported at seventy-five killed and wounded, five of the latter being officers.

Though defeated in this affair, Lafayette lost nothing in reputation. The criticism that he exposed his army to destruction, when so much depended upon keeping it intact, is hardly supported by the facts. As to his personal responsibility, while he had suffered Wayne to advance close to the enemy, under the impression that the latter was not in force, he proceeded to reconnoitre before precipitating an encounter. During his absence the responsibility rested with the dashing Wayne, whose appeal was always to the sword. By the joint efforts and gallantry of both leaders the nearly overpowered advance was extricated from its dangerous position. Nor, under the most unfavorable turn, could Lafayette have lost more than a third of his Continentals. Two-thirds of the Light Infantry were on the Green Spring side of the morass, and many of Wayne's men, even if driven in total rout, could undoubtedly have escaped to the same side, where, under cover of the night, safe retreat and junction with the militia were possible. The troops engaged were conscious that they had acquitted themselves well; and what Lafayette thought of them is a matter of record, expressed in his General Orders, as follows:

"Ambler's Plantation, opposite James River, July 8, 1781.

" The General is happy in acknowledging the spirit of the detachment commanded by General Wayne, in their engagement with the total of the British army, of which he happened to be an eye-witness. He requests General Wayne, the officers and men under his command, to receive his best thanks.

" The bravery and destructive fire of the riflemen engaged rendered essential service.

" The brilliant conduct of Major Galvan and the Continental detachment under his command entitle them to applause.

" The conduct of the Pennsylvania field and other officers are new instances of their gallantry and talents.

" The fire of the light infantry under Major Willis [Wyllys] checked the enemy's progress round our right flank.

" The General was much pleased with the conduct of Captain Savage, of the artil-

---

[1] See return of American loss in Appendix.

lery; and it is with pleasure, also, he observes that nothing but the loss of horses could have produced that of the field-pieces.

"The zeal of Colonel Mercer's little corps is handsomely expressed in the number of horses he had killed."[1]

When Greene heard of the affair he wrote this to Wayne: "It gives me great pleasure to hear of the success of my friends; but be a little careful and tread softly, for, depend upon it, you have a modern Hannibal to deal with in the person of Lord Cornwallis."[2]

There now came a pause in the Virginia Campaign, at least in daily operations and excitements. The State north of the James was relieved. Cornwallis crossed to the south side, at Cobham, on the 7th; and Lafayette, retiring up the river, encamped, about the 20th, on the now historic Malvern Hill, then described as one of the healthiest and best watered spots in the State. Wayne and Morgan, who had but just joined the American camp, manœuvred in the direction of Petersburg and Amelia County to threaten Tarleton, who, on the 9th, was despatched by Cornwallis to destroy magazines and private stores as far as New London, in Bedford County. Tarleton, however, accomplished nothing, and, after a march of four hundred miles, returned in a weakened condition to Suffolk, where Cornwallis remained with a portion of his force to receive him. The entire British army was soon after concentrated at Portsmouth, and preparations made to transport a considerable portion of it to New York.

Lafayette, meanwhile, at Malvern Hill, could only await developments. He thought of sending re-enforcements to Greene,[3] and asked Washington if, in case Cornwallis left Virginia, he might not return to the Northern army. His opinion as to results in his department is stated in a letter of the 20th: "That the subjugation of this State," he wrote to his chief, "was the great object of the ministry is an indisputable fact. I

---

[1] American accounts of the Green Spring action are generally based on that given in Lee's "Memoirs," who shares Tarleton's belief that Lafayette had a narrow escape. But, while Lee is to be accepted as good authority, he certainly was misled into several important errors in this case. He puts all Lafayette's Continentals in the action, whereas but little more than half were there. Nor was Steuben with the army, nor the militia near the battle-ground.

[2] From the Wayne papers, in *Casket*.

[3] "I am happy," wrote Lafayette to Steuben, July 10th, "that the north shore of James River is at length freed of the enemy. As soon as I am well ascertained of their motions I shall advise you. In my opinion it becomes every day more necessary to think seriously of supporting General Greene."—*Gates MS.*

think your diversion has been of more use to the State than my manœuvres; but the latter have been much directed by political views. So
long as my lord wished for an action, not one gun has been fired; the
moment he declined it, we have been skirmishing; but I took care never to
commit the army. His naval superiority, his superiority of horse, of regulars, his thousand advantages over us—so that I am lucky to have come
off safe. I had an eye upon European negotiations, and made it a point
to give his Lordship the disgrace of a retreat." And then he praises his
Light Infantry, not one of whom had deserted in Virginia, and whose
presence, he believed, had saved the State.

But while the marquis and Washington and Greene were speculating
on the future movements of Cornwallis, and were persuaded, from em-
barkations at Portsmouth, that he was to be deprived of a large part of
his force by Clinton, unexpected intelligence came to hand. Instead of
any part going to New York, the British force suddenly made its appearance, during the first days in August, at Yorktown, on the Virginia peninsula, which it had abandoned but three weeks before. Here again was
a new situation. Cornwallis, at last, at Yorktown—the spot he was not
to leave except as a prisoner of war!

Why he went there is a simple explanation. Clinton decided, upon
certain dissenting opinions expressed by Cornwallis respecting the situation in Virginia, not to withdraw the force in the Chesapeake which he
had called for, and which was about to sail for New York, but permitted
Cornwallis to retain the whole—all with which he had been pursuing
Lafayette and the large garrison at Portsmouth, a total of about seven
thousand, rank and file. His new instructions, conveyed at the same
time, were to the effect that his Lordship should abandon Portsmouth,
which both generals agreed was too unhealthy for the troops, and fortify
Old Point Comfort, where Fort Monroe now stands, as a naval station for
the protection of the British shipping. In addition, if it appeared necessary, for the better security of the Point, to occupy Yorktown also, that
was to be done. Obeying these instructions, Cornwallis ordered a survey
of Old Point Comfort; but, upon the report of his engineers, was obliged
to represent to Clinton that it was wholly unfit and inadequate for a
naval station, as it afforded little protection for ships, and could not command the channel, on account of its great width. Then, following what
he believed to be the spirit of his orders, Cornwallis, before hearing from
Clinton, moved up to Yorktown, and began to fortify it, in connection
with Gloucester, on the opposite shore, as the best available naval station.
Clinton made no subsequent objections, and there Cornwallis remained

until his surrender. His occupation of the place was simply an incident of the campaign—a move taken for convenience and in the interests of the navy and the health of his command.[1]

---

[1] Clinton afterward insisted that Cornwallis violated his orders in going to York-town, claiming that he was to occupy Yorktown only on condition he held Old Point Comfort also. He leaves the inference that, if the latter place could not be fortified, Cornwallis should have reported the fact, and not moved until receiving further orders from New York. It is a question whether Cornwallis, had he taken post at the Point, could not have escaped by crossing to Portsmouth the moment he learned of the arrival of the French fleet; in this case Clinton's charge that he disobeyed orders has some force.

CHAPTER IV.

WASHINGTON IN THE CAMPAIGN.—PLANS AND MOVEMENTS ON THE HUDSON.—
CO-OPERATION OF THE FRENCH.

BUT, to complete the chain of incidents which finally entangled Cornwallis in the fatal Yorktown meshes, we must change the scene four
hundred miles to the northward, and cross into the camps of the Americans and their "generous allies," the French. Something of consequence
is meantime going on there. An unexpected act unfolds in this military
drama.

Washington, who, with a wretchedly clothed and often but half-fed
army, had been sustaining the cause of the Revolution through six anxious years, never felt the embarrassments of his situation more keenly than
in the early part of the year 1781. He could do little to assist the South,
and saw no flattering prospects of achieving anything important in the
North. The long continuance of the war had produced a certain degree
of apathy in the States, and the army could with difficulty be kept at respectable numbers. Men were unwilling to serve for long terms; the
farmers dreaded camp life, and wished to be at home in the spring; the
population at large believed that the crisis was passed, and that peace
would eventually come by a show of opposition, or that in case of a great
emergency, like Burgoyne's invasion, the uprising of the militia would
carry the day. Moreover, the whole civil system, on which the support
of the military depended, was loose and vexingly slow in its operation.
The powers and resources of the Continental Congress were limited by
the willingness and alacrity of the State government to answer its calls.
There was no strong central authority, and the cause suffered from want
of it.

The almost ruinous effect of this absence of means and system is
vividly presented by Washington in his military journal. "Instead of
having magazines filled with provisions," runs the first entry in May,
1781, "we have a scanty pittance scattered here and there in the different

States.   Instead of having our arsenals well supplied with military stores, they are poorly provided, and the workmen all leaving them. . . . Instead of having a regular system of transportation upon credit, or funds in the quartermaster's hands to defray the contingent expenses of it, we have neither the one nor the other; and all that business, or a great part of it, being done by military impress, we are daily and hourly oppressing the people—souring their tempers and alienating their affection.   Instead of having the regiments completed to the new establishment, scarce any State in the Union has, at this hour, an eighth part of its quota in the field, and little prospect, that I can see, of ever getting more than half.   In a word, instead of having everything in readiness to take the field, we have nothing; and instead of having the prospect of a glorious offensive campaign before us, we have a bewildered and gloomy defensive one, unless we should receive a powerful aid of ships, land troops, and money from our generous allies; and these, at present, are too contingent to build upon."

It needs but a reference to the military situation to show how accurately Washington had described it.   While Sir Henry Clinton, at New York, notwithstanding the detachments sent to the Chesapeake, still retained a force of ten thousand five hundred men, both regulars and provincials, the American army on the Hudson, quartered around West Point, numbered scarcely three thousand five hundred Continentals.   These were mainly of the New England line.   The New York regiments were stationed above along the frontier, the New Jersey in their own State; and the greater part of the Pennsylvanians were with Lafayette.   The Continentals from the States to the southward composed Greene's army; while the French corps under Count Rochambeau, about four thousand effectives, was encamped at Newport, Rhode Island.   The single point against which offensive operations could be directed in the North was New York, and success there, with the force then available, appeared doubtful.   Through the clouded prospect the only ray of hope visible was a probable increase of the American army, and the possibility that in the course of the season a second division of French troops, accompanied by a large fleet, would appear upon the American coast, with whose assistance something might be effected.

A campaign, nevertheless, was arranged.   On the 22d of May, by previous appointment, Washington, in company with Generals Knox and Duportail, met Rochambeau and the Chevalier de Chastellux, one of his major-generals, in conference at Wethersfield, Connecticut, where, after discussing the general situation, a plan of operations was agreed upon, the

GEORGE WASHINGTON. [FROM THE ORIGINAL PORTRAIT BY TRUMBULL IN THE YALE ART GALLERY, NEW HAVEN.]

outlines of which were reduced to writing.[1] This plan was of an alternative character, subject to extensive modifications as circumstances might require. The hostile positions at that time each presented a prominent assailable point. The States, as already seen, were weakest at the South, where the enemy were operating with energy. On the other hand, the British were weak at New York—weaker, at least, than at any period during the war—and to a vigilant and active antagonist invited attack. Washington had long been anxious to re-enforce the Southern army, but was utterly powerless to do so if operations were to be undertaken by his own command in the North. Certain important considerations, furthermore, disinclined him either to lead or despatch troops to such a distance. The "insurmountable difficulty and expense of land transportation," the loss of men in long marches, objections to the Southern climate, the impossibility of filling up the regiments destined for such service, and the ease and rapidity with which the enemy could also re-enforce by water transportation, weighed against this plan of assistance. The only feasible method, in Washington's judgment, of relieving the pressure upon Greene and Lafayette was to unite the French forces to his own and make a serious demonstration against the weakened base at New York, where a combined attack might put the city and its garrison in his hands. This alone would be an important blow, whether the city were subsequently held or not; or, failing in this, it was confidently expected that, in view of the attempt, Clinton would recall to his defence a considerable part of the British detachments sent to the southward, which would also be an acceptable result. Or, again, future developments, such as a French naval superiority, might justify a general movement to the southward. These several contingencies were considered at Wethersfield, but, as a preliminary and definite basis of action, it was agreed between the respective commanders that the French should join the Americans on the Hudson at the earliest moment, and both move upon New York, to attempt operations as circumstances favored.

This was the Wethersfield plan. The claim, sometimes loosely asserted, that the campaign which ended in the splendid combination at

---

[1] From Washington's "Journal:" "May 18th.—Set out this day for the interview at Weathersfield with the Count de Rochambeau and Admiral Barras [the latter not present]—reached Morgan's Tavern, forty-three miles from Fishkill Landing, after dining at Colonel Vandeberg's. May 19th.—Breakfasted at Litchfield, dined at Farmington, and lodged at Weathersfield, at the house of Joseph Webb, Esq., the quarters which were taken for me and my suit." Washington's army head-quarters were at New Windsor, above West Point.

Yorktown was conceived and arranged four months before at this conference, cannot be sustained. That campaign was a development, not an inspiration. It presents Washington, not as a prophet, but as a general who conducted his movements upon the truest military principles. For it is to be observed, that at the time of the conference in question information was wanting upon two principal points. Although, from intercepted letters, suspicion may have been entertained that Cornwallis would sooner or later make his appearance in Virginia, there was no certainty in the matter, and intelligence of his actual invasion of the State did not arrive until two weeks after Washington and Rochambeau had returned to their respective armies. No definite campaign could thus have been devised against his Lordship. Furthermore, uncertainty existed in regard to the co-operation of a French naval armament to neutralize or overcome that of the enemy. It was known that a powerful fleet, under Admiral de Grasse, had recently sailed from France for her colonies in the West Indies, but Washington was ignorant of its future movements, or, in case it had been ordered to the American coast, of the time it might be expected. Much as he hoped for its assistance, he could base no projects upon it at Wethersfield—none, certainly, involving immediate co-operation. How far it was considered, and what, in fine, was decided at Wethersfield, appears with sufficient clearness in the closing interrogatory and answer given in the record of the interview:

ROCHAMBEAU.—Should the squadron from the West Indies arrive in these seas—an event which will probably be announced by a frigate beforehand—what operations will General Washington have in view, after a union of the French army with his own?

WASHINGTON.—The enemy, by several detachments from New York, having reduced their force at that post to less than one-half of the number which they had at the time of the former conference at Hartford, in September last, it is thought advisable to form a junction of the French and American armies upon the North River as soon as possible, and move down to the vicinity of New York, to be ready to take advantage of any opportunity which the weakness of the enemy may afford. Should the West India fleet arrive upon the coast, the force thus combined may either proceed in the operation against New York, or may be directed against the enemy in some other quarter, as circumstances shall dictate. The great waste of men . . . and other considerations too well known to Count de Rochambeau to need detailing, point out the preference which an operation against New York seems to have in the present circumstances over an attempt to send a force to the southward.[1]

---

[1] Sparks' "Washington," vol. viii., p. 518. In the same volume (p. 62), in a letter to Greene, June 1st, Washington writes: "I have lately had an interview with Count de Rochambeau, at Weathersfield. Our affairs were very attentively considered in every

This preliminary plan satisfactorily arranged, Rochambeau immediately returned to Newport, while Washington remained in Wethersfield one day longer—the 23d—and wrote urgent letters to the New England governors, emphasizing the necessity of filling their Continental regiments for the campaign, warning their militia to march at a week's notice, if called for, and calling for a liberal supply of provisions, powder, and wagons for transportation. Informing them in confidence of the meditated project against New York, and the impossibility of succeeding without an increase of force, he added : " The enemy, counting upon our want of ability, or upon our want of energy, have, by repeated detachments to the southward, reduced themselves in New York to a situation which invites us to take advantage of it; and should the lucky moment be lost, it is to be feared that they will, after subduing the Southern States, raise a force in them sufficient to hold them, and return again to the northward with such a number of men as will render New York secure against any force which we can at this time raise or maintain. Our allies in this country expect and depend upon being supported by us in the attempt which we are about to make, and those in Europe will be astonished should we neglect the favorable opportunity which is now offered." From the same place he also wrote to the Chevalier de la Luzerne, the French Minister, at Philadelphia, in regard to the destination of the fleet under De Grasse, upon which everything depended, requesting him in earnest terms, both in his own name and that of Rochambeau, to exert his influence in bringing the admiral to our coast in season to engage in offensive operations. Luzerne replied cordially, promising to communicate with De Grasse. " Be persuaded," he wrote to Washington, " that I shall use the most pressing motives to determine him, and I shall do it with so much the more zeal as I feel the necessity of it. I shall transmit to that general [the admiral] an extract of your letter ;

---

point of view, and it was finally determined to make an attempt upon New York, with its present garrison, in preference to a southern operation, as we had not the decided command of the water. You will readily suppose the reasons which induced this determination were the inevitable loss of men from so long a march, more especially in the approaching hot season, and the difficulty, I may say impossibility, of transporting the necessary baggage, artillery, and stores by land. If I am supported as I ought to be by the neighboring States in this operation, which you know has always been their favorite one, I hope that one of these consequences will follow : either that the enemy will be expelled from the most valuable position which they hold upon the Continent, or be obliged to recall part of their force from the southward to defend it. Should the latter happen, you will be most essentially relieved by it."

and nothing appears to me more likely to give weight to the demand which I shall make upon him." The fact is brought out in this correspondence that Washington, Rochambeau, and Chastellux were "perfectly" agreed that when it came, and while affairs remained as they were then, the French fleet should run to Sandy Hook, where it could be met with all the information requisite either to facilitate the operations in hand, or co-operate in any other more practicable. Luzerne was requested to present this opinion to De Grasse, as a guide in case he proposed coming to the American coast within a short time. Until De Grasse could be heard from, the land operations were to be pushed independently against New York.

Leaving Wethersfield in the forenoon of the 24th, Washington was back again at his head-quarters at New Windsor, on the Hudson, by sunset of the following day. His entire attention was now devoted to the preparations for the campaign. Knox and Duportail, the chiefs of artillery and engineers, were instructed to put their departments in the best train for the coming "siege" of New York; the troops were set to drilling, and afterward surprised the French with their proficiency and discipline; and outlying Continental detachments were ordered to hold themselves in readiness to join the main army. Congress was appealed to for renewed exertions, while encouragement came in the shape of news from France that, as the King could not at this juncture send more troops to America, he had made Congress a gift of six million livres, to be applied in part to the purchase of arms and clothing for the troops, with one million five hundred thousand of the surplus to be at Washington's disposal. Further relief was anticipated and experienced by the appointment of Robert Morris, of Philadelphia, as Superintendent of Finance, in whose resources and patriotism the chief had the greatest confidence, and to whom he wrote in congratulation: "My hand and heart shall be with you, and as far as my assistance can go, command it. We have, I am persuaded, but one object in view, the public good; to effect which I will aid your endeavors to the extent of my abilities and with all the powers I am vested with." Matters looked promising, but, what was not an unusual experience, when active movements began the promise had not been realized. The regiments had not been filled, and Washington's numbers were still sadly insufficient; while the generous grant from Louis XVI. did not arrive until too late in the season for the best use to which it might have been applied. Of all civilians Morris came nearest to fulfilling expectations; his skill and energy in providing ready money for pressing wants and obtaining supplies on credit, helped greatly in keeping the army on its feet, especially during the latter part of the campaign.[1]

But how slowly matters progressed! Five months between the Wethersfield interview and the Yorktown surrender! The French were to be at the Hudson "as soon as possible," but that meant six weeks. But two letters came from De Grasse throughout the entire summer. It took a month to hear from Greene; ten days from Lafayette. Recruiting, collection of supplies, and transportation went on pretty much at snail's pace, it would appear to us to-day. But it was a new country—a really immense field, a scattered population; and, besides, there was the sea to deal with, its storms, cross-winds, and, above all, the ponderous, slow-moving men-of-war of that period. It is rather to be wondered how, under such circumstances, extensive combinations succeeded as well as they did, and what we have to admire is the masterly patience of the men who undertook and carried them through.

Toward the middle of June certain new phases attached to the general situation, which, for the first time, brought a move from the Hudson to Virginia within the range of probabilities. Something more definite was known in regard to those two important points about which so little was known at Wethersfield. First: On the 13th of June letters reached Washington from Rochambeau containing the most welcome intelligence that De Grasse had finally been heard from, and would appear in American waters with a powerful fleet in midsummer. Here was all-important news, "very interesting communications," as Washington wrote back to Rochambeau, which he assured the latter he would keep perfectly secret. From this time all movements hinged on the assistance that could be given by this fleet. Second: The situation in the South had likewise changed. By letters received from Lafayette and others on the 4th, 7th, and 11th of June, there was no longer any doubt that Cornwallis, abandoning North Carolina for the time being, had undertaken the conquest of Virginia, and was then apparently carrying all before him. This was bringing the Southern contest nearer to the Northern field, and movements there would have a more direct influence upon movements around New York. Cornwallis had put himself where he was to be actively watched, not only by Lafayette and Greene, but, to a certain extent, by Washington as well. Indeed, as observed in connection with Lafayette's

---

[1] Writing to General Gates, September 5th, Dr. Rush, of Philadelphia, says: "Mr. Morris has become a new star in our American hemisphere. Our safety consists in the number of our great men."—*Gates MS.*

operations in Virginia, strong personal influences were brought to bear upon the commander-in-chief to send, or himself proceed with, immediate relief to his own State. Jefferson and Lee had written him pressingly on the subject, and very recently, on July 5th, Governor Rutledge, of South Carolina, had visited his head-quarters to appeal for aid for that State. These changes and incidents only served to impress more deeply upon Washington's mind the necessity of immediate active movements on his own part to help protect and quiet the section of country from which the cries of distress were coming up.

Under these new conditions the single question which presented itself to the allied commanders was, how best to utilize the expected fleet and the combined land-forces to relieve the burdened South, and, at the same time, win some additional great and permanent advantage for America.

The gradual solution of this question forms one of the most interesting features of the campaign. What De Grasse had written to Rochambeau—his letter being dated "at sea," as far back as March 29th—was little more than an announcement that after reaching the West Indies he should sail for North America, where he could not arrive, however, before the 15th of July, if as early as that; and that if his fleet was to co-operate, everything should be in readiness for immediate action upon his arrival, as his stay upon the coast must be short. For what point he should sail it was for the allied commanders to determine. This letter was received by Rochambeau on the 9th of June, and its contents, as stated, transmitted to Washington. A reply was despatched to De Grasse as soon as possible by the frigate *Concorde*, in which Rochambeau gave him full intelligence concerning "the plans in view, and also the strength, situation, and apparent designs of the enemy." He recommended him, further, "to enter the Chesapeake on his way, as there might be an opportunity of striking an important stroke there, and then to proceed immediately to New York, and be ready to co-operate with the allied armies in an attack upon that city."[1] This reply substantially reflected Washington's views, as it was, in fact, in accordance with the Wethersfield plan, and the land-forces proceeded to begin their part in the intended operations. At these, meanwhile, we may glance briefly until De Grasse is heard from again, and developments are reached of a still more positive character.

It was not until the first week in July that the Count de Rochambeau, with the French troops from Newport, formed a junction with the Amer-

---

[1] Sparks' "Washington," vol. viii., p. 76, note.

icans at the Hudson. They were an excellent corps, divided into four regiments of infantry, a battalion of artillery, and the Duke de Lauzun's Legion of horse and foot. The infantry, which had marched from Newport on the 9th of June, left Providence on the 18th–21st of the same month—the regiments following each other after a day's interval—and

COUNT DE ROCHAMBEAU.

took the direct route westward, passing through the Connecticut towns of Plainfield, Canterbury, Windham, Bolton, Hartford, Farmington, Southington, Newtown, and Ridgebury, and through Bedford and Northcastle to White Plains, in New York. Lauzun's Legion, which was quartered at Lebanon, Connecticut, followed a lower route, through Colchester, Middletown, Wallingford, Oxford, North Stratford, and Bedford. The march

6

was something of a holiday affair, and occasioned the liveliest scenes in the various towns and villages on the route. The inhabitants welcomed and cheered the allies, who in turn preserved the best of order and committed no depredations.

While the French were on the march Washington prepared his own army for the junction, and by the 24th of June had brigaded it anew and gone into camp near Peekskill. Here he had proposed to await Rochambeau's arrival, but on the 28th, the opportunity being favorable, he conceived the plan of opening operations by a sudden attack on the enemy's forts at the north end of New York Island, the possession of which would simplify subsequent movements. Major-general Lincoln was intrusted with its execution, with eight hundred good troops, including the select detachment of Light Infantry, four hundred strong, under Colonel Alexander Scammell, of New Hampshire, and Lieutenant-colonel Huntington, of Connecticut, and another battalion under Lieutenant-colonel Sprout, of Massachusetts. They were to descend in boats on the night of the 2d of July and surprise and hold the works in the vicinity of King's Bridge, even storming Forts Tryon and Knyphausen below, but not retaining them. At the same time the Duke de Lauzun, with his Legion, and General Waterbury, with Connecticut State troops, and Sheldon's Dragoons, were to cut off Delancey's and other bodies of the enemy posted north and east of the bridge. To take advantage of whatever success might be gained, Washington proposed to march down the river with all his remaining force to within supporting distance at Valentine's Hill, while Rochambeau was urged to hasten his march to the same point. Minute instructions were issued to the commanding officers of the detachments concerned, and the strictest secrecy enjoined as to the proposed attacks.

The surprise failed. Lincoln's orders required him not to make a landing below King's Bridge, if upon reconnoitring from the Jersey side he found the plan impracticable or his movement should be discovered, but to land above the bridge and be ready to co-operate with Lauzun's attack upon Delancey. The first part of Lincoln's plan was not attempted, as he found the enemy's ships in the way. He accordingly landed above the bridge. Lauzun, on his part, made a forced march during the night of the 2d to carry out his enterprise, but "the fatigue of his corps," says Washington, "prevented his coming to the point of action at the hour appointed," and in addition Lincoln had been attacked by a party of the enemy, which gave the alarm to those whom Lauzun was to surprise. The French duke thereupon promptly moved to Lincoln's support, but the skirmish, which proved a brisk one, was over, and the enemy were retiring. Every effort was made to renew the action on the part of the allies, but without success, and the rest of the day was devoted by the commander-in-chief to reconnoitring the ground and works around and below King's Bridge. On the following day the American troops fell back to Dobb's Ferry, where on the 6th the French army joined them and went into camp on their left.

While this could hardly have been regarded as an auspicious beginning of the movement against New York, it opened the eyes of the enemy to the fact that Washington had suddenly assumed an unusual boldness and confidence which was to be treated with respect. Sir Henry Clinton became more vigilant, and, indeed, discovered some uneasiness, especially as a little later—July 21st–24th—Washington made a thorough reconnoissance in force of all the northern defences of the island, indicating the prosecution of siege operations. But if nothing was accomplished before New York, as no fleet had arrived to co-operate, the very important and expected result was brought about, that Clinton was compelled to call for re-enforcements from the Chesapeake, and, for the time being, cripple Cornwallis in Virginia.

Thus matters stood in the early days of August—little done, and the future uncertain—when, on the 14th of the month, word came again from De Grasse, and the whole scene changed. From this moment a new and exciting interest attached to every movement. The news from the admiral put another face on the situation; for, instead of announcing his near approach to New York, and speedy co-operation with the land-forces against the city, he informed Rochambeau that he should sail for the Chesapeake Bay direct, on the 13th inst., with the view of undertaking or facilitating operations in that quarter, rather than at New York; and that he hoped that the troops would be ready upon his arrival for immediate activity, as he must return to the West Indies by the middle of October. Nothing remained, accordingly, but to fit everything to the new requirements of the situation and look—southward. Washington describes the change as follows in his " Journal:" " Matters having now come to a crisis, and a decided plan to be determined on, I was obliged — from the shortness of Count de Grasse's promised stay on this coast, the apparent disinclination of their naval officers to force the harbor of New York, and the feeble compliance of the States with my requisitions for men hitherto, and the little prospect of greater exertion in future—to give up all ideas of attacking

New York, and instead thereof to remove the French troops and a detachment from the American army to the head of Elk, to be transported to Virginia, for the purpose of co-operating with the force from the West Indies against the troops in that State."

So, finally, the army on the Hudson was to play its part directly in the Yorktown Campaign.

From the tone of the statement in his "Journal," and the somewhat mandatory character of the intelligence from De Grasse, it might be inferred that Washington had been forced, against his inclination, to make a radical change in his plans, and undertake a movement for which he was unprepared. The glory of his having conceived or been a principal organizer of the combination in the Chesapeake would be in a measure dimmed by such a reflection. But we reach here an interesting point. Had Washington, in fact, been surprised into this new movement? If so, who planned it? Who must have the credit of arranging the Yorktown net for the capture of Cornwallis? Or was it all a piece of blind fortune?

Whoever may have contributed in effecting the combination, it will be seen that the commander-in-chief had long regarded it as among the possibilities, and that he was entirely ready for it. His perfect understanding of the situation at the moment it was time to act, and his prompt decision to act as he did, prove the high order of his military talents. It was by the exercise of the same qualities that he executed his memorable retreat from Long Island in 1776, and, again, turned upon Trenton four months later. The present campaign, like all before it, was pre-eminently shaped by circumstances. If the commander-in-chief was only in part instrumental himself in shaping them, he watched, and at the right instant turned them to account. It is worth while to notice how he canvassed every contingency from the beginning, and how the development of the campaign had been a study which prepared him to take the closing decisive step.

The success of whatever movement might be undertaken hinged upon the co-operation of De Grasse. As the land and naval commanders were not subject to one controlling mind, it became of the first importance for them to be in perfect harmony as to the plan of operations. In the present case, as long as Washington and Rochambeau were agreed, there could be no question of De Grasse's cordial co-operation. But the difficulty lay here, that the field of operations could not be fixed upon any length of time in advance — clearly not two months or even one in advance. What might the enemy not do within that period? Was there any certainty that Cornwallis would be in Virginia in August, when De Grasse proposed to be there? That Washington was anxious to prosecute the siege of New York as late as the 1st of August, and expected De Grasse to assist, is not to be doubted. It was the plan he then regarded as the most feasible. But he had considered all contingencies. He had already thought of a possible move to Virginia, and so advised Lafayette, that he might hold himself in readiness for it. For instance, he wrote to him as follows on the 30th of July: "I am convinced that your desire to be with this army arises principally from a wish to be actively useful. You will not, therefore, regret your stay in Virginia until matters are reduced to a greater degree of certainty than they are at present, especially when I tell you that, from the change of circumstances with which the removal of part of the enemy's force from Virginia to New York will be attended, it is more than probable that we shall also entirely change our plan of operations. I think we have already effected one part of the plan of the campaign settled at Weathersfield—that is, giving a substantial relief to the Southern States, by obliging the enemy to recall a considerable part of their force from thence. Our views must now be turned toward endeavoring to expel them totally from those States, if we find ourselves incompetent to the siege of New York;" and he hinted at the expected arrival of De Grasse. By the 15th of August Washington had also sounded Robert Morris, at Philadelphia, as to the means of transportation from that point to Wilmington and beyond. From these and other expressions on the part of the chief, we may infer—as, indeed, one of his letters authorizes the inference—that even had De Grasse come to New York, Washington was ready to suggest his sailing back to the Chesapeake, while the army would move to the same point, if at that moment the situation in Virginia offered the most tempting prospects of success. In other words, the march upon Cornwallis was an alternative plan already maturing in Washington's mind, before word came from De Grasse that for good reasons he should sail immediately for the Chesapeake. When that word came Washington recognized that the situation was ripe for a change of plan, and at once decided to make it.[1]

---

[1] In regard to the plans of this campaign the simple fact is, that nothing could be settled until the French fleet was actually on the coast. Good generalship would then consist in being ready to make the right move the moment it came. This is all that could be claimed for any one, and it can all be claimed for Washington. President Sparks notices that Rochambeau, in his "Memoirs," takes the credit of bringing about

Follow, then, the fortunes of the army on the Hudson, as it suddenly moved, in part, to the southward, whither the commander-in-chief had finally resolved to lead it.

---

the combination at Yorktown himself. But on close examination it will be found that Washington's and Rochambeau's views were nearly identical from first to last. The latter general states that it was he who recommended De Grasse to sail to the Chesapeake and make Virginia the theatre of operations. Washington would have recommended the same, if he could have foretold what the position of the enemy would be there when De Grasse arrived. Suppose that Clinton had recalled the greater part of the force under Cornwallis, and the latter had returned to Charleston, as he proposed— De Grasse would have found but a mere handful of the enemy to blockade in the Chesapeake, and Washington would not have gone there. In that case Rochambeau's recommendations would have miscarried. The case seems to be properly stated by De Grasse in his letter to Rochambeau (Sparks' "Washington," vol. viii., appendix), where he explains that he had to decide for himself what point to sail to, and that the tenor of his letters from Rochambeau, Luzerne, *and* Washington inclined him to head for Virginia. They must necessarily have left him a large margin of discretion, as two months were to elapse between the date they wrote and the time he was to arrive. Nor could De Grasse have known positively himself where to co-operate until he was on the coast. By good fortune Cornwallis remained in the Chesapeake, and was just in the right position to be cornered when the French admiral made his appearance. Then the net was rapidly drawn around him by the fleet at sea, and Washington and Lafayette on land.

CHAPTER V.

THE MARCH UPON CORNWALLIS.—MOVEMENTS OF THE FRENCH AND ENGLISH FLEETS.

THE march now to be undertaken from the Hudson to the York ranks among the famous episodes of the Revolution. No movement on so grand a scale had as yet been attempted. Brilliant in results, it was equally bold and scientific as a military venture. To break up a base of operations, leave the vicinity of a powerful enemy, and enter a new field, more than four hundred miles distant, in order to engage in a single enterprise, is no ordinary effort. For the men of that time it was a great effort. With the limited, or at best uncertain, resources then at command, it is not to be wondered that Washington at first hesitated. Sir Henry Clinton, on the opposite side, seems to have entertained no suspicion of such a movement. Failure might have come—and there were those who looked for it, Hamilton among them—but, even with this result, adverse criticism must have been silenced before Washington's clear presentation of the political and military reasons in its favor. Convinced, after full reflection upon the demands of the country and his relations to the allies, and after canvassing every conceivable contingency, that it was his only as well as a promising alternative, he adopted the plan, and immediately proceeded to its execution. The energy of his measures seemed to be prophetic of success. The issue depended upon the exact coincidence of several movements, both by land and sea; and failure of co-operation on his part was not to be permitted. He pushed to the Chesapeake to be gloriously rewarded. That march was the centre-piece of the combination—*the* surprise of a campaign which abounded in surprises.

The force destined to the southward consisted of the French wing, four thousand strong, and two thousand men from the American army, including Scammell's Light Infantry, Lamb's Regiment of Artillery, the New York regiments, the two New Jersey, the Rhode Island, and Hazen's old Canadian regiment, and the small corps of Engineers, and Sappers and Miners. The remainder of the army—namely, ten Massachusetts regiments, five Connecticut, two New Hampshire, Crane's Third Artillery, Sheldon's Dragoons, and militia parties—a total of less than four thousand—were left, under General Heath, to guard West Point and the Highlands. General Lord Stirling took post at Saratoga above, and Lieutenant-colonel Willett upon the Mohawk, with New York Continentals and Eastern militia, to protect the Northern frontier against threatened incursions from Canada.

On the 19th of August the movement began. At first it was conducted under the guise of an attempt upon New York from the Jersey side. Above all was it necessary to conceal the real destination as long as possible from the enemy. The direction of the march favoring a feint toward Staten Island, the opportunity was fully improved. Clinton understood that the possession of that island by Washington would materially facilitate the latter's co-operation with the expected French fleet. The appearance of American troops in the vicinity of Springfield or Brunswick, New Jersey—an easy march from the lower end of the island —would thus be readily explained. To strengthen the impression of operations in that quarter, French ovens and storehouses were established at Chatham, near Springfield, where the Jersey line was encamped, and whither, on the 18th, Washington sent Hazen's regiment.[1] This indicated activity where Clinton would not be surprised to see it.

Breaking camp at Dobb's Ferry early on the morning of the date named—the 19th—the allied army faced about to cross the Hudson at King's Ferry above. Washington, with the Continentals, took the river route, while the French moved farther to the right by way of Northcastle, Pine's Bridge, and Crompond. At King's Ferry, where Quartermaster-general Pickering repaired to have everything in readiness, the American detachment, with its baggage and artillery, crossed first and rapidly on the 20th and 21st,[2] and encamped beyond—the Light Infantry at Kakeat. Muddy roads, poor horses, heavy guns, and much camp equipage delayed the French, and they were not all over until the 26th. Washington, who made his head-quarters at the Smith house, at Haverstraw, the scene of

---

[1] "Hazen's regiment, being thrown over at Dobb's Ferry, was ordered with the Jersey Troops to march and take Post on the heights between Springfield and Chatham, and cover a French Bakery at the latter place, to veil our real movement and create apprehensions for Staten Island."—*Washington's Journal*, August 18.

[2] "Monday 20th. . . . This morning the detachments from the American army reached King's Ferry and began to cross; and such despatch was used that day, the following night, and Tuesday morning, that the baggage, park, and American troops had crossed by noon of the 21st."—*Colonel Pickering's Journal.*

the complot of Arnold and André, superintended, in part, the crossing of the two armies. Claude Blanchard, commissary of the French corps, remembered his presence with them. "This crossing," he writes in his entertaining journal, "occupied much time, owing to the breadth of the river, which they were obliged to cross in ferry-boats, collected in great numbers, but still not enough. On the 25th I went myself to the spot, and saw many of the troops and much baggage cross. General Washington was there; they had provided a pavilion for him, from which he examined everything very attentively. He seemed, in this crossing, in the march of our troops toward the Chesapeake Bay, and in our reunion with M. de Grasse, to see a better destiny arise, when, at this period of the war, exhausted, destitute of resources, he needed a great success, which might revive courage and hope. He pressed my hand with much affection when he left us and crossed the river himself."

From the ferry the march was resumed without delay, and as far as Princeton three different routes were followed. The American wing, starting off early on the 25th, separated into two columns. The Light Infantry and the First New York, under

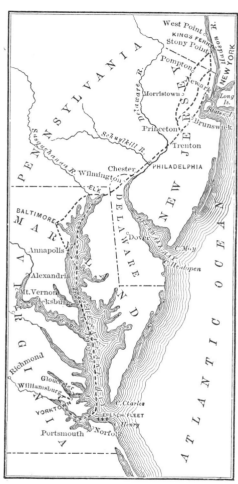

ROUTE OF WASHINGTON'S ARMY FROM THE HUDSON TO YORKTOWN.

the command of General Lincoln, keeping to the left, marched from Kakeat by way of Paramus and Second River, and encamped on the 27th at Springfield. The other column, including the remaining troops, with the artillery, baggage, and stores, marched by Pompton to Chatham; while the French, keeping to the right, passed through Suffrens and Pompton to Whippany. By these movements the entire force was encamped on the 28th in the vicinity of Chatham, within striking distance of the enemy.[1] Here, also, there was one day's halt; and, as Hazen's regiment and the Jersey line were already on the spot, the concentration seemed to point to the possible attempt upon Staten Island, or a march beyond to Sandy Hook, for the purpose, as Washington writes, of facilitating "the entrance of the French fleet within the Bay." On the 29th the troops were again in motion. One day's march more could be continued in the same general direction without exciting the enemy's suspicion, and on this date the left column, reorganized, proceeded to Brunswick, the centre to Boundbrook, and the French through Morristown to Bullion's Tavern. Then, on the following day, the columns, no longer inclining toward the enemy, headed directly away to Princeton and Trenton, and the march to the Chesapeake became an open movement.[2]

---

[1] Washington gave directions daily for the march of each column. The following, for the 29th, is one of General Lincoln's orders:

"Sir,—The general will beat at 3 o'clock to-morrow morning—the assembly at half-past three, and the march at 4 o'clock. General Hazin's regiment in front and the Sappers and Miners will cover your rear. You will march through the Scotch plains, Quibble Town, and Bound Brook. On the 30th to Princeton—31st to Trenton, where you will meet me and further orders. You will keep these orders a perfect secret.

"I am your very humble servant,
"August 28th, 1781.   "B. Lincoln.
"Colonel Lamb."
                                      [Lamb MS., N. Y. Hist. Soc.]

[2] "As our intentions could be concealed one march more (under the idea of marching to Sandy Hook to facilitate the entrance of the French fleet within the Bay), the whole army was put in motion in three columns; the left consisted of the light infantry, first York Regiment, and the Regiment of Rhode Island; the middle column consisted of the park, stores, and baggage, Lamb's Regiment of Artillery, Hazen's, and the Corps of Sappers and Miners; the right column consisted of the whole French army, baggage, stores, etc. This last was to march by the route of Morristown, Bullion's Tavern, Somerset Court House, and Princetown. The middle was to go by Boundbrook to Somerset, etc., and the left to proceed by the way of Brunswick to Trenton, to which place the whole were to march, transports being ordered to meet them there."—*Washington's Journal.*

The above is entered in the "Journal" under date of August 30th by mistake for the 29th. The Jersey line, omitted, marched with the left column, and the Second New York followed in the rear of the French, with thirty boats or "batteaux" on wheels, which had been built for the attack on New York, but which Washington took along for use in Virginia. Pickering states that he saw them safe as far as Suffrens on the 27th. The French army marched in two divisions—one following the other with a day's interval.

The feint, thus admirably preserved, had served its purpose. The true destination being kept a profound secret at head-quarters, no deserters could take the news to Clinton. Officers of rank in the allied army had not fathomed the movement, and were as ignorant of its object as the soldiers. Count Fersen, aide to Rochambeau, admits that he was not in the secret. Colonel Deuxponts was not favored with it until the 28th; and another French officer of the staff could only conjecture, on the 29th, that Virginia was the objective point. Surgeon Thacher, of Scammell's corps, states that curiosity in the matter remained at a high pitch in the American camp until Princeton was reached. And, as to the enemy, we have Sir Henry Clinton's own admission of his uncertainty and his unreadiness also to meet such a movement in time. " If I had as many reasons," he writes in his narrative of this campaign, "to believe that Mr. Washington would move his army into Virginia without a covering fleet as I had to think he would not, I could not have prevented his passing the Hudson under cover of his forts at Verplank's and Stoney Points. Nor (supposing I had boats properly manned) would it have been advisable to have landed at Elizabethtown, in the face of works which he might easily have occupied, as they were only seven miles from his camp at Chatham, without subjecting my army to be beat *en detail*. Nor could I, when informed of his march toward the Delaware, have passed an army in time to have made any impression upon him before he crossed that river."

Assured of their destination in facing southward, the troops marched on rapidly. The Americans, in the van, were at Princeton on the 30th, and at Trenton on the 31st. It was hoped that at the Delaware there would be boats and vessels enough to take them all down to Wilmington or Christiana Bridge; but, in spite of urgent letters from Washington and the efforts of Robert Morris and Quartermaster Miles, of Philadelphia, the number was insufficient to transport the whole, and the march by land was continued. The Second New York Regiment, with the batteaux and intrenching tools, the artillery, and Hazen's, alone went by water. Crossing the Delaware on the 1st of September, the Americans marched seventeen miles, to Lower Dublin; and on the 2d, after a twelve-miles march, reached and passed through Philadelphia, going into camp near the Schuylkill. The French followed on the 3d, keeping, from Princeton, a day behind.

Washington and Rochambeau, leaving Lincoln and Viomenil in charge of the respective wings of the army, hastened to Philadelphia in advance of the troops, reaching the city on the 30th. Quartermaster Pickering

reached it on the same day, after a hard ride of sixty miles from Brunswick landing. The commander-in-chief, of course, was received with
every honor and attention. A troop of light horse, meeting him in the
suburbs, escorted him into town, where he arrived at one o'clock. Robert
Morris, the Superintendent of Finance, was among the first to welcome
him. At the City Tavern, where the party alighted, he was received by
"the universal acclamations of the citizens," while many gentlemen called
to pay their respects. The general then adjourned, says Morris, in his
diary,[1] "to my house, with his suite, Count de Rochambeau, the Chevalier Chastellux, General Knox, General Moultrie, and others, to dinner."
There they drank toasts to the United States, to the Kings of France and
Spain, to the United Provinces, to the Allied Armies, and to the speedy
arrival of Count de Grasse, while several ships in the river thundered
salutes in response. In the evening there was a general illumination in
honor of his Excellency, who walked through some of the principal streets,
with devoted throngs pressing around him. The city was all astir on the
occasion; and, after these ovations to the chiefs, it was equally hearty in
its welcome of the troops, who came marching through a day or two later.
The American detachment appeared on the afternoon of September 2d,
but made no halt. Warm and dry weather it had been, and they raised
a dust "like a smothering snow-storm," which was not a little mortifying,
says Thacher, "as the ladies were viewing us from the open windows of
every house as we passed through this splendid city." The line of march,
he continues, including appendages and attendants, extended nearly two
miles. "The general officers and their aids, in rich military uniform,
mounted on noble steeds elegantly caparisoned, were followed by their
servants and baggage. In the rear of every brigade were several field-
pieces, accompanied by ammunition carriages. The soldiers marched in
slow and solemn step, regulated by the drum and fife;" and in the rear
followed a great number of wagons, loaded with tents, provisions, and
baggage. Gay and prosperous seemed the city to the bronzed Continentals, the heroes of hard service and privation; and if they grumbled
somewhat in the ears of Congress about their long-deferred pay, it
would have ill become that body or the civilian to blame them. Washington understood their discontent, and saw to it that they were speedily
satisfied.

Much more of a sensation was the entrance of the French army on
the following days. Philadelphia was the American capital. The same

---

[1] Extract from Robert Morris's diary, in "Diplomatic Cor.," vol. xi., p. 462.

honors were due to Congress that the King would receive at home. Uniformed in white, with colored trimmings, and dressed "as elegantly as ever the soldiers of a garrison were on a day of review," the army of our "gracious ally" marched into the city with Rochambeau, who had gone out to meet them, at their head. The first division entered on the 3d, the second on the 4th. They passed in review before Congress, the French minister, and the commanding generals, and from the accounts of

ROBERT MORRIS.

the day we learn that, as a special observance of etiquette, the President and delegates took off their hats at the salutes of the officers and standards, while Washington and Rochambeau stood uncovered. The crowded streets, the windows filled with spectators, the music of the bands, the brilliant array of troops, and the enthusiasm over the expected successes in the field, made these days historical for the city. French journals and letters enlarge upon the scene and the impression produced upon the American imagination by so much display and grandeur. Then, on the 5th, the regiment of Soissonnais gave an exhibition of the French drill in the presence of several thousand people, and Philadelphia settled down to await the more solid enjoyment that the coming victory was to bring.[1]

On move the troops, meanwhile, the Continentals halting but part of one day. The 3d, they marched ten miles from the Schuylkill to within three miles of Chester. On the 4th "through Chester, through Brandywine, through Wilmington," says Lieutenant Sanderson, of the Light Infantry, encamping one mile beyond—about twenty miles that day. The next day twelve miles, through Christiana, where the park of artillery and troops from Trenton had landed the day before; and on the 6th a march of ten miles brought them to the head of Elk, a short distance from the Chesapeake. It had been fifteen days since they left the Hudson, two hundred miles to the northward. On the 8th they were joined by the French troops. In spite of the fatigues of the march they were all in good spirits, with hardly a sick man among them, and seemed to realize the probably decisive results of the movement they were engaged in. " We shall soon look in upon Cornwallis as stern as the grave," wrote an officer to a friend in the North. From the same point wrote Pickering to his wife: " Here I am, my dearest, in perfect health. Presently I set out for Williamsburg by land. It will be a seven or eight days' journey, and give me an opportunity of seeing Maryland and Virginia. I hope, in a little time, to congratulate you on the capture of Cornwallis and his army. Should we succeed at all, the work, I think, will be short; and the only chance of ill-success will arise from this—that Cornwallis may possibly attempt to save himself by flight, by marching his army up the country, and then pushing to South Carolina. But a few days' delay will render this impossible, as our troops will soon surround them."

At Philadelphia, Washington confidently hoped to have the news of De Grasse's arrival in the Chesapeake. None came, and for a day or two the uncertainty clouded the prospect. What might not have stopped or delayed the fleet? The active Rodney and Hood, with good English ships, were in the West Indies, and would certainly do their best to harass the French. Had they encountered De Grasse and kept him back? All depended on that fleet. But, happily, the suspense was brief. Washington left Philadelphia for the Head of Elk on the 5th. At Chester, the same afternoon, he received despatches from General Gist, at Baltimore, with the welcome news that De Grasse was at last

---

[1] For particulars respecting the march of the French, and scenes in Philadelphia, see Deuxpont's " My Campaigns," Thacher's " Journal," and article and references in *Mag. of Am. History*, vol. v., pp. 1–20.

in the Chesapeake. Overjoyed at the intelligence, he sent it at once to Congress, and then pushed on to join the troops. "I never saw a man so thoroughly and openly delighted than General Washington," says the Duke de Lauzun. Reaching the Head of Elk on the next morning, he issued the following congratulatory order to the army:

"Head Quarters, Head of Elk, Sept. 6, 1781.

"It is with the highest pleasure and satisfaction that the Commander-in-chief announces to the Army the arrival of Count De Grass in the Chesapeak, with a very favourable Naval and Land force. At the same time he felicitates the army on the auspicious occasion, he anticipates the glorious events which may be expected from the combined operations now in contemplation. As no circumstance could possibly happen more opportunely in point of time, no prospect would ever have promised more opportunely of success. Nothing but want of exertion can possibly blast the pleasing prospect before us. The General calls upon the gentlemen officers, the brave and faithfull soldiers he has the honour to command, to exert their utmost abilities in the cause of their country, to share with him, with their usual alacrity, the difficulties, dangers, and glory of the enterprise." [1]

To this was added the gratifying announcement that abstracts for a month's pay were to be made out immediately for all the troops, excepting those who had been so "lost to all sense of honour, the pride of their profession and the love of their country, as to desert the Standard of Freedom at this critical period." Promptly, as soon as the pay-rolls were ready, Mr. Philip Audibert, Deputy Paymaster-general at Philadelphia, appeared in the camps with hard money, which Robert Morris had borrowed from the Intendant of the French army, with Rochambeau's consent, and succeeded in adding substantially to the good-humor of the soldiers.

Men, indeed, on every side seemed to feel that great events were at hand. "Before this reaches you," wrote Rush to Gates, on the 5th, "the fate of Great Britain and the repose of Europe will probably be determined in Chesapeake Bay. Heaven prosper our allies! I long to be satiated with revenge against *Scotch* Englishmen. Heyder Ali is the standing toast of my table. The enemies of Great Britain *anywhere* and *everywhere* should be the friends of every American. Virtue, justice, and humanity have exhausted their tears in weeping over her depredations upon human nature." "Everything," said Governor Howley, of Pennsylvania, "conspires to complete the destruction of British hopes in our Southern world." "General Washington and the army," wrote William Clajon, "are gone to take Lord Cornwallis in his mouse-trap." [2]

---

[1] Lieutenant Sanderson's MS. Diary.　　　　[2] Extracts from the Gates MS.

Leaving the allies, now, for a moment, at the head of the Elk, preparing to sail down the Chesapeake, what was the situation below? How came Cornwallis to remain quietly at Yorktown when he discovered that he must soon be cooped up there? How had the French suddenly acquired a naval supremacy on this coast? What was Lafayette doing?

As to the latter, when he learned that Cornwallis had sailed from Portsmouth up the Bay, instead of to New York, he broke up camp at Malvern Hill, and "cut across," with the Light Infantry, toward Fredericksburg, under the supposition that Baltimore was the enemy's destination. Finding that they brought up at Yorktown, he took position on the Pamunky, near West Point. As he supposed that field movements were to begin again, he called loudly for cavalry. "Push on every dragoon," he wrote to Steuben on the 3d; on the 9th again: "Tarleton is arrived at York. I dread the consequences of such a superiority of horse;" on the 13th, from Montock Hill: "Unless I immediately receive two hundred dragoons the consequences will be fatal, not only to this State and army, but to the whole system of our campaign." Singularly enough, he could get very few—one hundred in all, sixty of whom represented the Fourth Regiment, which came from Pennsylvania. Virginia should have supplied the demand, but the State had no equipments. Fortunately, Tarleton and Simcoe kept quiet at York and Gloucester.

Presently Washington communicated to Lafayette the possible land and naval combination in the Chesapeake, and the marquis was happier. On the 25th of August he was elated with word from his chief that De Grasse was certainly coming to Virginia, and that he himself was about to move down with part of the Northern army to his assistance. The point was now of great importance to keep Cornwallis ignorant of these movements as long as possible, and also to prevent his retreat, should he attempt it, into North Carolina. Lafayette, accordingly, exerted himself with new vigor under the pleasing prospect. Wayne, with the Pennsylvanians, was on the south bank of the James, under instructions to join General Greene in South Carolina. They were stopped at once, Lafayette explaining the reason to Wayne, on the 25th, as follows: "I am happy in this safe opportunity to open my heart to you; there is an important secret which I communicate to you alone, and which I request you to keep from everybody's knowledge. There is great reason to hope for an immediate aid by water. In the last letter from the General he communicates this intelligence, which I am bound upon honor to keep secret. He directs me to keep you here until further orders; and, above all, recommends that every measure be taken to prevent the enemy's retreating to Carolina. . . .

I would therefore wish you to take an healthy position, near Westover; to make every preparation; to collect the means of helping to keep up the idea of a southern destination; and to improve your situation upon James River, in having your men well supplied."[1] At the same time Governor Burke, of North Carolina, was requested to destroy the fords and boats on the rivers that the enemy would have to cross, and post his militia at the passes and advantageous points to delay them.

This, then, was the general situation at the close of August: Cornwallis fortifying leisurely at Yorktown; Lafayette in a camp of observation at Holt's Forge, on the Pamunky, near the White House; Wayne on the James, about opposite Harrison's Landing; Washington's troops marching down through Trenton; De Grasse entering the Chesapeake. Cornwallis did not yet know about Washington or the French admiral.

The next point is the naval co-operation. From the beginning of the war Great Britain had retained complete control of the American waters. By unexpectedly losing it at this crisis she lost her colonies. Fox and other members of the Opposition in Parliament insisted that the failure of the British plans in 1781 was to be laid at the door of the Navy and its Secretary, Lord Sandwich. It was a vital question: Why had France been permitted suddenly to acquire such decisive naval superiority on the American coast? Cornwallis, otherwise, would have been saved from ruin.

Briefly reviewing the facts in the case, and it appears that while the British navy, which, in 1781, included about eighty ships-of-the-line in commission, was superior to that of France, it was far inferior to the combined navies of France and Spain, whose courts were then in alliance. The protection of many points necessitated the dispersion of her fleets. One covered Gibraltar. Admiral Darby, with thirty sail-of-the-line, watched the English Channel. Sir George Rodney, seconded by Sir Samuel Hood, cruised in the West Indies; while Admiral Arbuthnot, soon succeeded by Graves, guarded New York with eight ships. The French fleet in American waters, before the campaign opened, was also of eight ships, and lay at Newport, Rhode Island, under the command of the newly-arrived Admiral de Barras.

France had long hoped to render America more effective assistance than her first land and naval contingent of 1780, under Rochambeau, could offer, but it was not until eight months later that her promise could

---

[1] Wayne papers, in *Casket*, August 25, 1781.

be realized; and then only a fleet could be spared, with conditional instructions respecting operations on the Northern coast. This was placed under the command of Admiral de Grasse, a sailor of reputation; and, on the 22d of March, it started, with a large convoy, from Brest, with the primary object of serving French and Spanish colonial interests in the West Indies. Toward the close of April De Grasse, with twenty-four ships, appeared off Martinique, in the Little Antilles, skirmished with Hood, and, in the first days of May, took Tobago from the English. Rodney, who with Hood had twenty-two ships, did not engage seriously, for fear of becoming entangled "among the Grenadillas" and decoyed into the rapid currents off the coast of Venezuela. De Grasse then sailed to Cape François—the present Cape Haytien, on the northern coast of Hayti—where he found the frigate *Concorde* awaiting him with the despatches from Washington and Rochambeau urging his co-operation with them at whatever might prove the most favorable point on the coast. Concluding, as we have seen, that the Chesapeake was that point, he collected as many ships as possible, borrowed three thousand troops, under the Marquis St. Simon, and fifteen hundred thousand livres at Havana, as the allied commanders had requested, and, heading northward on the 13th of August, anchored on the 31st in Lynnhaven Bay, outside of Hampton Roads. He had brought a noble fleet of twenty-eight sail-of-the-line and six frigates—his own flag-ship being the *Ville de Paris*, carrying one hundred and twenty guns, and regarded with pride in the French navy as the grandest hull afloat on all the seas.

Thus the several lines were drawing together with singular good-fortune. One further step, however, remained to be taken, and that cautiously. Should Cornwallis suddenly realize his danger, he might leave Yorktown, move up the peninsula, cross the James at or above Richmond, and put himself in the Carolinas again. Lafayette, accordingly, concerted with the Marquis St. Simon, as soon as the fleet arrived, to have the troops, brought from the West Indies, land at Jamestown Island on the 5th of September, while he should move his own troops from the Pamunky to the same vicinity at about the same time, and Wayne move his to the island down the south bank of the James. This simultaneous junction was effected without interruption, and on the evening of the 7th the entire force, with Lafayette in command, took up a strong position across the peninsula at Williamsburg, a dozen miles north of Yorktown. Cornwallis subsequently reconnoitred Lafayette's camp, with a view of breaking through, but he seems to have counted the hazard great, and preferred to await the movements of the British admirals, who, he supposed and was encouraged to believe, would sooner or later be able to raise De Grasse's blockade and bring him relief.

Finally, in this connection, what were Rodney, and Hood, and Graves about, that they permitted De Grasse to preoccupy the Chesapeake and hold his own there until Cornwallis fell? Fatality attended them at every step. It was Rodney's duty to see that the French fleet was neutralized in these waters, and as early as May 3d he warned Arbuthnot, at New York, of its arrival—"that you may be upon your guard," are his words, "should they visit the coasts of America, in which case I shall send every assistance in my power." Graves had succeeded Arbuthnot, but soon after receiving this intelligence he sailed off on a cruise to the eastward. When Rodney heard that De Grasse had repaired to Cape François, he promptly sent a second despatch to Graves, recommending him to unite his squadron with that which he should send or lead himself to Virginia, and requesting him to have frigates looking out for him with the latest information as to affairs in America. This despatch never reached Graves. The captain of the sloop-of-war which carried it arrived safely at New York, but not finding the admiral, sailed in search of him to the eastward. On the way he fell in with three American privateers, which compelled him to run his vessel ashore on Long Island. The despatches he sunk! not suspecting their importance.[1] Meanwhile Rodney, pleading ill-health, decided to return to England, and sent Hood northward to join Graves and head off De Grasse. Sailing up the coast, Hood looked into the Chesapeake on August 25th, but found no French there; nor was there any frigate or any word from Graves. Continuing his course, therefore, with the fourteen sail-of-the-line, six frigates, and one fire-ship, which he brought from the West Indies, he reached Sandy Hook, and reported the situation to Graves, who had lately returned to New York; and this was the first that Graves knew of the approach of De Grasse and the threatened danger in Virginia. He realized the necessity, however, of immediate action, and joining his ships to Hood's, assumed the command and bore down to the Chesapeake. As it had just been ascertained that De Barras, with the French fleet at Newport, had sailed, presumably, for the same point, haste was made to get there before him, and at least prevent his junction with De Grasse.

Graves and Hood were too late, for De Grasse had entered the Chesapeake. He was but five days behind Hood on the way from the West

---

[1] These facts appear in "Two Letters Respecting the Conduct of Rear-admiral Graves," etc. Edited by Mr. H. B. Dawson.

Indies. But the English admirals determined to attempt his dislodgement by fighting, and on the 5th of September, the day St. Simon's troops were landing at Jamestown Island, the two fleets hove in sight of each other and prepared for action.   De Grasse slipped his cables and stood out to sea for more room.   His line of battle numbered twenty-four ships of the

COUNT DE GRASSE.

line, carrying seventeen hundred guns and nineteen thousand seamen. Le Sieur de Bougainville and Le Sieur de Monteil commanded the two main divisions of the fleet. Opposed to him, Graves presented the lighter armament of nineteen ships-of-the-line, with fourteen hundred guns and thirteen thousand seamen. The three divisions of his fleet were commanded by Sir Samuel Hood, Sir Francis Samuel Drake, and himself. At a quarter-past four in the afternoon the action began, and at half-past six it was over, with advantage to the French, but not decisive. The English lost ninety men killed and two hundred and forty-six wounded, and had sixteen guns dismounted. On the part of the French the loss was something more; but the English admiral found that two or three of his ships were badly damaged, and after manœuvring four days returned to New York, leaving De Grasse master of the Chesapeake.

"The 5th of September was, I confess, a moment of ambition for me," wrote Graves at a later day; and well it might have been. Could he have gained one of those memorable victories over De Grasse which so often grace the records of England's navy, the Yorktown Campaign would have had a different termination. The secret of the British failure there was either the ministry's neglect in immediately securing absolute naval supremacy on this coast, after De Grasse sailed from France, or the over-confidence or carelessness of the admirals in command. It is the British naval administration that is to be charged with the Yorktown catastrophe. The blunders of Clinton and Cornwallis contributed only in a minor degree.[1]

It only remained now for Washington's troops to reach Lafayette's force at Williamsburg, and march down upon Cornwallis. From the head of the Elk the advance of each army embarked in light transports. The main body of the French and the New York and New Jersey troops kept on to Baltimore and Annapolis, and embarked in frigates sent up by De Grasse. By the 18th (September) they were all off, heading down the Chesapeake for the landings nearest Williamsburg on the James. Scammell's light infantry were the first to arrive, and they disembarked at the College Landing, about a mile from Williamsburg, on College or Archer's Hope creek.[2] The French landed in the vicinity, at Jamestown

---

[1] Clinton claims that the home authorities assured him of Rodney's ability to take care of De Grasse, relieving him of anxiety on that point. As to Hood and the action of September 5th, Clinton says this: "When Mr. Graves sailed, Sir Samuel Hood was clear of opinion La Grasse would bring no more than 16 of the line at most. Barras tho' at sea was far to the Eastward; there, therefore, was every probability that Mr. Graves would beat them en detail, and even should they join, Sir Samuel Hood said he thought they were a match."—*Clinton's explanation in "New York in the Revolution,"* pp. 183–84.

[2] The original name of what is usually called College Creek is "Archer's Hope." Chaplain Evans, of Scammell's corps, says, September 20th: "We proceeded up James'

Island, and at Burwell's Ferry, the present King's Mills Wharf, one mile below the mouth of Archer's Hope. The stores and artillery were unloaded at Trebell's, or the present Grove Wharf, three miles below Burwell's, and six miles from Yorktown, these points being precisely located on the accompanying map, made by Major Kearney in 1818. On the 26th all the troops—Washington's, the French, and Lafayette's—were concentrated in front of Williamsburg.

As to the commander-in-chief—not waiting for the embarkation of the troops at the head of Elk, he pushed on to Baltimore with Rochambeau, and then, riding sixty miles a day, reached his home at Mount Vernon, which he had not visited for six years. Here he remained three days, the 9th to the 12th, and on the 14th arrived at Lafayette's headquarters, at Williamsburg, in advance of his army. As he approached the latter's camp the troops turned out on their parades, a salute of twenty-one guns was fired, and later in the afternoon the Marquis St. Simon gave a sumptuous entertainment, at which the chiefs and all the officers were present. "To add to the happiness of the evening," says Colonel Butler, "an elegant band of music played an introductive part of a French opera, signifying the happiness of the family when blessed with the presence of their father, and their great dependence upon him. About ten o'clock the company rose up, and after mutual congratulations and the greatest expressions of joy, they separated."

On the 27th Washington issued marching orders for the next morning, and all was made ready for the final grapple with the enemy.

The situation thus presented was the great surprise of the Revolution. It appears as one of the few grand relieving features in an otherwise comparatively tedious war, for here we have a piece of strategy on Washington's part which involved for the first time extensive and critical operations, and whose details were carried out with singular precision and success. Clinton is quietly left in the lurch at New York; Washington boldly marches four hundred miles away, and suddenly falls upon his famous lieutenant at a point where assistance cannot reach him.

In the following chapter we reach the glorious termination of these rapidly developing movements.

river with a fair wind until our vessel ran on ground, where we continued till 8 o'clock this morning, when we left that vessel, and went on board of a smaller one. The wind was against us this day, and very violent; nevertheless, by tacking frequently and contending with the wind, we arrived at this place, which is called the landing of Archer's Hope. . . ."

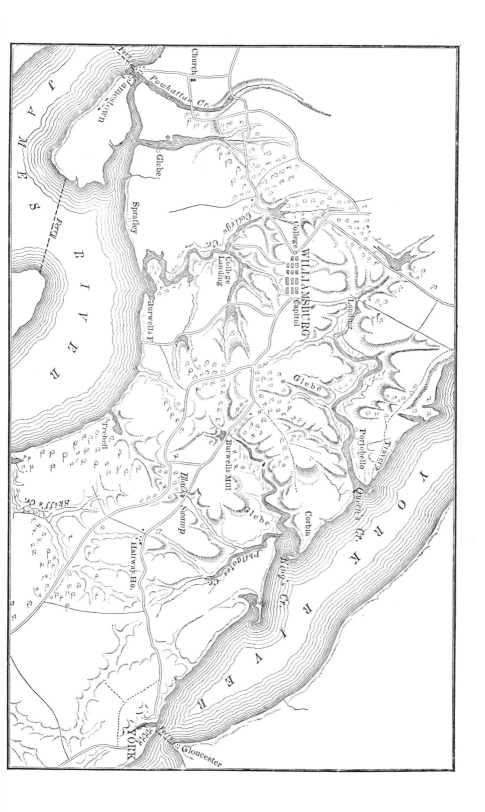

CHAPTER VI.

THE SIEGE OF YORKTOWN.

EARLY on the morning of the 28th the expectant troops moved forward from Williamsburg to the scene of their coming triumph. It proved to be a leisurely march of eleven miles under a fair sky. Taking the "great road" down the peninsula, the main body of Continentals and French, the former in advance, passed the Half-way House in single column; then, following separate routes—the Americans filing to the right —halted at noon within two miles of the enemy's position in front of Yorktown. The militia, marching farther to the right, by Harwood's Mills, joined the Continentals at a point known as Munford's Bridge. Muhlenberg's Light Infantry Brigade, preceded by Moylan's dragoons and Colonel Lewis's riflemen, formed the van of the Americans; while the volunteers of Baron St. Simon and chasseurs and grenadiers, under the Marquis de Laval, led the French. The troops all moved in light marching order, ready for action at a moment's notice, and were doubtless eager for the opportunity to fulfil the instructions of the commander-in-chief issued the day before. "If the enemy should be tempted to meet the army on its march," ran the order, "the General particularly enjoins the troops to place their principal reliance on the bayonet, that they may prove the vanity of the boast which the British make of their peculiar prowess in deciding battles with that weapon. He trusts a generous emulation will actuate the allied armies; that the French, whose national weapon is that of close fight, and the troops in general, that have so often used it with success, will distinguish themselves on every occasion that offers. The justice of the cause in which we are engaged, and the honor of the two Nations, must inspire every breast with sentiments that are the presage of victory."

To this approach of the allies no resistance was offered. For Cornwallis it would have been a waste of men; and as the combined columns appeared in sight his pickets fell back. Those of Abercrombie's light infantry, which covered the British right, were the first to give the alarm. Rochambeau sent forward Baron Viomenil, who, with De Laval's chasseurs

and two field-pieces, cleared the way for an examination of the ground
in that quarter. Tarleton's Legion covered the enemy's left, but the in-
tervention of a marshy rivulet prevented more than the firing of a few
cannon-shot at his videttes, and at sunset his command withdrew to the
Moore House, below Yorktown. No casualties occurred in this advance;
and the allied army, forming in line of battle from the York River, above
the town, through the woods and fields to the Beaverdam, or Warwick
Creek, the French on the left, the Americans on the right, rested within
a mile of the British posts. Washington's brief order in the evening indicated the proximity of the combatants: "The whole army, officers and
soldiers, will lay on their arms this night." [1]

The position of the enemy, now to be invested by the allies, was not
especially favorable for defence. In taking post at Yorktown Cornwallis
never anticipated the contingency of a siege. The place might answer
as a naval station, and works would be necessary to protect it in case the
garrison should be reduced, but otherwise it was a bad selection. "Nothing but the hope of relief," said Cornwallis afterward, "would have induced me to attempt its defence." The town stood on the bank of the
river, thirty or forty feet above the water, but possessed no commanding
features as against a land attack. Cornwallis surrounded it with a line
of earthworks. Of the ten redoubts in this line two covered the right,
facing the river-road to Williamsburg; three stood back of the town, and
three on the left, looking down the river; the two remaining redoubts,
known as Nos. 9 and 10, stood disconnected in advance of, and as an additional strength to, the left. A projecting redoubt, called the Horn-work,
commanded the road to Hampton. In the fourteen batteries constructed
along the line sixty-five guns had been mounted, none of which were
larger than eighteen-pounders, and to obtain some of these the frigate
Charon, in the river, had been stripped of her armament.

These were the immediate defences of Yorktown; but as the ground
beyond, especially on the left, would favor a besieging force, and as the
defences themselves were not complete when the place was threatened,
Cornwallis determined to take up a good outer position also, about a
half a mile in advance of his inner line. He describes it as "a
strong position out of the town." Above Yorktown a ravine extended from the river nearly half-way around the inner works; below,

---

[1] The incidents of the 28th are gathered from Washington's "Journal," "Orderly
Book of the Siege of Yorktown," Tarleton's "Campaigns," Deuxpont's "Campaigns,"
"Journal," in Martin's Gazetteer of Virginia, Pickering's "Journal," etc.

Wormley Creek sets up. These two natural obstructions protected the flanks, and contracted the distance to be fortified in solid ground between them to little more than half a mile. This site was somewhat elevated, and a few works would be sufficient to secure it. It is mentioned as the "gorge" or throat of land between ravine and creek, over which ran the road to Hampton and the main road to Williamsburg.

BRITISH OFFICERS RECEIVING THE NEWS OF WASHINGTON'S APPROACH.

Here the engineers laid out three redoubts, one on each side of the latter road, in what was then known as Pigeon Quarter, and the third, a field work, on the left, commanding the Hampton Road. "Trees were felled," says Tarleton, "flèches were thrown up, and batteries were constructed at the points which were deemed most vulnerable." There were intrenchments at Moore's Mill, near the head of Wormley Creek, while on the extreme right, beyond the ravine, and on the bank of the York, "close to the river-road from Williamsburg," a large star-shaped work was constructed, known as the Fusileers' Redoubt, which was garrisoned by a portion of the Royal Welsh Fusileers—Twenty-third

Foot—under Captain Apthorpe, and a body of marines. The officer second in command was Captain Thomas Saumaurez, who lived long enough to be promoted to the rank of lieutenant-general in the British army on the day of Queen Victoria's coronation. Opposite this redoubt and the mouth of the ravine the frigate *Guadaloupe* was moored, whose guns could also protect that flank.[1] Across the river, there a mile wide, the village of Gloucester had been fortified before Yorktown, and the defences consisted of a line of intrenchments, with four redoubts and three batteries, mounting nineteen guns.

Here, too, we may stop to notice the composition of the two hostile armies, on whose operations so much depended. In the opposing lines we should have found representatives of those four leading groups of people who claim superiority in arms, and each of whom, at different periods of their history, have displayed extraordinary tenacity in supporting their national cause—the English and Germans, the French and Americans. It was no indifferent collection of soldiers that had now gathered within and around Yorktown, but bodies of tried troops, who were, for the most part, the veterans of many fields, both on this and the European continent.

The allied army was composed of three parts—American Continentals, American militia, and French auxiliaries; the two former constituting the right, the latter the left wing. The Continentals had been organized at Williamsburg, on the 27th, into three divisions of two brigades each, with Major-generals Lincoln, Lafayette, and Steuben as division commanders. Lincoln, in addition, was given the temporary command of the American wing. Lafayette's division, which took the right of the entire line, included the select troops of the army, or the corps

---

[1] Before the Revolution Yorktown was quite an emporium—the only port from which the Virginia planters shipped their tobacco to England. Baltimore and Norfolk gradually reduced it by competition. Some two centuries or more ago we first hear of it as one of the few outposts or forts in the colony. In 1725 it was the centre of a thriving county—an Episcopal parish of sixty communicants, with a church. Williamsburg, the capital, with its House of Burgesses and growing college, attracting thither the wisdom and fashion of the Dominion, was but a dozen miles away. Until Cornwallis stationed himself there, the town had escaped the ravages of war on the Virginia coast, and after its surrender it still contained about seventy houses, not more than two or three having been wholly destroyed. Fifteen years later it had not extended its limits, and we find its population, more than half of which was composed of negroes, numbering about eight hundred souls. The last war, it need hardly be said, left it in a depressed condition, almost beyond recovery; and to-day it contains less than three hundred inhabitants, among whom are to be found but few descendants of the ancient proprietors.

of Light Infantry. General Muhlenberg commanded the First Brigade, General Hazen the Second. The three battalions of the First were led by Colonel Vose, of Massachusetts, Lieutenant-colonel Gimat, aide to Lafayette, and Lieutenant-colonel Barber, of New Jersey; those of the Second by Lieutenant-colonel Huntington, of Connecticut, Lieutenant-colonel Alexander Hamilton, of New York, and Lieutenant-colonel Laurens, of South Carolina, aide to Washington. Brigaded with these, also, was Hazen's old Canadian regiment, some two hundred and fifty strong. Excluding the latter, the Light Infantry numbered about fourteen hundred men, nearly all of whom had been detached from the New England lines. The First Brigade, which had been with him through the Virginia campaign, was Lafayette's favorite, and he used to say of it that finer troops could not be found the world over. Steuben's division included the brigades under Generals Wayne and Gist. In the former were two Pennsylvania regiments, commanded by Colonels Butler and Stewart, and a lately raised Virginia Continental detachment, under Lieutenant-colonel Gaskins; while two Maryland regiments, also recently recruited, under Colonel Adams and Major Roxburgh, composed Gist's brigade. In Lincoln's division we have the First and Second New York regiments, under Colonels Van Schaick and Van Cortlandt, forming one brigade, commanded by General James Clinton, and Colonel Olney's full Rhode Island regiment, with the two New Jersey regiments, under Colonels Dayton and Ogden, making up the remaining brigade under Colonel Dayton.

Detachments of artillery, with siege and field pieces, including Colonel Lamb's Second Artillery, and a few companies from Proctor's Fourth Regiment, formed the Artillery Brigade, under General Knox. Three or four companies of Sappers and Miners, with artificers; two companies of Delaware recruits, and about one hundred dragoons, under Colonel Moylan, completed the Continental force, which mustered five thousand five hundred strong.

The militia, who all came from Virginia—those of North Carolina, as already noticed, being posted at the passes and fords in their own State—numbered over three thousand men, and were commanded by their patriotic Governor, General Thomas Nelson; General Weedon, formerly a Continental officer; and Generals Lawson and Stevens, who had lately done good service at Guilford Court House. Colonel William I. Lewis, of Campbell County, brought down a corps of riflemen, or " Sons of the Mountains," and Lieutenant-colonel Dabney commanded what is described in orders as the " Virginia State Regiment."

For the French contingent we have seven regiments of infantry, averaging nine hundred men each; a corps of six hundred artillerists, and a legion of horse and foot, also six hundred in number—altogether

GENERAL PETER MUHLENBERG.

a noble body of troops. Their commander-in-chief, Lieutenant-general Count de Rochambeau, brought with him an enviable military reputation, based upon personal bravery and skilful leadership. His four major-generals were the Baron de Viomenil, the Count de Viomenil, the Chevalier de Chastellux, and the Marquis de St. Simon, with Brigadier M. de Choisy. The regiments of infantry were those described by the titles of Bourbonnois, Royal Deuxponts, Saintonge, Soissonois, Touraine, Agenois, and Gatenois, commanded respectively by the Colonels Marquis de Laval, M. Guillaume de Deuxponts, M. Custine, the Viscount de Noailles, Viscount de Pondeux, the Marquis d'Audechamp, and the Marquis de Rostaing. Lieutenant-colonel d'Aboville commanded the artillery, and the Duke de Lauzun the legionary corps. An able and brilliant staff attended the general officers, one of whose members was Berthier, afterward marshal under Napoleon; and we may notice that the major of the regiment

Saintonge was M. Fleury, who had previously served in the American army with so much distinction, as at Mud Island and Stony Point.

Of the British troops in Yorktown it will suffice to say that they formed the *élite* of the King's army in America. The veterans who came with Cornwallis from the South yielded the palm to no one, though in numbers they were terribly reduced. In the command were to be found the Brigade of Guards, mustering scarcely five hundred men; the Twenty-third, Thirty-third, Seventy-first Foot, the light company of the Eighty-second, Tarleton's Legion, some North Carolina volunteers, and the German regiment, under Colonel de Bose. Including the troops sent under Arnold and Phillips—two battalions of light infantry, the Seventeenth, Forty-third, Seventy-sixth, Eightieth, Simcoe's Rangers, Anspachers, under Colonels de Voit and de Seybothen; the Hessian regiment, Prince Hereditaire; small detachments of light dragoons, yagers, artillery, and light companies—and we have a total of about seven thousand five hundred officers and men, besides eight or nine hundred marines, cooped up in Yorktown. A noticeable fact was the dearth of superior officers. O'Hara was Cornwallis's only brigadier, and his list of field-officers showed but two colonels, twelve lieutenant-colonels, and twelve majors in the entire force.[1]

In round numbers, we may put sixteen thousand besiegers against seven thousand five hundred besieged, exclusive of eight hundred marines engaged on land on each side, as the strength, on the rolls, of the combatants at Yorktown.

Adding further details, and the organization of the opposite armies can be presented as follows—that of the American wing showing the final arrangement after changes made to the 8th of October:

---

[1] Many of these English officers rose to distinction. Cornwallis became Lord-lieutenant of Ireland and Governor-general of India, where he died in 1805. O'Hara was with the English in Toulon when it surrendered in 1793; after that he became governor of Gibraltar. Colonel Abercrombie, who commanded the left wing of the Yorktown defences, died a general in the British service. The same rank was attained by Captains Samuel Graham, of the Seventy-sixth; Charles Asgill, of the Guards; and Saumaurez, of the Twenty-third. Major Needham, of the Seventy-sixth, and Major Ross, aide to Cornwallis, also became generals; so, also, Tarleton and Simcoe, the latter being governor of Upper Canada in 1791-4. General Philips, who died at Petersburg, just before Cornwallis entered Virginia, in May, 1781, was an accomplished officer, whose advice would have been invaluable to the former in this campaign. Arnold, who brought the second expedition to Virginia, was recalled to New York by Clinton before Cornwallis started after Lafayette. Clinton himself returned to England in May, 1782, and was graciously received by his sovereign.

ALLIED ARMY.

GEORGE WASHINGTON,

COMMANDER-IN-CHIEF.

AMERICAN WING.

CONTINENTALS.[1]

GENERAL GEORGE WASHINGTON, of Virginia.[2]

SECRETARY.

Colonel Jonathan Trumbull, Jr., of Connecticut.

AIDES-DE-CAMP.

Lieutenant - colonel Tench Tilghman, of Maryland; *Lieutenant - colonel* David Humphreys, of Connecticut; *Lieutenant - colonel* David Cobb, of Massachusetts; *Lieutenant-colonel* William S. Smith, of New York; *Lieutenant-colonel* John Laurens, of South Carolina.

ADJUTANT-GENERAL.

Brigadier-general Edward Hand, of Pennsylvania.

QUARTERMASTER-GENERAL.

Colonel Timothy Pickering, of Massachusetts.

ASSISTANT QUARTERMASTER-GENERAL.

Lieutenant-colonel Henry Dearborn, of New Hampshire.[3]

COMMISSARY-GENERAL.

Colonel Ephraim Blaine, of Pennsylvania.

CHIEF PHYSICIAN AND SURGEON.

Doctor James Craik, of Virginia.

CHIEF OF ENGINEERS.

Brigadier-general Chevalier Du Portail.[4]

SUPERINTENDENT OF MATERIALS IN THE TRENCHES.

Colonel Samuel Elbert, of Georgia.

---

[1] Official rolls and records show that the officers named in this roster were present at the siege.

[2] Washington, while at the head of the entire army, retained active command of the American wing, issuing to it daily orders as usual. Lincoln, next in rank, had his tent on the right of the line, as the nominal head, but took his turn on duty with the other division commanders.

[3] Colonel Pickering requested Washington to appoint Dearborn his assistant, at Peekskill, June 19th, 1781; and the appointment was made.—*Sparks' MS. Collection,* Harvard College Library.

[4] General Du Portail, Lieutenant-colonel Gimat, and Major Galvan were French officers, holding commissions in the Continental Army.

ARTILLERY BRIGADE.

BRIGADIER-GENERAL HENRY KNOX, of Massachusetts.

Rank and File.[1]

Second Regiment [N. Y. & Conn.] { *Colonel* John Lamb, of New York . . . . } *Lieutenant-colonel* Ebenezer Stevens, of Massachusetts . } 225 *Major* Sebastian Bauman, of New York . . . . . }

Detachments.[2]

First Regiment.
Lieutenant-colonel Edward Carrington, } of Virginia . . . 25
Captain Whitehead Coleman . . . }

Fourth Regiment.
Captains Patrick Duffy, William Fer- } of Pennsylvania . 60
guson, and James Smith . . . . }

CAVALRY.

Fourth Regiment Dragoons.[3]—*Colonel* Stephen Moylan, of Pennsylvania . 60
Armand's Legion 40

INFANTRY.

LAFAYETTE'S DIVISION—LIGHT INFANTRY.

MAJOR-GENERAL MARQUIS DE LAFAYETTE.[4]

Division Inspector, Major William Barber, of New Jersey.

FIRST BRIGADE.

BRIGADIER-GENERAL PETER MUHLENBERG, of Virginia.

Brigade Major, Captain John Hobby, Tenth Massachusetts.

---

[1] In the absence of official rolls, the figures representing the strength of the several Continental regiments and detachments are given as approximately correct. See, in Appendix, "Strength of the Armies at Yorktown."

[2] The detachment from Proctor's Fourth Regiment included the companies which came with Wayne to Virginia. Lieutenant-colonel Carrington, of Harrison's First, had not served with his regiment for some time. He acted as quartermaster for Greene in his North Carolina campaign, and proved very efficient. He appears to have been alone again "on command" at Yorktown, with Captain Coleman's company from the First. Coleman is given in the detail of artillery officers.

[3] In Penn. Archives, O. S., vol. ix. General Orders, of September 26th, 1781, mention dragoons from "Colonel Moylan's command."

[4] The names of all the aides of the division commanders do not appear. In the early Virginia movements Lafayette had Majors George Washington (nephew of the chief), Richard C. Anderson, and William Archibald, of Virginia. With Steuben were Captains North and Walker. Major William Popham served with General James Clinton.

8

Three Battalions.

Rank and File.

1. $\left\{\begin{array}{l} \textit{Colonel} \text{ Joseph Vose, of Massachusetts} \dots \\ \textit{Major} \text{ Caleb Gibbs, of Rhode Island}^1 \dots \end{array}\right\}$ 8 Mass. Companies.   250

2. $\left\{\begin{array}{l} \textit{Lieutenant-colonel} \text{ Gimat} \dots \dots \dots \\ \textit{Major} \text{ John Palsgrave Wyllys, of Connecticut} \; . \end{array}\right\}$ $\left.\begin{array}{l} 5 \text{ Conn., 2 Mass., 1} \\ \text{R. I.} \dots \dots \end{array}\right\}$ 250

3. $\left\{\begin{array}{l} \textit{Lieutenant-colonel} \text{ Francis Barber, of New Jersey} \\ \textit{Major} \text{ Joseph R. Reid [of Hazen's]} \; . \; \dots \dots \end{array}\right\}$ 5 N. H., N. J., &c.   200

SECOND BRIGADE.

BREVET BRIGADIER-GENERAL MOSES HAZEN, of Canada.

Brigade Major, Captain Leonard Bleeker, First New York.

Four Battalions.[2]

1. $\left\{\begin{array}{l} \textit{Lieutenant-colonel} \text{ Ebenezer Huntington, of Conn.} \\ \textit{Major} \text{ Nathan Rice, of Massachusetts} \dots \end{array}\right\}$ 4 Mass., Conn. . .   200

2. $\left\{\begin{array}{l} \textit{Lieutenant-colonel} \text{ Alexander Hamilton, of N. Y.} \\ \textit{Major} \text{ Nicholas Fish, of New York} \dots \dots \end{array}\right\}$ 2 N. Y., 2 Conn. .   200

3. $\left\{\begin{array}{l} \textit{Lieutenant-colonel} \text{ John Laurens, of South Carolina} \\ \textit{Major} \text{ John N. Cumming, of New Jersey} \; . \; . \; . \end{array}\right\}$ 4 N. H., Mass., Conn. 200

4. $\left\{\begin{array}{l} \textit{Lieutenant-colonel} \text{ Edward Antill} \dots \dots \\ \textit{Major} \text{ Tarleton Woodson} \dots \dots \dots \end{array}\right\}$ $\left.\begin{array}{l} \text{Hazen's \quad Canadian} \\ \text{Regiment . . .} \end{array}\right\}$ 200

LINCOLN'S DIVISION.

MAJOR-GENERAL BENJAMIN LINCOLN, of Massachusetts.

Division Inspector, Major —— ——.

CLINTON'S BRIGADE.

BRIGADIER-GENERAL JAMES. CLINTON, of New York.

Brigade Major, Captain Aaron Aorson, First New York.

First Regiment, New York . $\left\{\begin{array}{l} \textit{Colonel} \text{ Goose Van Schaick} \dots \dots \\ \textit{Lieutenant-colonel} \text{ Cornelius Van Dyke} \; . \; . \\ \textit{Major} \text{ John Graham} \dots \dots \dots \end{array}\right\}$ 325

Second Regiment, New York. $\left\{\begin{array}{l} \textit{Colonel} \text{ Philip Van Cortlandt} \dots \dots \\ \textit{Lieutenant-colonel} \text{ Robert Cochran} \dots \dots \\ \textit{Major} \text{ Nicholas Fish (with Light Infantry) .} \end{array}\right\}$ 350

---

[1] Major Galvan, who had been with this battalion, was relieved, and Major Gibbs, of Washington's Guards, appointed in his place.

[2] The battalions 1 and 3 had lately composed the full regiment, under Colonel Scammell. Divided by General Orders, October 8th.

DAYTON'S BRIGADE.

COLONEL ELIAS DAYTON, of New Jersey.

Brigade Major, Captain Richard Cox, First New Jersey.

Rank and File.

First and Second New Jersey Regiments (united) . . . { *Colonel* Mathias Ogden . . . . / *Lieutenant-colonel* William De Hart . . . > 600 / *Major* John Hollinshead . . . . }

Rhode Island Regiment . . { *Lieutenant-colonel Com'dant* Jeremiah Olney / *Major* Coggeshall Olney . . . . > 450 / *Major* John S. Dexter . . . . }

STEUBEN'S DIVISION.

MAJOR-GENERAL BARON STEUBEN.

Division Inspector, Major Galvan.

WAYNE'S BRIGADE.

BRIGADIER-GENERAL ANTHONY WAYNE, of Pennsylvania.

Brigade Major, Lieutenant Richard Fullerton, of Pennsylvania.

First Battalion, Pennsylvania. { *Colonel* Walter Stewart . . . . / *Major* James Hamilton . . . . > 275 / *Major* William Alexander . . . . . . }

Second Battalion,[1] Penn. . . { *Colonel* Richard Butler . . . . / *Lieutenant-colonel* Josiah Harmar . . . . > 275 / *Major* Evan Edwards . . . . }

Virginia Battalion . . . . *Lieutenant-colonel* Thomas Gaskins . . . 350

GIST'S BRIGADE.

BRIGADIER-GENERAL MORDECAI GIST, of Maryland.

Brigade Major, Captain Lilburn Williams, Third Maryland.

Third Regiment, Maryland . *Lieutenant-colonel Com'dant* Peter Adams . 550

Fourth Regiment, Maryland . *Major* Alexander Roxburg 450

SAPPERS AND MINERS.

Captain James Gilliland, New York. . . . .)
Captain David Bushnell, Connecticut . . . . > 50
Captain-lieutenant David Kirkpatrick, New Jersey (?) . . . .)

Delaware Recruits . . . . *Captain* William McKennan 60

---

[1] A third Pennsylvania battalion arrived just as the operations came to an end. It was under Colonel Craig and Lieutenant-colonel Mentges. Major-general St. Clair also reported, but had no command at the siege.

MILITIA.

GENERAL THOMAS NELSON, Governor of Virginia.

BRIGADES.

Rank and File.

BRIGADIER-GENERAL GEORGE WEEDON 1500

BRIGADIER-GENERAL ROBERT LAWSON 750

BRIGADIER-GENERAL EDWARD STEVENS 750

State Regiment . . . . . *Lieutenant-colonel* Dabney 200

FRENCH WING.[1]

LIEUTENANT-GENERAL COUNT DE ROCHAMBEAU.

AIDES-DE-CAMP.

Count de Fersen ; Marquis de Vauban ; Marquis de Damas ; Chevalier de Lameth ; M. Dumas ; De Lauberdière ; Baron de Clozen.

MARECHAUX-DE-CAMP.

Major-general Baron de Viomenil ; *Major-general* Marquis de St. Simon ; *Major-general* Viscount de Viomenil ; *Major-general* Chevalier de Chastellux.

M. de Choisy, Brigadier-general.

INTENDANT.

M. de Tarlè.

QUARTERMASTER-GENERAL.

M. de Béville.

COMMISSARY-GENERAL.

Claude Blanchard.

MEDICAL DEPARTMENT.

M. de Coste, Physician-in-chief ; M. Robillard, Surgeon-in-chief ; M. de Mars, Superintendent of Hospitals.

ENGINEERS.

Colonel Desandrouins ; *Lieutenant-colonel* de Querenet ; *Major* de Palys ; and nine line-officers.

ARTILLERY.

Rank and File.

Colonel Commandant d'Aboville ; *Adjutant* Manduit.   Director of the Park, M. Nadal. 600

---

[1] This roster of French officers is taken from the lists printed in the *Mag. of Am. Hist.*, vol. iii., No. 7 ; and by Blanchard in his "Journal." Many staff-officers, assistants, etc., are here omitted.

CAVALRY.

Rank and File.

Lauzun's Legion, or Volunteers . . . .

Duke de Lauzun . . . .
Count Arthur Dillon . . . .

600

INFANTRY.

Brigade Bourbonnois.

Regiment Bourbonnois . .

Colonel Marquis de Laval . . . . . .
Second-colonel Vicomte de Rochambeau .
Lieutenant-colonel de Bressolles . . . .
Major de Gambs . . . .

900

Regiment Royal Deuxponts

Colonel Count de Deuxponts . . . . .
Second-colonel Count Guillaume de Deux-
ponts . . . .
Lieutenant-colonel Baron d'Ezbeck . . .
Major Desprez . . . .

900

Brigade Soissonois.

Regiment Soissonois . . .

Colonel Marquis de St. Maime . . . . .
Second-colonel Vicomte de Noailles . . .
Lieutenant-colonel d'Anselme . . . . .
Major d'Espeyron. . . . .

900

Regiment Saintonge . . .

Colonel Marquis de Custine . . . . .
Second-colonel Count de Charlus . . . .
Lieutenant-colonel de la Vatelle . . . .
Major M. Fleury . . . .

900

Brigade Agenois.

Regiment Agenois . . . .

Colonel Marquis d'Audechamp . . . .
Lieutenant-colonel Chevalier de Cadignau .
Major Pandin de Beauregard . . . . .

1000

Regiment Gatenois. . . .

Colonel Marquis de Rostaing . . . . .
Lieutenant-colonel de l'Estrade. . . . .
Major de Tourville . . . .

1000

Regiment Touraine[1] (not brigaded) . . . .

Colonel Vicomte de Pondeux . . . . .
Lieutenant-colonel de Montlezun . . . .
Major de Ménonville . . . .

1000

[1] The regiments Agenois, Gatenois, and Touraine are those which St. Simon brought from the West Indies in De Grasse's fleet.

BRITISH ARMY.[1]

LIEUTENANT-GENERAL EARL CHARLES CORNWALLIS.

AIDES-DE-CAMP.

Lieutenant-colonel Lord Chewton; *Major* Alexander Ross; *Major* Charles Cochrane, Acting Aide.

DEPUTY ADJUTANT-GENERAL.

Major John Despard.

COMMISSARY.

—— Perkins.

DEPUTY QUARTERMASTER-GENERAL.

Major Richard England.

DEPUTY QUARTERMASTER-GENERAL'S ASSISTANTS.

Captain Campbell, *Captain* Vallancy, *Lieutenant* Oldfield, and *Ensign* St. John.

MAJORS OF BRIGADE.

Edward Brabazon, —— Manley, J. Baillie, Francis Richardson.

ENGINEERS.

Lieutenant Alexander Sutherland, commanding; *Lieutenants* Haldane and Stratton.

ROYAL ARTILLERY.

Rank and File.

Captain George Rochfort, commanding . . . . } 193
Captain-lieutenant Edward Fage . . . . }

CAVALRY.

Queen's Rangers—*Lieutenant-colonel* J. Graves Simcoe 248
British Legion —*Lieutenant-colonel* Banistre Tarleton 192

INFANTRY.

BRIGADE OF GUARDS.

BRIGADIER-GENERAL CHARLES O'HARA 467

---

[1] This list is compiled from copies of the MS. rolls of the Surrender signed by Major Despard, and from Gaines's Army Register for 1782. All the officers named were present at the siege. The figures are taken from the official return of the American Commissary of Prisoners, in Appendix.

LIGHT INFANTRY.

Rank and File.

Lieutenant-colonel Robert Abercrombie. . . . . }
Major Thomas Armstrong . . . . } 594

LIEUTENANT-COLONEL YORKE'S BRIGADE.

Seventeenth—*Lieutenant-colonel* Henry Johnson. 205

Twenty-third—*Captain* Apthorpe (?) 205

Thirty-third—*Lieutenant-colonel* John Yorke 225

Seventy-first. { *Lieutenant-colonel* Duncan McPherson . . . . }
{ *Major* Patrick Campbell . . . . } 242
{ *Major* James Campbell . . . . }

LIEUTENANT-COLONEL DUNDAS'S BRIGADE.

Forty-third—*Major* George Hewett (?) 307

Seventy-sixth—*Major* Francis Needham 628

Eightieth. { *Lieutenant-colonel* Thomas Dundas . . . . }
{ *Major* James Gordon . . . . } 588

GERMAN TROOPS.

Two Anspach Battalions. { *Colonel* de Voit . . . . }
{ *Colonel* de Seybothen . . . . } 948

HESSIAN.

Prince Hereditaire—*Lieutenant-colonel* Matthew de Fuchs 425

Regiment De Bose—*Major* O'Reilly 271

Yagers—*Captain* John Ewald 68

North Carolina Volunteers—*Lieutenant-colonel* John Hamilton 114

Pioneers 33

These were the troops who lay on their arms on the night of the 28th within a mile of each other, just outside of Yorktown, and whose exertions were to determine the control of this continent.

The investment of the place so auspiciously opened by the allies was more securely established in the course of the two following days. On the 29th the American wing moved to the right, and nearer to the enemy, and the entire army spread out into permanent camps, forming a semicircle from the banks of the York, above the town, around to Wormley Creek, an arm of the York below. About the centre of this line the ground is intersected with marshes, running out in the shape of a bird's claw, whose rivulets unite to form what at that time was known as Beaverdam Creek, or the head-waters of Warwick River. This creek was made the dividing line of the allied army—the American wing upon the right, and the French upon the left.

LIEUTENANT-COLONEL DAVID HUMPHREYS—
AIDE TO WASHINGTON.

A bridge or causeway had been thrown across it the night before, and on the following morning, the 29th, parties of light infantry and riflemen reconnoitred the ground within cannon-shot of the enemy's outworks, and skirmished successfully with the pickets of the Anspach battalions, on the right. About four o'clock in the afternoon the American troops encamped on the selected site.[1]

The morning of the 30th opened with a surprise and an advantage for the allied forces. It was discovered at an early hour that the enemy had quietly abandoned their outer position during the night and retired, with their guns, to the immediate defences of Yorktown. With the besiegers the motive or necessity for this move was a matter of speculation. Both French and American officers pronounced it unmilitary, upon the ground that for the besieged the position was a defensible point, which should have been held as long as possible, to gain time, in view of possible

---

[1] Washington's memorandum for the 29th is as follows: "Moved the American troops more to the right, and encamped on the east side of Beaverdam Creek, with a morass in front, about cannon-shot from the enemy's lines—spent this day in reconnoitering the enemy's position, and determining upon a plan of attack and approach which must be done without the assistance of the shipping above the Town, as the admiral (notwithstanding my earnest solicitation) declined hazarding any vessels on that station."

"29th.—The American army marched over a bridge, and took a position extending from the morass, which separated us from the French army, to beyond the Hampton road from York."—Col. Pickering's Journal.

Rochambeau says, in his "Memoirs:" "On the 29th the American army crossed the marshes, leaving its left on their borders, and its right on the York river. The investing of this place was now as complete and restrained as it possibly could be." The point of crossing was a short distance above the present Wynn's Mill, on Beaverdam Creek. It was this creek, better known as the Warwick, that was made the Confederate line of defence in McClellan's campaign of 1862.

relief.[1] Sir Henry Clinton likewise criticised it with some severity; but that was at a later date, when his controversy with Cornwallis had taken a somewhat bitter turn. It appeared to him extraordinary that the latter should have quitted "such works in such a position without a conflict," especially as, in a previous letter, he had led the commander-in-chief to infer that it would be held. In addition, several officers of rank, who had seen the ground, had given it as their opinion, before a council of war, in New York, that "his Lordship might defend that position twenty-one days, open trenches, against 20,000 men and a proportionable artillery."[2] Cornwallis, however, was, at that moment, the best judge of the situation. He was obliged to regard his reduced force, the formidable aspect of the besiegers, and the fact that his left flank could be turned by the passage of Wormley Creek. Despatches, too, from Clinton had reached him the day before, announcing the probable departure of a relieving fleet about the 5th of October, in which case, until its arrival, Yorktown could be held at the inner line. The contents of Clinton's letter were certainly assuring, twenty-three sail-of-the-line and five thousand men being expected to sail " in a few days," to relieve, and afterward co-operate with, Cornwallis. This intelligence gave the latter the "greatest satisfaction," and he immediately replied : " I shall retire this night within the works, and have no doubt, if relief comes in time, York and Gloucester will be both in the possession of his Majesty's troops." Perhaps Cornwallis was too hopeful, and forgot the perversity of fortune where the navy was concerned. Clinton seems to have thought so.

But, as the event proved, the abandonment of the outer works was immaterial. It only hastened the end. The allies accepted the move with satisfaction, as greatly simplifying future operations. " On the 30th, in the morning," wrote Washington to the President of Congress, " we discovered that the enemy had evacuated all their exterior works, and withdrawn themselves to those near the town. By this means we are in possession of very advantageous grounds, which command their line of works in a very near advance." The abandoned position was occupied by the allies on the same forenoon. French chasseurs and grenadiers took possession of the two redoubts at Pigeon Quarter, while the American Light Infantry held the ground on their right, where, at night, fatigue

---

[1] Wayne, Deuxponts, Butler. Tarleton, on the British side, regarded the move as premature, and declared that it " unexpectedly hastened the surrender of the British army."

[2] Clinton's " Observations on Stedman's History of the American War," p. 29.

parties began a new redoubt, and proceeded to change the battery on the
right of the Hampton Road into a fourth enclosed work.[1]

On the same morning French light parties—the "volunteers" of
Baron St. Simon—drove in the enemy's pickets on the extreme left, in
front of the Fusileer redoubt, and a sharp skirmish occurred, with the
loss of one killed and two or three wounded, including among the latter M. de Bouillet, an officer of the regiment Agenois. This enabled
the left brigade of the French to occupy a more advantageous position.
The redoubt itself was bravely defended.

By this change in the situation the generals and engineers, who had
spent most of the 29th in reconnoitring, were given the opportunity
of making a closer examination of the immediate defences of Yorktown. Washington and other general officers rode to Pigeon Quarter
at an early hour and surveyed the works, which were in full view.
The group, attracting the enemy's attention, were complimented with
a discharge of cannon-shot, which struck into the trees above them, but
the chief remained under fire until he had finished his observations.[2]
The engineers went the rounds, and noted the topography, which was
found very favorable for the prosecution of the siege. Means of shelter, small commanding knolls and ravines, were conveniently situated.
Vigilance, energy, and skilful management would bring success., The
outlook was eminently promising, and under its inspiration Washington again reminded his troops of their duty, as follows: ". . . The advanced season and various conditions render it indispensably necessary
to conduct the attacks against York with the utmost rapidity. The
General therefore expects and requires the officers and soldiers of this
army to pursue the duties of their respective departments and stations
with the most unabating ardor. The present moment offers, in prospect, the epoch which will decide American Independence, the glory
and superiority of the allies. A vigorous use of the means in our
power cannot but insure success. The passive conduct of the enemy

---

[1] Writing to Hon. David Jameson, at Richmond, from "Camp before York," October
1st, Governor Nelson says: " Our progress has been more considerable for the time than
could have been expected, and attended with less opposition and loss. Yesterday
morning it was discovered that the enemy had evacuated their outposts at Moore's
Mill, Pigeon Quarter, and every other place beyond the creek, except at Nelson's
Farm. Our troops are to-day working on grounds they relinquished. The French
took possession of Pigeon Hill. There have been two men killed and six wounded."
—*Pub. Va. Hist. Soc.*

[2] Autobiography of Colonel Van Cortlandt.—*Am. Mag. of Hist.*, May, 1878.

argues his weakness and the uncertainty of his councils. The liberties of America, and the honor of the Allied Arms are in our hands. Such objects must excite a patriotic emulation in the greatest actions and exertions; their consequences will amply compensate every danger and fatigue. . . ."[1]

This favorable prospect was clouded only by the fall, early on the 30th, of the brave and much-loved Colonel Alexander Scammell, of New Hampshire. When the pickets reported the evacuation of the enemy's outer position he went forward, with a small party, as field-officer of the day, to reconnoitre the deserted works. Proceeding alone a short distance toward Yorktown, he was suddenly surprised by some troopers of Tarleton's Legion, under Lieutenant Cameron, and mortally wounded the moment after his surrender.[2] One of the troopers, coming up behind, shot him in the back, although it must have been evident that he could not escape. His captors hurried him roughly into Yorktown, where his wound was dressed, and on the same day he returned on parole to Williamsburg. There he lingered until the evening of the 6th, when he sunk rapidly and died. One of the heroes of Saratoga, lately adjutant-general of the army, a noble and gifted soul, with an enviable future before him, his fall was hardly less than a public loss.[3]

---

[1] Orders for Sept. 30.—*Yorktown Orderly Book.*

[2] That Scammell was shot after his surrender is well established—an accident, perhaps, in the haste of the surprise.

[3] Colonel Scammell's death was universally regretted in the army. Quartermaster-general Pickering says of the wounding that it was "barbarously done." "After two dragoons had him their prisoner, a third came up and shot him through the side. Of this wound he died the 6th inst., at Williamsburg, lamented by all who knew him, and who valued friendship, integrity, and truth." Colonel Harry Lee eulogizes him in his "Memoirs." Colonel Humphreys wrote an epitaph for his monument, and, in his "Address to the Armies of America," remembers him with a feeling tribute:

> "Ripe were thy virtues, though too few thy days,
> Be this thy fame—through life of all approv'd,
> To die lamented, honor'd, and belov'd."

The letters of Colonels Lamb and Dearborn, in the Appendix, are of interest; also the letter from Colonel Smith, quoted in *Mag. of Am. Hist.*, Jan., 1881, p. 21. Chaplain Evans, of Scammell's regiment, has this entry in his "Journal:" "Sunday, 30th . . . Colonel Scammel, being officer of the day, and reconnoitring the situation of the enemy, was surprised by a party of their horse, and after being taken prisoner was inhumanly wounded by them."

Of course the enemy were not silent observers of the investment. Upon discovering that their abandoned works at Pigeon Quarter were occupied by the allies, they opened a well-sustained fire, and directed it especially at the American parties who were constructing the two new redoubts. A few casualties occurred—in one case four men of the Pennsylvania line being killed by a single shot—but the work was not interrupted. On the 2d, according to Colonel Butler, the enemy fired three hundred and fifty-one shot between sunrise and sunset, the Americans making no reply, but digging away until the redoubts were finished. With their completion, in the course of four days, what had just been Cornwallis's outer line of defence became Washington's first fortified offensive-defensive position, extending from the ravine above to the head of Wormley Creek below.

The first week of October was now devoted by the allies to preparations, such as the making of gabions, fascines, and stakes, bringing up of guns, and careful surveying for nearer approaches. It was a busy interval—no man busier than Washington himself. On the 1st he was in the saddle again, reconnoitring on the right. " This afternoon, three o'clock," says Lieutenant Feltman, who was on picket at Moore's Mill, head of Wormley Creek, " his Excellency General Washington, General Duportail, and several other engineers crossed at the mill-dam to take a view of the enemy's works. His Excellency sent one of his aides-de-camp for Captain Smith and his guard of fifty men, to march in front of his Excellency as a covering party, which we did, and went under cover of a hill, where we posted our guard, when his Excellency General Washington and General Duportail with three men of our guard advanced within three hundred yards of the enemy's works, which is the town of York." The French engineers were equally active.

The main delay in opening the approaches arose from lack of transportation for the siege-pieces which were at the James. " Much diligence," writes Washington, " was used in debarking and transporting the stores, cannon, etc., from Trebell's Landing (distant six miles) on James River to camp ; which for want of teams went on heavily." The teams had been

---

The place of the colonel's capture was in the vicinity of the Confederate " White Redoubt," in or near the Williamsburg Road.

Detail of officers for the 29th :

Major-general for the day—Marquis Lafayette.
Colonel   "   " —Scammell.
Lieutenant-colonel   " —Van Dyck.
Brigade Major   " —Bleeker.

GENERAL HENRY KNOX. [GILBERT STUART.]

sent around by land from the head of Elk, and on their arrival there was more despatch. So urgent was the commander-in-chief in the matter, that he sent his own baggage wagons over, and in the morning orders of the 2d requested all the general, field, and other officers to send theirs, as it was "of the utmost importance that the Heavy Artillery should be brought up without a moment's loss of time." General Knox, chief of artillery, also displayed his usual energy on the occasion.[1]

---

[1] Knox's orders to the artillery brigade, dated "James River, Virginia, 29th September, 1781," run as follows:

"The troops are immediately to disembark at Trebell's Landing and encamp as contiguous to the shore as convenient. The officers will be particularly attentive to prevent the soldiers from plundering or doing the inhabitants any other injury. Any

Nor were the infantry idle. Twelve hundred men were detailed from the American wing, on the 30th and the 1st, to gather wicker material in the woods; and by subsequent orders these were always to be kept complete in camp, each regiment furnishing its proportion—at least six thousand stakes, two thousand fascines, six hundred gabions, and six hundred saucissons. To prevent confusion during the siege, clear and minute regulations were issued, on the 6th, respecting its conduct. Fifty-four in number, they provided for every variety of service and precaution. Absolute system was to be maintained at the trenches when opened. General Elbert, of Georgia, superintendent of the materials, was to take charge of all the sand-bags, fascines, gabions, hurdles, and tools at the points selected by the engineers, and keep an accurate account of them. Fatigue parties were to be counted as they went in and out; no straggling; "greatest silence" during the digging; covering parties to sit down, musket in hand. General officers in command at the trenches were to examine carefully " all the avenues, places of arms, and advantageous angles," for the proper disposition of troops in case of attack. All troops, whether relieving or relieved, to march with drums beating and colors flying, though this was countermanded when the second parallel was opened. Sentries were to be posted at proper intervals in the lines, protected by sand-bags, to give notice of the approach of any one from the town, and to shout when the enemy fired shells, but not when they fired shot. In case of a sortie the fatigue parties were to retire briskly to the rear, and not embarrass the troops under arms; while the artillerists were directed to concentrate their fire upon and break up the fronts of the attacking columns. When the enemy were repulsed pursuit was not to be permitted; and so on, many details.

The care and discipline, too, of the army were strictly enjoined. "The health of the troops," say the orders of the 1st, " is an object of such infinite importance, that every possible attention ought to be paid to the preservation of it." Quartermasters and commissaries were directed to furnish straw, good bread, and one gill of rum per man daily. Again, in orders of the 29th: " Our ungenerous enemy having, as usual, propagated the small-pox in this part of the country, the commander-in-chief forbids

---

soldier who shall be detected in such malpractice may depend on being punished without being tried by a court-martial. An officer with a party of twenty men to be sent without delay to Colledge Creek, to collect all the Batteaus and scows for the purpose of landing the ordnance and stores. An officer will remain on each Powder vessel till further orders. The vessels loaded with shott and shells will go as near the shore as possible."—*Order Book, Lamb's Reg't.,* N. Y. Hist. Soc. Collection.

the officers or soldiers of the army having any communication with the houses or inhabitants in the neighborhood, or borrowing any utensils from them." For obvious reasons officers and men were strictly forbidden "to wear red coats." Two or three men having been base and foolhardy enough to go over to the British, there came, on the 4th, the peremptory order that "every deserter from the American troops, after this public notice is given, who shall be found within the enemy's lines at York, if the place falls, will be instantly hanged." No subsequent desertions are mentioned; but, on the contrary, the highest spirit prevailed in camp, and the daily work was carried on with vigor and cheerfulness. "Our troops," wrote Chaplain Evans, on the 5th, "vie with one another in the performance of duty and the love of danger." The general sentiment during these few days of preparation was doubtless reflected by Wayne in the following striking letter he addressed to President Reed, of the Pennsylvania Executive Council:

"Lines before York, 3d Oct., 1781.

"DEAR SIR,—The investiture of the British army under Lord Cornwallis was effected the 29th ultimo. The enemy abandoned their advanced chain of works the same evening, leaving two enclosed redoubts almost within point-blank shot of their principal fortification; this was not only unmilitary, but an indication of a confused precipitation; these works were immediately possessed by the allied troops, and we are now in such forwardness that we shall soon render his Lordship's quarters rather disagreeable.

"However, the reduction of that army will require time and some expense of blood, for we cannot expect that Lord Cornwallis will tacitly surrender 6000 combatants, without many a severe *sortie*—his political and military character are now at stake—he has led the British king and ministry into a deception by assuring them of the subjugation of the Carolinas, and his manœuvre into Virginia was a child of his own creation, which he will attempt to nourish at every risk and consequence—he is now in full as desperate a situation as his namesake *Charles* was at *Pultowa*. I have for some time viewed him as a fiery meteor that displays a momentary lustre, then falls—to rise no more.

"That great officer Genl. Greene first eclipsed his glory—he next met a Fabius in that young nobleman the Marquis Lafayette, and is now encompassed by a Washington, which renders his ruin certain.

"I was going chatting on, but am called to take charge of the covering troops. Adieu; and believe me yours most sincerely, ANTY. WAYNE.

"HIS EXCELLENCY JOS. REED, ESQR.,
  Prest. Pennsylvania.

"We are much distressed for shoes, shirts, and overalls—some needles and thread would tend to make our coats something longer. A. W."[1]

---

[1] From Sparks' MS. collection, Harvard College Library; also in Reed's "Life of Reed."

Meantime there was activity and excitement upon the Gloucester side. Although no attempt was to be made to reduce that position by regular approaches, the nec ssity of checking foraging expeditions and shutting the door of escape to the enemy required the presence there of a large detachment from Washington's army. The force which had been previously stationed in Gloucester County consisted of about fifteen hundred militia under General Weedon. By the 28th of September it had been re-enforced by the Duke de Lauzun's Legion, six hundred strong, half cavalry, half infantry; and a few days later by eight hundred marines from the French fleet. Brigadier-general M. de Choisy was assigned to the command of the whole. On the 3d, as Weedon's camp at Dixon's Mill was too far from the enemy, Choisy moved forward to take a nearer position. This led to a brisk encounter, a touch of warfare the besiegers had seen little of—a collision of horse—and, as a success for their side, it put them in the best of humor. It seemed to hint at the greater success to come.

General Choisy himself, with the main body, the Legion and militia, marched toward Gloucester by the Severn Road, while one company of the Legion dragoons, under Dillon, and a small but excellent corps of militia grenadiers—mostly old soldiers—commanded by Lieutenant-colonel John Mercer (now again in the field), took the York River Road. These two roads united in "a long lane nearly four miles from Gloucester," which emerged upon an open plain on the right and a piece of woods on the left. It was at this lane that the two parts of Choisy's force formed a junction.

On the same morning, as it happened, the British were also upon the Gloucester Road. They had come out for "a grand forage"—nearly the entire garrison, with Lieutenant-colonel Dundas, commanding, at their head. Simcoe's Rangers had frequently been the rounds of the country, taking what they wanted, but this was to be the last excursion of the kind. Without molestation Dundas scoured the fields, loaded down his wagons and "bat-horses" with Indian corn, and before ten o'clock in the forenoon was on the return march for Gloucester. Part of the Rangers and Tarleton's Legion, which had crossed from Yorktown the evening before, followed leisurely as the covering body, unsuspicious of Choisy's near approach. In fact, the latter entered one end of the lane described at about the moment the enemy were moving out at the other. The parties were now too close to escape discovery, and both immediately prepared for action. The experienced Tarleton quickly formed in the woods, some distance beyond the lane, and then advanced in person with part of his Legion cavalry to reconnoitre and skirmish. On the other hand, the Duke de Lauzun with his advance dragoons dashed through the lane, and riding on to the open ground beyond, charged upon Tarleton without halting. This was just the opportunity these ambitious leaders had been courting. So much they had both confessed to the occupant of a little farm-house on the road that very morning. As Lauzun was passing by he rode up to the woman in the door-way and questioned her as to the enemy. "Oh," she replied, "Colonel Tarleton left this place only a few minutes ago; he said he was very eager to shake hands with the French Duke." "Ha, ha!" laughed Lauzun, "I assure you, madam, I have come on purpose to gratify him." A little later he was riding, full speed, upon Tarleton. A skirmish followed at close quarters. Lauzun and Tarleton very nearly met hand-to-hand, an accident to the latter alone preventing. As he was moving forward the horse of one of his dragoons, which had been struck with a spear by a French trooper, plunged suddenly and threw both Tarleton and his horse to the ground. About this moment the main body of the British cavalry appeared upon the scene, but could make no impression upon Lauzun's corps, when Tarleton, escaping from his critical situation and mounting another horse, sounded a retreat and re-formed his men under cover of Captain Champagne's infantry company, which had just come up to his assistance. This timely arrival saved Tarleton. The French pushed him vigorously, but in turn retired on meeting the enemy's infantry. No further collision occurred between the cavalry, for when Tarleton attempted to renew the conflict, by advancing again, he was met by Lieutenant-colonel Mercer's militiamen, who also had just arrived upon the ground, and was effectually checked by their steady fire. "No regular corps," says Lee, "could have maintained its ground more firmly than did this battalion of our infantry." During this encounter Lauzun drew up in Mercer's rear, prepared for another charge, when the enemy left the field, with the loss of twelve men and Lieutenant Moir, of the infantry, who was killed close to the militia line. The laurels of this little affair rested with Lauzun and Mercer, who were congratulated and thanked by Washington in General Orders on the following day.[1]

Upon the field of the skirmish Choisy fixed his main camp, throwing out strong advanced posts within a mile and a half of Gloucester, and remained in this position until the close of the siege, the enemy sticking close within their lines.

[1] The details of this affair are given in Lee's "Memoirs," and by Tarleton.

Crossing back again to the Yorktown front, we shall find that Washington's army had urged on the siege preparations with such industry and energy that, by the evening of the 6th, everything was in readiness for the opening of the regular approaches. The guns were up; the materials prepared; the enemy's works carefully reconnoitred; the ground in their front minutely surveyed. At once a novel and exhilarating sensation must the Continental soldiers have felt as they drew up in the face of a hitherto dreaded enemy to reduce him by purely scientific methods of warfare. To anything like siege operations they were nearly all perfect strangers. The war, for them, had been little more than years of patience and stout endurance; a war of hard camp life, of marching and countermarching, of advances and retreats, with an occasional battle, and a war in which the continued lack of means and supplies was only made good by their own hopefulness and resolution. These men were now to have their reward in an unexpected way. If they were greatly assisted by military science in this instance, and a triumph fell to them without costly sacrifices, it is to be remembered that their sacrifices had already been made in the tedious years before.

This, now, is the situation just before the combatants look each other closely in the face. Cornwallis has posted his army compactly along the works around the town. Guarding the front, looking up the river, is part of Yorke's brigade, and the regiment Prince Hereditaire, with the brigade of Guards in reserve. Looking down the river are the brigade of Dundas and the Seventy-first. Along the lines back of the town are the Anspachers; facing the river, in detached works, are the Thirty-third and the regiment De Bose; while in the Horn-work, the salient point, the light infantry have the post of honor. Cornwallis has made his head-quarters at the conspicuous and elegant mansion of Secretary Nelson, standing outside the town and just within the works, not far from the light infantry. General O'Hara takes command of the right of the defences; Lieutenant-colonel Abercrombie of the left. Over on the Gloucester side are Simcoe's and Tarleton's troopers, Ewald's yagers, two British light companies, and the North Carolina provincials. Dundas having been recalled to Yorktown, Simcoe is left in command. Then, as to the allies, we shall see an imposing array of camps encircling the besieged. The quarters farthest on the right are those of General Lincoln, at the head of the American wing. According to the maps of the engineers, his tent stood close to the right bank of Wormley Creek, six or seven hundred yards below the mill-dam

The troops on his left, holding the right of the entire line, are Lafayette's light infantry. Lafayette's marquee is in their rear, east of the Hampton Road. Forming a second line behind the infantry are General Nelson and his militia. Next to the left, and on the second line, is Lincoln's division; and on its left, on the front line, is Steuben's. Some distance beyond the Beaverdam Creek is the French wing, reaching to the York above; while in the rear of the centre of the entire line, half a mile north-west of Wynne's Mill, and two and a half miles back from the Yorktown works, will be found the head-quarters of the commander-in-chief, with those of Rochambeau a little to the east. The investment is complete; the enemy cannot escape; and the next step is to tighten the lines and force a surrender.

The final advance upon Yorktown was made by parallels, and the nature of the ground determined the direction of approach. As the ravine in front of the upper half of the town prevented operations in that quarter, the attack was directed against the lower part, or the enemy's left. For the allies this was a valuable advantage, since it contracted their front and lessened their labors. The line for the first parallel, as marked out by the engineers, and now to be opened, extended from Pigeon Quarter, nearly opposite the British centre, around to the bank of the York below. Its length was two thousand yards; its distance from the enemy on the left, six hundred yards; and on the right, something more than eight hundred yards—this increase of distance on the right being necessitated by the position of the enemy's two redoubts, which stood in advance of their left, near the river. The entire line was established with great care, in view, as a French engineer remarks, of "the strength and reputation" of the besieged. "The forces," says Rochambeau, "which the place contained, and the disposition of the men who commanded it, required us to conduct these attacks with much science and precaution."

On the evening of the 6th the work began. Four thousand three hundred men, French and Americans, paraded at dusk and marched to the designated ground. Major-general Lincoln commanded the American detachment, which consisted of six regiments—one from the right of each of the six brigades—and took the right half of the line. His brigadiers were Clinton and Wayne. The French detachment, under Baron Viomenil, took the left. Fifteen hundred of the troops were to act as the fatigue party and do the digging, while twenty-eight hundred lay under arms to repel attacks. Colonel Lamb, of the artillery, writing to Governor

Clinton, of New York, on the evening of the 6th, mentions the movement, and adds: "You may depend on its being a night of business." Such it proved to be, but not as exciting as anticipated. The troops, as they came up, were placed by the engineers at proper intervals along the projected line, when they fell to digging, in reliefs, with a will, and in "the greatest silence." Part of the materials — gabions, hurdles, and what not—had been previously taken to the spot under cover, and, as the soil was sandy and easily thrown up, progress was rapid. The night, too, was "the most favorable in the world"—dark and cloudy, with a gentle rain.

Complete success attended this first important step. The enemy neither heard nor saw what was going on until daybreak revealed the long line of embankment rising ominously in their front. The eight hours' work had been altogether satisfactory, for the trenches, though not completed, were high enough to protect the parties who were to continue the digging the next day. Washington, who in his diary notices all the important occurrences of the siege, says of this move, with evident gratification: "Before morning the trenches were in such forwardness as to cover the men from the enemy's fire. The work was executed with so much secrecy and despatch that the enemy were, I believe, totally ignorant of our labor till the light of the morning discovered it to them. Our loss on this occasion was extremely inconsiderable, not more than one officer (French) and about 20 men killed and wounded, the officer and 1⁸ of which were on our left, from the corps of the Marquis de St. Simon who was betrayed by a deserter from the Hussars that went in and gave notice of his approaching his parallel."[1] Along the American line, in

---

[1] Nearly all the diaries or journals of the time refer to the opening of the siege proper on the night of the 6th. *Lieutenant-col. Tilghman*, aide to Washington, says "The 6th at night the trenches were opened between 5 and 600 yards from the enemy' works and the 1st parallel run—commencing about the centre of the enemy's work opposite the Secretary's House and running to the right to the York river. The par allel supported by 4 redoubts. These approaches are directed against the 4 works o the enemy's left. The enemy kept up a pretty brisk fire during the night; but as ou working parties were not discovered by them, their shot were in a wrong direction. *Count Fersen*, aide to Rochambeau: "At 8 o'clock in the evening we opened a trench a 300 fathoms from the works. . . . The ground, which is very much cut up by little ra vines, greatly facilitated our approach, and enabled us to reach our trenches under cov er without being obliged to cut a tunnel." *Gen. Wayne:* "Six regiments, *i. e.*, one fro the right of each brigade, marched at 6 o'clock P.M. under the command of Maj. Ge Lincoln and Brigadiers Clinton and Wayne, and opened the 1st parallel within 55 yards of the enemy." *Chaplain Evans:* "The night was the most favorable in th

PLAN OF THE SIEGE OF YORKTOWN.

References: A, Works at Cornwallis's outer position, evacuated night of September 29th. —B, B, First parallel.—C, American battery on extreme right, from which Washington fired the first shot.—D, Captain Machin's American battery.—E, American mortar battery.—F, French battery on extreme left, first to open fire October 9th.—G, G, French grand and mortar batteries.—H, Zigzag to second parallel.— I, M, Second parallel.—O, N, N, French batteries.—K, Redoubt stormed by Americans night of October 14th.—Q, Redoubt stormed by French.—P, P, French and American batteries attacked by enemy, night of October 15th.—S, British Fusileers' Redoubt.--T, Frigate *Charon* and transports on fire.—R, R, R, French ships approaching after the surrender.

fact, not a man had been either killed or wounded. Nor did the loss referred to by Washington occur in this part of the field, but on the extreme left, where the French regiment of Touraine instituted, at the same time, a false attack upon the British Fusileers' redoubt, just above Yorktown. The object of constructing a parallel and battery opposite that work was to threaten an approach from that quarter and drive off the men-of-war, which might take the main trenches, as well as the camps, in reverse. M. de la Loge, of the artillery, was the French officer wounded. The garrison of the Fusileers' redoubt maintained their post, reports Cornwallis, with "uncommon gallantry." From the French accounts, however, it does not appear that they made any serious attempt upon it beyond a cannonade from their battery.

For ten days, now, until the closing scene, the siege was conducted with the greatest system and activity. The first Continental troops to occupy the trenches on the forenoon of the 7th were Lafayette's Light Infantry. They marched in with the tread of veterans, colors flying, drums beating, and planted their standards on the parapet.[1] The enemy saluted them with a few shot without effect. Digging went on. It was proposed to make the parallel safe against sorties, and four palisaded redoubts and five batteries had accordingly been marked for construction at proper intervals along the line. Upon these and the trenches the fatigue parties worked incessantly under the enemy's fire, which at times was severe; but casualties were few. The duty proved taxing, and many soldiers were taken down with the ague, French especially. In the enemy's camp over one thousand were reported on the sick-list. They were digging there defensively quite as hard as the allies offensively.

On the 7th and 8th much was accomplished.[2] Batteries approached completion; and the allies were surprised at the little interruption from the opposite side. "The enemy," says Colonel Butler, "seem embarrassed,

---

world. Providence seemed very evidently to have drawn the curtains of darkness around us on purpose to conceal us from our enemies until the time of our greatest danger had passed by. Not a man killed or wounded in the American Camp, and but a few in the Camp of the French." See *Deuxponts, Butler, Pickering, Thacher, Tarleton*, etc., for further details.

[1] Diary in "Martin's Gazetteer of Virginia," title, Yorktown.

[2] "The night of the 7th four new works were commenced advanced of the 1st parallel, scarce any annoyance from the enemy. 1 man of ours killed by the firing of one patrole upon the other and 1 man had his foot shot off---2 men wounded in the French trenches.—8th. Still employed completing the advanced redoubts—fire of the enemy very slack—this night 1 American killed—1 wounded, 1 French killed—4 badly wounded."—*Tilghman.*

confused, and indeterminate; their fire seems feeble to what might be expected, their works, too, are not formed on any regular plan, but thrown up in a hurry occasionally, and although we have not as yet fired one shot from a piece of artillery, they are as cautious as if the heaviest fire was kept up." The truth was that Cornwallis, little dreaming that he should be compelled to stand a siege, was unprepared for it. On the 8th, to follow details a little farther, Steuben's division relieved Lafayette's at the trenches, and on the 9th Lincoln relieved Steuben. This order was preserved during the siege. In the French wing, M. de Chastellux, the Marquis St. Simon, Viscount Viomenil, and the Baron Viomenil succeeded each other at the trenches as "Maréchal de Camp." Their detachments were made up of "bataillons," "auxilliaires," and "travailleurs de nuit."[1]

As Steuben was the only general officer in the American wing who had been present at a siege before, his word was doubtless taken as law on many points. He seems to have been the only division commander who issued orders to the parties on the lines. On the 8th, for example, he gave them some practical advice as to defending a parallel. "The general of the trenches," he said, "enjoins it in the strictest manner, on the officers, to remain constantly with their respective commands. The officers commanding platoons are, particularly during the night, to keep their men together, with their arms in their hands. In case the enemy should sally, the whole of the troops are to form eight paces in the rear of the trench; and as the enemy come into the trench, the respective platoons will rush on them with the bayonet; when they are repulsed and retiring, then, and not before, the troops will occupy the banquette, and fire at them in their retreat. Experience has proved the efficacy of this method of defence, and from the General's knowledge of the troops he has the honor to command, he has not the least doubt but that the enemy will pay dearly for their temerity, should they think proper to sally. . . ."

Knox, too, was in his element. This was the opportunity for his guns and gunners, and under his active direction they fully improved it. The

---

[1] Washington's and Rochambeau's daily details ran in this form—those of the 8th, for instance:

"For the trenches to-morrow:
"MAJOR-GENERAL LINCOLN, GENERAL CLINTON,—Major-general Lincoln's division will mount in the trenches to-morrow."

"Marechal de Camp: le Marquis de Saint Simon.
"Brigadier: de Custine; Gatinais: deux bataillons; Royal Deux-Ponts: deux bataillons; Auxiliaires: les grenadiers de Soissonnais et de Saintonge; Travailleurs de nuit: huit cents hommes."

artillery was already regarded as the most efficient arm in the Revolutionary service, and now it was to add to its high reputation. Not only was Knox himself an accomplished chief of artillery, but many of his officers would have done honor to the profession in any service. Such, among others, were Colonel Lamb, Lieutenant-colonels Stevens and Carrington, and Major Bauman, who took turns as superintendents of the batteries and directors of the park. We get a glimpse of the strictness and precision required of the officers in the performance of their duties from Knox's orders of the 8th, as follows:

BARON STEUBEN.

"A Field officer of artillery will be appointed every day to command in the Trenches, to be relieved every twenty-four hours. He will pointedly attend that the firing is well directed according to the object, and that the utmost coolness and Regularity is observed. Upon every occasion where it shall be practicable, the Recochet firing of shott and shells must be practiced. This mode has a vast superiority over all others, and is much more œconomical. The officers of Artillery in the Batteries are to level every piece themselves. As soon as the Field officer of the Trenches shall be relieved, he will make a written report of the occurrences which have happened during his Command, specifying the number and species of shott and shells expended with the apparent effect on the enemy's Works, and a Return of the killed and wounded. . . ."[1]

In this branch of the service at the siege the Americans were in no way inferior to the French, and observably superior to the British.

Industrious digging on the part of the allies continued night and

---

[1] Artillery Brigade orders, "MS. Orderly Book," N. Y. Hist. Soc. Papers.

In camp and guard duties the artillery corps was assisted as indicated in the following general order of the 6th : "Lt. Coll Dabney's Regt [Va.] the Delaware Detachᵗ now doing duty with the Third Mary^ld and one hundred & sixty men which his Excellency Genl Nelson is requested to have selected from the militia for the Purpose, are to assist the Artillery During the present operations—they will encamp in the park, and take their orders from Genl Knox."

day, until by the afternoon of the 9th a sufficient number of batteries had been erected to open the bombardment of Yorktown. The first to fire, at three o'clock, was the French battery on the extreme left, opposite the British Fusileers' redoubt. It had been erected by the regiment Touraine, and mounted four twelve-pounders and six howitzers and mortars. Its fire compelled the frigate *Guadaloupe* to retire to the Gloucester shore.[1] At five o'clock the American battery on the extreme right, on the river bank below, which appears to have been under the charge of Captain Ferguson, of the Fourth Artillery, followed with discharges from six eighteen and twenty-four pounders, four mortars, and two howitzers, and the serious work of the siege had begun.

The journal of more than one American officer mentions the fact that the first shot from the American battery was fired by Washington himself.[2] Colonel Cortlandt remembered that he distinctly heard it crash into some houses in Yorktown. If Captain Samuel Graham, of the Seventy-sixth Regiment, whose station was directly in the line of fire, was not mistaken as to the particular discharge he refers to in his "Memoirs," this first shot was singularly fatal. A party of officers from the Seventy-sixth were then at dinner in a neighboring building. The British Commissary-general Perkins was with them. One of the officers was an old Scotch lieutenant, who, when the allies first invested the place, was heard to soliloquize as he buckled on his sword: "Come on, Maister Washington. I'm unco glad to see you. I've been offered money for my commission, but I could na think of gangin' home without a sight of you. Come on." Poor fellow! Washington fell upon him in a way that was quite unexpected, for that first ball struck and wounded him terribly. It also wounded the quarter-master and adjutant of the Seventy-sixth, and killed the commissary-general. Another marked casualty of the siege was the death of Major Cochrane, who arrived at Yorktown on the 10th, with despatches from Clinton to Cornwallis. Two days after, in company with the British general, he went to the lines, and fired one of the guns himself; but as he looked over the parapet to see its effect *en ricochet*, a ball from the American works carried away his head, narrowly missing Cornwallis, who was standing by his side.[3]

---

[1] Note on Captain Fage's map of Yorktown, published 1782, London.

[2] Colonel Butler, of Penn., states positively that Washington fired the first shot.

[3] Statement made by Captain Mure in letter published in appendix to vol. vii. of Lord Mahon's "History of England."

THE SIEGE OF YORKTOWN.

One of the principal objects fired at by the besiegers was Secretary
Nelson's house, where Cornwallis was quartered, and it soon became
untenable. His Lordship withdrew from it on the 10th, as did Mr. Nelson, who received permission to pass into the American lines. "By
report of Mr. Secretary Nelson," says Colonel Tilghman, the American
shells did "a good deal of damage." Fifteen years after the war the
mansion still stood unrepaired, "pierced in every direction with cannon-shot and bomb-shells."[1]

On the 10th two new batteries opened—the "Grand French Battery,"
on the left of the parallel, mounting ten eighteen and twenty-four pounders and six mortars, and the American battery of four eighteen-pounders
and two mortars, under command, as Tilghman says, of Captain Thomas
Machin, of the Second Artillery. On this date Lafayette was general
officer of the day, and he invited Governor Nelson to be present at the
opening of the fire from Machin's guns, not only as a compliment, but because of his accurate knowledge of localities in Yorktown. "To what
particular spot," he asked, "would your Excellency direct that we should
point the cannon?" "There," replied Nelson, "to that house. It is

---

[1] The British maps of the siege distinctly mark the Secretary's house as the head-
quarters. The fact is given also in Chastellux's "Travels" and those of Rochefoucauld
and Weld, in 1795–'96. The latter, an Englishman, says: "York is remarkable for having been the place where Lord Cornwallis surrendered his army to the combined forces
of the Americans and French. A few of the redoubts, which were erected by each
army, are still remaining, but the principal fortifications are almost quite obliterated;
the plough has passed over some of them, and groves of pine trees sprung up about
others, though, during the siege, every tree near the town was destroyed. The first
and second parallels can just be traced when pointed out by a person acquainted with
them in a more perfect state. In the town the houses bear evident marks of the
siege, and the inhabitants will not, on any account, suffer the holes perforated by the
cannon-balls to be repaired on the outside. There is one house in particular, which
stands in the skirt of the town, that is in a most shattered condition. It was the
habitation of a Mr. Neilson, a Secretary under the regal government, and was made
the head-quarters of Lord Cornwallis when he first came to the town; but it stood
so much exposed, and afforded so good a mark to the enemy, that he was soon forced
to quit it. . . . The walls and roof are pierced in innumerable places, and at one cor-
ner a large piece of the wall is torn away." This mansion is not now standing.
   In what house Cornwallis took up his quarters next does not appear—possibly
Governor Nelson's, in the town. More likely he pitched his tent under the bank,
which gave rise at the time to the story that he made a cave his head-quarters. Pickering says, on the 11th: "Yesterday Secretary Nelson came out of York. He was put
under no restraint by the enemy. He says our shells had great effect. The enemy
retired for shelter under the bank of the river, but the shells annoyed them there."

mine, and, now that the Secretary's is nearly knocked to pieces, is the best one in the town. There you will be almost certain to find Lord Cornwallis and the British head-quarters. Fire upon it, my dear marquis, and never spare a particle of my property so long as it affords a comfort or a shelter to the enemies of my country."[1] Nelson's patriotism was conspicuous all through this campaign. How earnestly and actively he was engaged in urging the public officers throughout the State to forward everything they could collect in the shape of provisions for the allied army appears from his letters published in 1874 by the Virginia Historical Society. Although serving but a brief term, he proved himself a "War Governor," like George Clinton, of New York, and Trumbull, of Connecticut, but, unfortunately, failed, in the midst of private claims brought against him for necessary impressments made in the public service, to receive the same hearty and grateful appreciation upon his retirement.

Nor could the British shipping in the river remain at the usual anchorage off the town. A number of vessels had been scuttled and sunk by order of the British commander, while the *Charon* was set on fire on the night of the 10th by hot shot from the French battery on the extreme left, and destroyed. An officer who witnessed the sight writes: "The *Charon* was on fire from the water's edge to her truck at the same time. I never saw anything so magnificent." Two transports close to her were also burned.

By the 11th fifty-two pieces were playing from the allied batteries upon the enemy, and had succeeded in nearly silencing their fire. At noon of this day Cornwallis wrote to Clinton: "We have lost about seventy men, and many of our works are considerably damaged. With such works, on disadvantageous ground, against so powerful an attack we cannot hope to make a very long resistance." In a postscript at 5 P.M. he adds: "Since my last letter was written we have lost thirty men."

But vigorously as the siege was prosecuted, the turning-point and the end came even sooner than expected. The incident which largely determined matters occurred in connection with the construction by the allies of a second parallel from three to five hundred yards in advance of the first, thus bringing both wings within storming distance of the British lines. This parallel was opened on the night of the 11th by detachments from the 'two armies, Steuben's division furnishing the American detail.

---

[1] "Recollections and Private Memoirs of Washington," Custis, p. 336.

The parties moved out at dusk, every second man carrying a fascine and shovel, and every man "a shovel, spade, or grubbing hoe," and by morning they had thrown up an intrenchment seven hundred and fifty yards long, three and a half feet deep, and seven feet wide.[1] It was an exciting and busy night, with its alarms of sorties by the enemy, and the whizzing of shot and shell from the first parallel over the heads of the diggers. Two men were killed by the premature bursting of French shells in this cross-fire. Both Steuben and Wayne were exposed as well as their men, and the story is told that once, when a shell fell near them, Steuben threw himself into the trench, and Wayne followed, stumbling over him. "Ah ha, Wayne," laughed Steuben, "you cover your general's retreat in the best manner possible." This was coming to close quarters, but the increasingly effective fire from the French and American batteries continued to keep the British gunners very quiet, and work on the second line went on two days longer without many casualties. It had been ob-

---

[1] Baron Steuben's Order in the Trenches, October 11th, 1781 : "The Soldiers not to be allowed to lay down in the night, but remain as in the day time with their arms in their hands. Officers to remain at their respective posts. No Fashines to be untied nor made use of in any manner whatsoever but for the construction of the works."—*Col. Febiger's MS.*

In his congratulatory orders to his division, October 21st, Steuben tenders the officers and men his "best thanks for the good conduct shown in opening the second parallel, which he considers as the most important part of the siege. He takes pleasure in assuring them it was performed with a degree of bravery and despatch that exceeded his most sanguine expectations."

From the "Journal" in Martin's Gazetteer : "11th.—In the evening, the second parallel opened by B. Steuben's division. This parallel was carried on with amazing rapidity, at 360 yards' distance from the enemy's batteries, under a very heavy fire of the enemy's shot and shells going over our heads in a continual blaze the whole night. The sight was beautifully tremendous." . . .

From Deuxponts' "Campaigns," describing the part taken by the French on this occasion : "On the 11th of October, the regiments of Gatenois and of Royal Deuxponts relieved the trenches, and the same night we constructed a second parallel within short musket range of the town, to be ready against a vigorous sortie. Several companies were ordered in consequence as auxiliary grenadiers and chasseurs, and the Chevalier de Chastellux, general officer of the trenches, made such disposition of the troops as to receive the enemy in the most advantageous manner. At eight o'clock in the evening we began the work; at ten o'clock we heard a score of musket-shots; everybody thought that it was the beginning of an attack, but it was only an English patrol. There were several small volleys of this kind during the night, and it is to this all the outside attempts of the enemy are confined. Nevertheless, they fire many cannon, bombs, and howitzers; but the fire of our artillery preserves its superiority, and the fire of the enemy has little effect."

served, however, that the new parallel would not form a sufficiently com-
pact investment unless it was extended on the right to the river-bank.
But here there was a serious obstacle, for the ground near the river was
occupied by the two outer British redoubts, Numbers 9 and 10, which
must first be taken. The resolution to storm them was accordingly formed the moment the necessity was obvious, and the capture of the two
forts stands out as the incident which more than any other marked the
energy of the siege, and which, upon his own admission, hastened the surrender of Cornwallis. We have no "great" assault here, no storming of
the Malakoff or Redan; but the work was done so well, was so highly
praised at the time, and was, moreover, the last piece of fighting on the
part of any of Washington's troops, that some of its details may be
recalled.

The assault was assigned to the choice corps of the allied army—the
work upon the right, on the high bank of the York, to the American
light infantry; the other, nearly a quarter of a mile to the left, to the
French chasseurs and grenadiers. The martial pride of these soldiers,
excited by what amounted to a friendly challenge to do their best, carried
them along to complete success, both redoubts being gallantly taken at
nearly the same moment.

The time selected was the night of the 14th. For the storming party
on the side of the French the grenadiers and chasseurs of the regiments
Gatenois and Royal Deuxponts, four hundred strong, were detailed. The
work they were to take was the bastion redoubt "Number 9," standing
across the road running from Yorktown to the Moore house below, and
was held by Lieutenant-colonel McPherson and about one hundred and
twenty British and Hessians. Colonel William Deuxponts, a brave, enthusiastic spirit in the French army, commanded the detachment, with
Lieutenant-colonel Baron de l'Estrade, an officer of forty years' service,
as second. As the detachment moved out of the lines into position everybody wished Deuxponts success and glory, and expressed regret at not
being able to go with him. "That moment," he writes in his journal,
"seemed to me very sweet, and was very elevating to the soul and ani-
mating to the courage. My brother, especially, my brother—and I shall
never forget it—gave me marks of a tenderness which penetrated to the
bottom of my heart." At the given signal—the firing of six shells in
rapid succession—about eight o'clock, just after dusk, the force advanced
in columns by platoons, the first fifty chasseurs carrying fascines, to fill
the ditch, and eight carrying ladders. Two trusty sergeants—who, with
Deuxponts and L'Estrade, had previously reconnoitred the ground with

great care—led the way. The second battalion of the regiment Gatenois, under Count de Rostaing, remained in reserve, with Baron de Viomenil commanding the whole. Deuxponts moved on silently, when, at a hundred and twenty paces from the redoubt, a Hessian sentinel discovered them. " Wer da ?"—" Who goes there?" he shouted. No answer coming, the enemy instantly opened fire. Unluckily, the strong abatis, twenty-five paces in front of the fort, stopped the French several minutes, and there they lost men while the pioneers cut away a passage; but, the obstructions once cleared, the chasseurs dashed on, and began mounting the parapet. The first to reach the top was the Chevalier de Lameth; but, receiving a point-blank discharge from the Hessian infantry, he fell back shot through both knees. L'Estrade while climbing was tumbled into the ditch by a soldier falling from above him. Rising badly bruised, he scolded the man roundly for making such bungling work of it. Deuxponts also fell, when young Lieutenant de Sillegue, of the chasseurs, pulled him up the parapet, to be fatally wounded in doing so. Finding the French actually on the edge of their redoubt, the enemy charged upon them; but Deuxponts ordered his men to fire and countercharge, and the work was theirs. The Hessians threw down their arms; the French raised the shout of " Vive le roi!" They had carried the redoubt in less than half an hour, with the loss of fifteen killed and seventy-seven wounded, the enemy losing eighteen killed and fifty prisoners. For his conduct on this occasion Deuxponts received the title of Chevalier in the Military Order of St. Louis as a special distinction. In his journal he has this appreciative word for his comrades: " With troops so good, so brave, and so disciplined as those I have the honor to lead against the enemy, one can undertake anything, and be sure of succeeding, if the impossibility of it has not been proved. I owe them the happiest day of my life, and certainly the recollection of it will never be effaced from my mind." The grenadiers of the regiment Gatenois behaved so well that Rochambeau, at their entreaty, before the assault, petitioned the King to restore their old honored name and motto of "Auvergne sans tache." " Good for Royal Auvergne!" wrote the King upon the petition, when he read of their exploit.

Not less brilliant was the success of the Americans at the other redoubt. The praise bestowed by Lafayette upon his light infantry, that they were equal to the best troops in the world, proved to be well-grounded. Viomenil added to the compliment when he referred to them in his official report as behaving on this occasion "like grenadiers accustomed to difficult things." These light infantry troops, it may be repeated, were in truth, both officers and men, tried veterans of the war, half of whom, in addition to previous service, had just completed the campaign in Virginia under Lafayette. The battalions selected for the present assault were Gimat's, Alexander Hamilton's, and half of Laurens's— the whole under the immediate command of Hamilton, whose own corps was led by his major, Nicholas Fish, of New York. As in the case of the French, the detachment was four hundred strong. The command at first

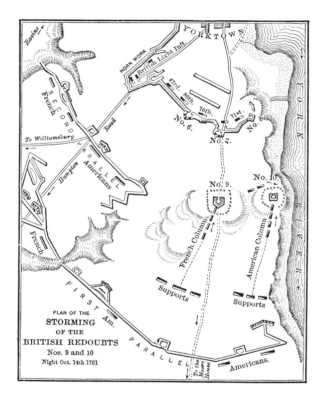

was a matter in dispute. Lafayette, as chief of the Light Division, had intended the honor for Gimat, lately his aide, who had entered the American service in 1777, and served two campaigns with the light infantry, with the brevet rank of lieutenant-colonel. On that date, October 14th, Hamilton was field-officer of the day. At once he protested against Gimat's appointment for command during his own tour of duty. Being informed by Lafayette that the assignment had already been made, and approved at head-quarters, he wrote a spirited letter to Washington, who, upon inquiring into the claim, decided in favor of Hamilton, much to the latter's gratification.[1]

Gimat's battalion, however, as the oldest and one of the three that had been in Virginia from the first, retained the post of honor in the van of the assaulting party. It was composed of companies, it will be recalled, drawn mainly from the Connecticut line, and was the regiment which protected Wayne's right flank at the action of Green Spring Farm. John Palsgrave Wyllys, of Hartford, was its major, and its original captains were Barker, Douglass, Heart, St. John, and Welles, from Connecticut,[2] Hunt, and another from Massachusetts, and Olney, from Rhode Island. Hamilton's battalion was composed of two New York and two Connecticut companies; and of Laurens's two companies, which were part of Scammell's old corps, one was from Connecticut, under Captain Stephen Betts, of Stamford, and the other, under Captain Ebenezer Williams, of Massachusetts. With the detachment went also a party of sappers and miners, under Captains Gilliland and Kirkpatrick; while for a reserve corps Lafayette drew up the remainder of the Light Division, under Generals Muhlenberg and Hazen, and in their rear Wayne posted two Pennsylvania battalions.

The work to be stormed was a square redoubt, "Number 10," somewhat smaller than the one captured by the French, standing within twenty feet of the river-bank, and held by the British Major Campbell and about seventy men. It was upon the site of this work—the "Rock Redoubt," as it was afterward called—that the triumphal arch was erected in honor of Lafayette, upon the occasion of his visit to Yorktown in 1824, and under which he paid a feeling tribute to the worth and valor of his "dear light infantry" of 1781.

At the given signal—the six shells—Hamilton and his column advanced rapidly, with unloaded muskets, Laurens having first been detached to take the redoubt in reverse, and prevent the escape of the garrison. Under the almost perfect discipline of these troops every order was executed with precision. As they neared the work they rushed to the charge without waiting for the sappers to remove the abatis, and thereby saved themselves the delay and loss which befell the French. Climbing

---

[1] Colonel Harry Lee, who was at the siege, apparently as bearer of despatches from General Greene, states that he had this incident from Hamilton himself.—*Memoirs*, vol. ii., p. 342, note.
[2] Revolutionary MS., State Library, Hartford. The composition of the rest of the command is ascertained from Order Books and Hamilton's Report.

over or breaking through the obstructions, they reached the ditch, enveloped the work, and scaling the parapet, made the capture within ten minutes after the start. The forlorn hope of twenty men, under Lieutenant John Mansfield, of the Fourth Connecticut, led the column without wavering. Mansfield, who entered the work among the first, receiving a bayonet wound, was reported by Hamilton as deserving particular commendation for his "coolness, firmness, and punctuality."[1] Stephen Olney, of the Rhode Island regiment, perhaps the oldest captain in the service, marched with his company at the head of the detachment; but in attempt-

ALEXANDER HAMILTON.

ing to climb into the fort two of the enemy struck at him with their bayonets, which slid down his spontoon, or spear, and wounded him severely in the side and arm. Hamilton thought him entitled to "peculiar applause." Captain Hunt was also wounded, as well as Kirkpatrick, of the Sappers. Hamilton himself behaved with conspicuous gallantry in the front. Colonel Armand and three officers of his troop accompanied him as volunteers, and stimulated the troops by their example. Gimat was wounded in the foot just as the obstructions were reached, and retired. Laurens meanwhile had conducted his two companies with his usual skill and nerve, and succeeded in coming in at the right moment to make Major Campbell his prisoner. With him was Captain Betts, who was also honored with a wound. A Sergeant Brown, of the Fifth Connecticut, was subsequently awarded a special " badge of merit " for his coolness and gallant conduct as one of

---

[1] See Hamilton's account of this affair—a model of a military report.— *Works*, vol. i., p. 270.

The entry in the "Journal" in Martin for the 14th is this: "About 2 o'clock P.M. the out defences of two redoubts that were advanced on the left 250 yards in their front were thought sufficiently weakened to attempt them that evening by storm. The light infantry were relieved and directed to refresh themselves with dinner and a nap. About dusk they moved on under the Marquis, and were in possession of one in nine minutes. The other was carried by the French grenadiers and light infantry under Baron Viomenil, nearly about the same time, when the second parallel was continued on and enveloped these two redoubts, and finished a line of communication between the rights of the first and second parallel of upwards of a mile, before daylight next morning. The whole of this was performed under a very incessant and heavy fire from the enemy, with amazing steadiness and expedition."

Hamilton's forlorn hope. So well had every movement been timed, that Major Fish's battalion, which followed Gimat's, inclining to the left, participated in the assault; and Lieutenant-colonel Barber's battalion, which Lafayette sent forward at the last moment to support Hamilton, was on hand after the assault to help hold the position in case of a counter-attack by the enemy. The American loss in the affair was nine killed and twenty-five wounded.[1]

Washington could not conceal his enthusiasm over the success of these brilliant feats, and in General Orders he praised the troops unstintedly—officers and men alike.[2] What also redounded to the credit of the Americans was their forbearance, under aggravating circumstances, in the hour of victory. The brutality of Arnold's conduct at New London was fresh in their minds, and Scammell's fate at the opening of the siege could not be forgotten; but, on the night of this assault, no retaliation was encouraged or indulged in.[3]

---

[1] Compare Hamilton's return of the casualties, in Appendix. In addition to the officers mentioned above, Lieutenant-colonel Barber and Major Barber, Division Inspector, were slightly wounded; also, according to Gordon, Major Gibbs, of Vose's battalion in reserve. Lafayette's report may be found in his " Memoirs " and Sparks' " Correspondence of the Revolution."

[2] " The Commander-in-chief congratulates the army on the success of the enterprise against the two important works on the left of the enemy's line. He requests the Baron Viomenil, who commanded the French Grenadiers and Chasseurs, and Marquis De La Fayette, who commanded the American Light Infantry, to accept his warmest acknowledgments, for the excellency of their dispositions, and for their own gallant conduct on the occasion; and he begs them to present his thanks to every individual officer, and to the men of their respective commands, for the spirit and rapidity with which they advanced to the attacks assigned them, and for the admirable firmness with which they supported them, under the fire of the enemy, without returning a shot.

" The General reflects with the highest degree of pleasure on the confidence which the troops of the two nations must hereafter have in each other. Assured of mutual support, he is convinced there is no danger which they will not cheerfully encounter —no difficulty which they will not bravely overcome."—General Orders, October 15th, 1781.

[3] In this connection, Lafayette's brief speech at the " Rock Redoubt," in 1824, will be read with interest. He was welcomed by General Taylor, who closed his address with presenting him a laurel wreath. As he was about to fix it upon Lafayette's brow the latter took it in his hand, and made the following reply:

" I most cordially thank you, my dear General, and your companions in arms, for your affectionate welcome, your kind recollections, and the flattering expressions of your friendship. Happy I am to receive them on these already ancient lines, where the united arms of America and France have been gloriously engaged in a Holy Al-

No sooner were the redoubts taken than the supports fell to digging, and by morning both works were included in the second parallel, which thus became complete, and unpleasantly menacing to the besieged. To Clinton, who was making hurried efforts to rescue him, Cornwallis wrote on the 15th: " Last evening the enemy carried two advanced redoubts on the left by storm, and during the night have included them in their second parallel, which they are at present busy in perfecting. My situation now becomes very critical; we dare not show a gun to their old batteries, and I expect that their new ones will open to-morrow morning. Experience has shown that our fresh earthen works do not resist their powerful artillery, so that we shall soon be exposed to an assault in ruining works, in a bad position, and with weakened numbers. The safety of the place is, therefore, so precarious that I cannot recommend that the fleet and army should run any great risk in endeavoring to save us."

It would have been quite contrary to the custom of a besieged force, and rather a reflection upon the British troops in particular, had no sortie been made by them upon the besiegers ; and, accordingly, on the night of the 15th, we find them dashing out at the second parallel with their wonted courage, and repeating what the French and Americans had done two nights before. Cornwallis's object was to cripple some unfinished batteries, whose fire, when opened, would prove too destructive, and thus gain a little more time for still possible relief. The party, which was led by Colonel Abercrombie, numbered about

---

liance to support the right of American Independence, and the sacred principle of the sovereignty of the people. Happy, also, to be so welcomed on the particular spot where my dear light infantry comrades acquired one of their honorable claims to public love and esteem. You know, sir, that in this business of storming redoubts, with unloaded arms and fixed bayonets, the merit of the deed is in the soldiers who execute it; and to each of them I am anxious to acknowledge their equal share of honor. Let me, however, with affection and gratitude, pay a special tribute to the gallant name of *Hamilton*, who commanded the attack, to the three field-officers who seconded him, *Gimat*, *Laurens*, and *Fish*, the only surviving one, my friend now near me. In their name, my dear General, in the name of the light infantry, those we have lost as well as those who survive, and only in common with them, I accept the crown with which you are pleased to honor us, and I offer you the return of the most grateful acknowledgments."

Turning to Colonel Fish, who was with him, he exclaimed, "Here, half of this wreath belongs to you." "No, sir, it is all your own," was the reply. "Then," said Lafayette, putting it into the colonel's hand, "take it and preserve it as our common property."—From the account by an eye-witness entitled "*The Siege of York in* 1781; *and the Celebration of the Capture of Cornwallis, the* 19th *October*, 1824." Pamphlet, 26 pp.

four hundred men, half of them light infantry, under Major Armstrong, and the other half, the grenadiers of the Foot-guards and Captain Murray's company of the Eightieth, under Lieutenant-colonel Lake. Moving forward about three o'clock in the morning, they rushed upon a French battery, drove off the guards, spiked four cannon, and then attacked Captain Savage's battery to its right. Entering it, they quickly spiked his three guns with bayonet-points and challenged, " What troops?" " French," came the answer; on which Abercrombie shouted, "Rush on, my brave boys, and skin the hounds!" But just then the Count de Noailles, who had command of the supports that night, distinctly hearing Abercrombie's cry, ordered his grenadiers to the charge, when they instantly met the British with the shout of "Vive le roi!" killed eight of them, took twelve prisoners, with the loss of twenty officers and men on their part, and one American sergeant, and prevented the assailants from doing further mischief.[1] It was altogether a gallant sortie, but it proved of no avail, and in six hours the spiked guns were playing upon Yorktown. When some British officers visited the spot, after the surrender, the French feelingly showed them the grave of a brave sergeant of the Guards, whom they had buried in the parapet where he fell.

Cornwallis now thoroughly appreciated his critical position, but determined to make a desperate effort to escape before surrendering. On the night of the 16th he began to transfer his troops to the opposite side, at Gloucester Point, with the design of breaking through the besiegers there with his whole force, and by rapid marches push northward to New York.[2]

---

[1] Colonel Butler's "Journal."

[2] On the next morning, October 17th, Governor Nelson wrote to Hon. Geo. Webb: "Since my last we took by storm two of the enemy's redoubts. The loss on both sides was nearly equal, and did not exceed 100. Our batteries are now playing on their works at the distance of about 200 yards. By noon, I am informed, we shall have seventy pieces of heavy cannon planted against them, which must soon reduce them to terms, unless they take a flight to Gloucester, which may delay their capture a few days. Yesterday morning, a little before daybreak, they made a sally and got into one of our batteries. They spiked eight cannon, which were immediately unspiked, and killed and wounded about sixteen men. They were repulsed, and suffered nearly the same loss."

In regard to his projected escape, Cornwallis says, in his answer to Clinton: "The success of this attempt would, no doubt, have been precarious, and I cannot say that it would have been practicable to reach New York; but, in our desperate situation, I thought it well deserved a trial." Clinton replied that he could not see "the least daylight" in it.

It is scarcely possible that he could have succeeded; and the elements interposed to stop him.   At midnight a storm arose, preventing the crossing of all the troops, and at dawn those who had already crossed returned to their old stations at the works, which were now crumbling away under the point-blank fire of the new batteries opened on the second parallel.

Further resistance would have been madness.   "We at that time could not fire a single gun, . . ." reports Cornwallis.   "I therefore proposed to capitulate."

CHAPTER VII.

THE SURRENDER.

SO, at length, on the 17th of October—a date vividly remembered by our soldiers, as the anniversary of Burgoyne's surrender—the end came. At ten o'clock that morning a drummer in red mounted the enemy's parapet on the left and began to beat a "parley." As for being heard, he might have played till doomsday; but he could readily be seen, and the cannonading stopped. An ensign at the American lines imagined that he never listened to music so delightful as the sound of that drum.[1] No one could have misunderstood its meaning. In fact, the drummer in that particular rôle was somewhat of a momentous figure. He seemed to publicly confess the end of British domination in America, and proclaim the success of the "rebel" Revolution.

With the drummer appeared an officer waving a white handkerchief. He was met and blindfolded by an American officer, and conducted to the rear of our lines. The message Cornwallis had sent by him to Washington was to the effect that hostilities be suspended for twenty-four hours, and joint commissioners appointed to determine the terms of surrender. To this Washington replied that he should prefer, before the meeting of commissioners, to have his Lordship's proposals submitted to him in writing, and that for the purpose he would grant a suspension of hostilities for two hours. Cornwallis complied, and sent in the terms on which he proposed to capitulate. Among his demands he included the inadmissible condition that his troops should be sent to England upon a parole not to serve against either France or America during the continuance of the war unless regularly exchanged. Again the flag returned, and this time with an ultimatum from Washington, who had good reasons for wasting as little time as possible in the negotiations. There existed all through the siege the possibility of the British fleet's appearance off the Capes, and the breaking up of De Grasse's blockade of the York, which

---

[1] Ensign Denny, Penn. Line.

might prove fatal to the success of the siege operations. Every day's delay increased the danger. The situation might change any hour, and Cornwallis be encouraged to hold out in the hope of immediate relief. Washington's terms included the surrender of the British army as prisoners of war, upon the basis of the Charleston capitulation in 1780, to which Cornwallis yielded. This result was effected by the night of the 17th, and on the 18th commissioners met to digest and embody the articles.

THE MOORE HOUSE.

On the part of the British appeared Lieutenant - colonel Dundas and Major Ross, and for the French and Americans the Viscount de Noailles and Lieutenant-colonel Laurens. They met at the Moore house, which still stands on the bank of the York, a short distance in the rear of the American lines, and drew up fourteen articles, providing for the surrender of the garrison, and the disposition of the ordnance, stores, ships, and Loyalists. On the morning of the 19th these were submitted to Cornwallis, accompanied by a note from Washington intimating his expectation that the terms would be signed by eleven o'clock that morning, and that the troops would march out to surrender their arms at two in the afternoon.[1]

Toward eleven o'clock the articles were signed " in the trenches," and Cornwallis and his army, which had been the scourge of the South for fourteen months, were prisoners of war.[2] The British " Hannibal " had found his Zama in Yorktown.

---

[1] For the correspondence and articles of capitulation, with Cornwallis's report of the siege and surrender, see Appendix.

[2] Clinton attempted to relieve Cornwallis, but arrived off the Chesapeake only to hear of the surrender. The fleet under Graves and Hood was detained for repairs, when every moment was precious. It was proposed that the fleet should offer battle to De Grasse and get him out to sea, which would give the frigates and transports, with seven thousand troops, the opportunity of running in and up the York River to Yorktown. In case this could not be effected, the troops were to be landed at or near the Severn River and push on to Gloucester; and, for a third alternative, a landing was to be attempted at Jamestown Island, in the rear of the allies. Had the relieving fleet appeared as early as the 5th, it might have proved a very disturbing factor in the situation.

Article 14th

No Article of the Capitula
tion to be infringed on pre
text of Reprisal, & if there be
any doubtfull Expressions
in it, they are to be inter=
preted according to the common Meaning & Acceptation
of the Words.

Done at York in Virginia
this 9th day   October 1781

Cornwallis
Thos: Symonds:

FAC-SIMILE OF ONE OF THE ARTICLES OF CAPITULATION.

At noon of the 19th we have the first act of surrender. Yorktown changed hands. Two redoubts on the left of the enemy's works were at that hour taken possession of by detachments from the allied army. Colonel Richard Butler commanded the American, and the Marquis Laval the French party, each of one hundred men. At two o'clock we reach the closing scene. The army of Cornwallis marched out as prisoners of war, grounded their arms, and then marched back. Accounts agree in describing the display and ceremony on the occasion as quite imposing. The British appeared in new uniforms, distributed among them a few days before, and it only required the flying of their standards to give their march the effect of a holiday parade. But their colors were cased, and they were prohibited from playing either a French or an American tune. This was the return of a compliment—a piece of justifiable as well as poetic retaliation on the part of the Americans for what the enemy were pleased to command when General Lincoln was compelled to surrender at Charleston the year before. The matter came up at the meeting of the Commissioners:

"This is a harsh article," said Ross to Laurens.

"Which article?" answered the latter.

"'The troops shall march out, *with colors cased, and drums beating a British or a German march.*'"

"Yes, sir," returned Laurens, with a touch of *sang-froid*, "it is a harsh article."

"Then," said Ross, "if that is your opinion, why is it here?"

Whereupon Laurens, who had been made prisoner at Charleston with Lincoln's army, proceeded to remind Ross that the Americans on that occasion had made a brave defence, but were ungallantly refused any honors of surrender other than to march out with colors cased and drums *not* beating a British or a German march.

"But," rejoined Ross, "my Lord Cornwallis did not command at Charleston."

"There, sir," said Laurens, "you extort another observation: it is not the individual that is here considered; it is the nation. This remains an article, or I cease to be a commissioner."

Nothing more was to be said; the article stood, and the enemy marched out with colors cased, while the tune they chose to follow was an old British march with the quite appropriate title of "The World Turned Upside Down."[1]

---

[1] Garden's "Anecdotes of the Revolution."

As the prisoners moved out of their works along the Hampton Road they found the French and American armies drawn up on either side of the way—the Americans on the right, and extending for more than a mile toward the field of surrender. The French troops presented a brilliant spectacle in their white uniforms, with plumed and decorated officers at their head, and gorgeous standards of white silk, embroidered with golden fleur-de-lis, floating along the line. The Americans were less of an attraction in outward appearance, but not the less eagerly eyed by their antagonists. Among the war-worn Continentals there was variety of dress, poor at the best, distinguishing the men of the different lines; but, to compensate for lack of show, there was a soldierly bearing about them which commanded attention. The militia formed in their rear presented a less martial sight, so far as clothing and order were concerned. But all these men were conquerors, and their very appearance bespoke the hardships and privation they and their States had undergone to win in the struggle. At the head of the respective lines were the commanding generals, nobly mounted — Washington, Rochambeau, Lincoln, Lafayette, Steuben, Knox, and the rest. Leading the British came General O'Hara instead of Cornwallis. The latter pleaded illness, but he sent his sword by O'Hara to be given up to Washington. As O'Hara advanced to the chief, he was referred to Lincoln, who, upon receiving the sword as a token of the enemy's submission, immediately returned it to the British general, whose troops then marched between the two lines to a field on the right, where they

GENERAL BENJAMIN LINCOLN.

grounded their arms. For the proud and veteran soldiers, who were the heroes of repeated Southern victories, this was a humiliating ceremony, but it was done in good order. In the field a squadron of French hussars had formed a circle, and within it each regiment marched and deposited their arms. There were sad hearts in the column. The colonel of the Bayreuthian regiment, Von Seybothen, led his men into the circle and gave the commands: "Present arms! Lay down arms! Put off swords and cartridge-boxes!" his cheeks wet with tears. A corporal in the Seventy-sixth feelingly clasped his musket to his breast and then threw it down, with the words, "May you never get so good a master!" Writes a captain, "We marched out reluctantly enough." Trumbull's painting in the Rotunda at the Capitol represents the surrender of the enemy's standards.[1]

Returning to their tents through the same lines, the British were permitted a few days of rest, when the rank and file, with a number of officers, were marched off to prison-camps at Winchester, Virginia, and Frederick, Maryland, guarded chiefly by militiamen. Their route lay through Williamsburg, Fredericksburg, Red House, and Ashby's Gap, into the Shenandoah Valley.[2] Cornwallis and his principal officers were allowed to return to New York on parole, though not till they had been hospitably entertained by their victors. Both Washington and Rochambeau invited the distinguished prisoners to their tables, and for several days camp dinners were the fashion, at which the English were the guests. "The Amer-

---

[1] See, in Appendix, a letter from Colonel Fontaine, an eye-witness, describing the surrender. Surgeon Thacher, Colonel Harry Lee, and others also give details of the scene. "The most pleasing sight I ever beheld, to see those haughty fellows march out of their strong fortifications and ground their arms," wrote Captain Welles, of Gimat's Light Infantry, to his father, four days after. In a note dated 8 A.M. the morning of the surrender, Knox wrote gayly to his wife: "I have detained William [his brother] until this morning, that I might be the first to communicate *good news* to the charmer of my soul. A glorious moment for America! This day Lord Cornwallis and his army march out and pile their arms in the face of our victorious army. . . . They will have the same *honors* as the garrison of Charleston; that is, they will *not* be permitted to unfurl their colors or play *Yankee Doodle*. We know not yet how many there are. The General has requested me to be at head-quarters instantly, therefore I cannot be more particular."—DRAKE'S *Memoir of General Knox*.

[2] When the prisoners were passing through the Gap two or three of the English officers rode up to Mrs. Ashby's tavern, and asked if she could get them up a dinner. She stared at their uniforms, and ejaculated at the spokesman,

"A militiaman, I guess?"

"No," said the officer.

"Continental, mayhap?"

Another negative.

"Oho!" she exclaimed again, "I see; you are one of the sarpints—one of old 'Wallis's men. Well, now, I have two sons; one was at the catching of Johnny Burgoyne, and the other at that of you, and next year they are both going to catch Clinton at New York. But you shall be treated kindly: my mother came from the old country."— GENERAL GRAHAM'S *Memoirs*.

ican, French, and English generals," says Lafayette, in his "Memoirs," "visited each other, and everything passed with every possible mark of attention, especially toward Lord Cornwallis, one of the most estimable men of England, who was considered their best general." The American wing of the allied army took up the return march to the Hudson about November 1st, while the French remained around Yorktown until the following spring, when they returned to Rhode Island. In December, 1782, they embarked from Boston for the West Indies, after a stay in this country of nearly two years and a half.

Comparing the statistics of the siege, we find that the total number of British, officers and men, surrendered on October 19th and taken during the operations, was officially reported to Congress by Washington as seven thousand two hundred and forty-seven, and eight hundred and forty seamen. Their losses, as published by themselves, were one hundred and fifty-six killed, and three hundred and twenty-six wounded. Over fifteen hundred were reported as sick or unfit for duty at the time of the capitulation. Of the twenty-four regimental standards surrendered, eighteen were German and six British, the latter belonging to the Forty-third, Seventy-sixth, and Eightieth regiments; while two hundred and forty-four pieces of artillery were captured, seventy-five of which were brass. The American loss during the siege was twenty killed and fifty-six wounded; that of the French, fifty-two killed and one hundred and thirty-four wounded. According to an unofficial statement, the number of sick and unfit for duty in the allied camps on the day of the surrender was fourteen hundred and thirty.

In America the news of the surrender was everywhere received with the profoundest joy. Lieutenant-colonel Tilghman, Washington's aide, who had been with him since the battle of Long Island, rode with the official despatches for Congress as fast as horse could carry him, reaching Philadelphia soon after midnight of the 24th. He roused the President, Thomas McKean, and the great news was soon spread through the city by the watchmen.[1] Congress met in the morning, and, after hearing the

[1] "ANECDOTE.—A watchman of this city, after having conducted the express rider to the door of his Excellency the President of Congress, on Monday morning last, the honest old German continued the duties of his function, calling out, 'Basht dree o'glock, und Gorn—wal—lis isht da—ken.'"—*Penn. Freeman's Journal; N. Y. Packet,* Nov. 1, 1781.

despatches read, proceeded in a body, at two o'clock in the afternoon, to the Lutheran church, where services were held by the Rev. Mr. Duffield, one of the chaplains of the body. Later they passed resolutions of thanks to the army, and for the erection of a monument at Yorktown in commemoration of the event. A grand illumination of the city in the evening ended the day's rejoicings, which were then continued throughout the country.[1] The army in the Highlands, under Heath, devoted nearly a week to salutes and camp banquets, with Continental *menu;* and at Harvard and Yale there were orations and bonfires. The students of the latter college sung "a triumphal hymn;" and its president, Dr. Stiles, was afterward moved to write to Washington in terms like these: "We rejoice that the Sovereign of the Universe hath hitherto supported you as the deliverer of your country, the Defender of the Liberty and Rights of Humanity, and the Mæcenas of Science and Literature. We share the public Joy, and congratulate our Country on the Glory of your arms, and that eminence to which you have ascended in the recent Victory over the Earl of Cornwallis and his army in Virginia." Nor are we to forget that our generous ally Louis XVI. of France, upon hearing of the surrender, ordered a "Te Deum" to be sung in the Metropolitan church in Paris, on the 27th of November, while the *Bureau de la Ville* issued an ordinance directing "all the *bourgeois* and inhabitants" of the city to illuminate the fronts of their houses, "in order to celebrate with due

---

[1] The *New York Journal* of Nov. 12th, 1781, says: "This very important and remarkable event, the capture of a whole British army, the second time, just four years after the first, both under commanders of the most approved characters and ability—an event in which the hand of heaven has been visibly displayed—has been celebrated, in various expressions of thankfulness and joy, by almost every town and society in the thirteen United States, at the different times when the news came to their knowledge."

The Connecticut Delegates in Congress announced the news to Governor Trumbull as follows:

"Phila., Octr. 25, 1781.

"SIR:—We have the honor now to transmit to your Excellency an official account of the surrender of Lord Cornwallis and the army under his command. The despatches from Gen. Washington were rec'd yesterday morning and at two o'clock in the afternoon Congress went in a body to the Lutheran Church, where divine service (suitable to the occasion) was performed by the Rev. Mr. Duffield, one of the chaplains of Congress. The Supreme Executive Council and Assembly of this State, the Minister of France and his secretary, and a great number of the citizens attended. In the evening the city was illuminated. This great event we hope will prove a happy presage of a compleat reduction of the British forces in these States and prepare the way for the Establishment of an honorable Peace. . . .	ROGER SHERMAN.
RICHARD LAW." .
[From the Trumbull Manuscripts, Mass. Hist. Society.]

respect a great victory gained in America, both by land and sea, over the English, by the armies of the King combined with those commanded by General Washington."

Even in Great Britain the disappointment was not universal. Bancroft tells us that " Fox—to whom, in reading history, the defeats of armies of invaders, from Xerxes' time downward, gave the greatest satisfaction—heard of the capitulation of York-

town with wild delight." The King, of course, was still firm and uncompromising, and declared that he should never be " in the smallest degree an instrument " in making peace at the expense of separation from America.[1] To Lord North he wrote, November 28th : " I have no doubt when men are a little recovered of the shock felt by the bad news, and feel that if we recede no one can tell to what a degree the consequence of this country will be diminished, that they will then find the necessity of carrying on the war, though the mode of it may require alterations."[2] Many good Englishmen be-

LOUIS XVI.

lieved as the King did, and the gentle poet Cowper was only avowing his loyalty to his sovereign and his nation when he inserted this passage in a letter to his friend the Rev. John Newton : " It appears to me that the King is bound, both by the duty he owes to himself and his people, to consider himself with respect to every inch of his territory as a trustee, deriving his interest in them from God, and invested with them by Divine authority for the benefit of his subjects. As he may not sell them or waste them, so he may not resign them to an enemy, or transfer his right to govern them to any, not even to themselves, so long as it is possible for him to keep it. If he does, he betrays at once his own interest and that of his other dominions. Viewing the thing in this light, if I sat on his Majesty's throne, I should be as obstinate as he."

Opinion in Parliament rapidly changed after the disaster, and early in 1782 the Commons voted to authorize the King to make peace with America.

---

[1] An interesting extract from Wraxall's " Memoirs," describing the reception of the news by the home government, is given in the Appendix.

[2] " Correspondence with Lord North." Donne.

At the session held in November and December, 1781, the majority on the side of the Government showed a significant falling off; and after the holidays, on February 22d, 1782, General Conway in the Commons, moved an address to the throne in favor of a discontinuance of the war, and "a happy reconciliation with the revolted Colonies." The motion was lost by a single vote—193 against 194. But, on the 27th, Conway introduced the subject again before a fuller house, and after the defeat, by nineteen votes, of the Government's motion for adjournment, carried his address to the King without a division. On the 4th of March another resolution was passed "that the House would consider as enemies to his Majesty and the Country all those who should advise, or by any means attempt, the further prosecution of offensive war on the Continent of North America, for the purpose of reducing the revolted Colonies to obedience by force." These resolutions were received by the English public with "general demonstrations of joy," and afterward in America with thankful gratitude and relief. Peace was assured.

On the 30th of November, 1782, the provisional articles were signed by commissioners from both countries, and on September 3d, 1783, the definitive treaty formally ratified. The struggle from Lexington to Yorktown had been crowned with the final achievement—independence recognized.

APPENDIX.

I.—*General Return of Officers and Privates Surrendered Prisoners of War, the General Washington — taken*

REGIMENTS OR CORPS.	Lieutenant-general.	Brigadier-general.	Colonels.	Lieutenant-colonels.	Majors.	Captains.	Lieutenants.	Ensigns and Cornets.	Chaplains.	Adjutants.	Quartermasters.	Surgeons.	Mates.	Sergeants.	Drummers and Trumpeters.	Rank and File.	Town Major.
General and Staff	1	1	...	1	2	5	2	...	2	...	...	...	...	...	...	...	1
Artillery	...	...	...	...	...	2	9	...	...	...	...	1	1	1	4	193	...
Guards	...	...	...	3	...	12	...	1	...	2	1	1	3	25	12	467	...
Light Infantry	...	...	...	1	1	10	16	1	...	...	...	2	...	33	13	594	...
17th Regiment	...	...	...	1	1	3	8	4	...	...	...	1	...	9	13	205	...
23d Regiment	...	...	...	...	...	3	6	...	...	1	...	1	1	16	...	205	...
33d Regiment	...	...	...	1	...	3	5	1	...	...	...	1	...	15	9	225	...
43d Regiment	...	...	...	...	1	3	5	3	...	...	1	1	...	22	16	307	...
71st Regiment	...	...	...	1	1	1	11	4	...	...	1	1	1	28	9	242	...
76th Regiment	...	...	...	...	1	6	16	4	...	1	1	1	1	38	18	628	...
80th Regiment	...	...	...	1	2	5	17	3	...	1	1	1	1	49	20	588	...
2 Battalions Anspach	...	...	2	1	2	8	32	...	1	...	2	2	10	32	25	948	...
Prince Hereditary	...	...	...	1	1	5	5	4	1	...	1	...	4	19	11	425	...
Regiment De Bose	...	...	...	...	2	...	5	2	...	1	1	1	3	46	16	271	...
Yagers	...	...	...	...	...	1	3	...	...	...	...	1	...	...	1	68	...
British Legion	...	...	...	1	...	6	8	3	...	...	6	1	...	17	7	192	...
Queen's Rangers	...	...	...	1	1	10	15	11	...	...	3	2	...	24	5	248	...
North Carolina Volunteers	...	...	...	1	...	5	9	8	...	...	...	...	...	7	...	114	...
Engineers	...	...	...	...	...	...	2	...	...	...	...	...	...	...	...	...	...
Pioneers	...	...	...	...	...	2	3	...	...	...	...	...	...	4	...	33	...
Loyal Foresters	...	...	...	...	...	2	1	...	...	...	...	...	...	...	...	2	...
3d New Jersey Volunteers	...	...	...	...	...	1	1	...	...	...	...	...	...	...	...	...	...
New York Volunteers	...	...	...	...	...	1	...	1	...	...	...	...	...	...	...	...	...
Virginia Volunteers	...	...	...	...	...	1	...	...	...	...	...	...	...	...	...	1	...
King's American Regiment	...	...	...	...	...	...	1	...	...	...	...	...	...	...	...	1	...
Gen. Delancey's Battalion	...	...	...	...	...	...	2	...	...	...	...	...	...	...	...	2	...
North Carolina Ind. Com'y	...	...	...	...	...	...	1	...	...	...	...	...	...	...	...	...	...
	1	1	2	14	15	95	178	53	4	6	18	18	25	385	179	5963	1
Taken 14th and 16th inst.	...	...	...	...	1	2	2	1	...	...	...	...	...	2	...	76	...

Camp near Yorktown, 27th October, 1781.

N.B.—Since finishing the above Return I find unaccounted for—1 Ensign Loyal Foresters,

October 28, 1781.

[*From Archives, State Dept.*

19th of October, 1781, to the Allied Army under Command of his Excellency from the Original Muster-rolls.

Commissary of Prisoners.	Assistant Quartermaster.	HOSPITAL DEPARTMENT.								COMMISSARY DEPARTMENT.							COMMISSARY MILIT'Y STORES DEPARTM'T.				WAGON DEP'T.					
		Surgeon and Field Inspector.	Surgeons.	Mates.	Purveyors.	Stewards.	Ward Masters.	Assistants.	Carpenters.	Deputy Commiss'y.	Dep. Com. Forage.	Ass't Commissary.	Clerks.	Issuers.	Coopers.	Laborers.	Commissary of Military Stores.	Conductors.	Cond'tors of Horse.	Artificers.	Wagon Master.	Wagoners.	Provost Marshal.	Assistant.	Total belonging to the Army.	Followers of the Army.
1	1	1	3	10	2	4	2	19	2	5	1	5	2	3	2	1	...	...	...	...	...	...	...	...	79	80
...	...	...	...	...	...	...	...	...	...	...	...	...	...	...	...	...	1	3	5	11	...	11	...	...	242	...
...	...	...	...	...	...	...	...	...	...	...	...	...	...	...	...	...	...	...	...	...	...	...	...	...	527	...
...	...	...	...	...	...	...	...	...	...	...	...	...	...	...	...	...	...	...	...	...	...	...	...	...	671	...
...	...	...	...	...	...	...	...	...	...	...	...	...	...	...	...	...	...	...	...	...	...	...	...	...	245	...
...	...	...	...	...	...	...	...	...	...	...	...	...	...	...	...	...	...	...	...	...	...	...	...	...	233	...
...	...	...	...	...	...	...	...	...	...	...	...	...	...	...	...	...	...	...	...	...	...	...	...	...	260	...
...	...	...	...	...	...	...	...	...	...	...	...	...	...	...	...	...	...	...	...	...	...	...	...	...	359	...
...	...	...	...	...	...	...	...	...	...	...	...	...	...	...	...	...	...	...	...	...	...	...	...	...	300	...
...	...	...	...	...	...	...	...	...	...	...	...	...	...	...	...	...	...	...	...	...	...	...	...	...	715	...
...	...	...	...	...	...	...	...	...	...	...	...	...	...	...	...	...	...	...	...	...	...	...	...	...	689	...
...	...	...	...	...	...	...	...	...	...	...	...	...	...	...	...	...	...	...	...	...	1	8	2	1	1077	...
...	...	...	...	...	...	...	...	...	...	...	...	...	...	...	...	...	...	...	...	...	...	6	1	...	484	...
...	...	...	...	...	...	...	...	...	...	...	...	...	...	...	...	...	...	...	...	...	...	...	1	...	349	...
...	...	...	...	...	...	...	...	...	...	...	...	...	...	...	...	...	...	...	...	...	...	...	...	...	74	...
...	...	...	...	...	...	...	...	...	...	...	...	...	...	...	...	...	...	...	...	...	...	...	...	...	241	...
...	...	...	...	...	...	...	...	...	...	...	...	...	...	...	...	...	...	...	...	...	...	...	...	...	320	...
...	...	...	...	...	...	...	...	...	...	...	...	...	...	...	...	...	...	...	...	...	...	...	...	...	142	...
...	...	...	...	...	...	...	...	...	...	...	...	...	...	...	...	...	...	...	...	...	...	...	...	...	2	...
...	...	...	...	...	...	...	...	...	...	...	...	...	...	...	...	...	...	...	...	...	...	...	...	...	42	...
...	...	...	...	...	...	...	...	...	...	...	...	...	...	...	...	...	...	...	...	...	...	...	...	...	5	...
...	...	...	...	...	...	...	...	...	...	...	...	...	...	...	...	...	...	...	...	...	...	...	...	...	4	...
...	...	...	...	...	...	...	...	...	...	...	...	...	...	...	...	...	...	...	...	...	...	...	...	...	3	...
...	...	...	...	...	...	...	...	...	...	...	...	...	...	...	...	...	...	...	...	...	...	...	...	...	2	...
...	...	...	...	...	...	...	...	...	...	...	...	...	...	...	...	...	...	...	...	...	...	...	...	...	2	...
...	...	...	...	...	...	...	...	...	...	...	...	...	...	...	...	...	...	...	...	...	...	...	...	...	4	...
...	...	...	...	...	...	...	...	...	...	...	...	...	...	...	...	...	...	...	...	...	...	...	...	...	2	...
1	1	1	3	10	2	4	2	19	2	5	1	5	2	3	2	1	1	3	5	11	1	25	4	1	7073	80
...	...	...	...	...	...	...	...	...	...	...	...	...	...	...	...	...	...	...	...	...	...	...	...	...	84	...
																									7157	

THOMAS DURIE,
Deputy Commissary of Prisoners.

1 Wagon Master, 6 Conductors, 5 Artificers, 1 Clerk to the Deputy Quartermaster-general.

(Signed) THOMAS DURIE, D.C.P.

Library, Washington, D. C.]

II.— *Washington's Journal.*

28th.—Having debarked all the troops and their baggage, marched, and encamped them in front of the City [Williamsburg], and having with some difficulty obtained horses and wagons sufficient to move our field Artillery—Intrenching Tools—and such other articles as were indispensably necessary, we commenced our march for the Investiture of the enemy at York.

The American Continental and French Troops formed one column on the left, the first in advance the Militia composed the right column & marched by the way of Harwoods Mill—half a mile beyond the half way house the French and Americans separated, the former continued on the direct road to York by the Brick House, the latter filed off to the right for Munfords bridge, where a junction with the Militia was to be made. About noon the head of each column arrived at its ground & some of the enemy's Picquets were driven in at the left by a corps of French Troops advanced for the purpose, which afforded an opportunity of reconnoitering them on their right, the enemy's Horse on the right were also obliged to retire from the ground they had encamped on, & from whence they were employed in reconnoitering the right column.

The line being formed all the Troops—officers and men lay upon their arms during the night.

29th.—Moved the American Troops more to the right, and encamped on the East side of Bever dam Creek, with a morass in front, about cannon shot from the enemy's lines, spent this day in reconnoitering the enemy's position and determining upon a plan of attack and approach which must be done without the assistance of shipping above the Town as the Admiral (notwithstanding my earnest solicitation) declined hazarding any vessels on that Station

30th.—The enemy abandoned all their exterior works, & the position they had taken without the town, and retired within their Interior works of defense in the course of last night immediately upon which we possessed them, and made those on our left (with a little alteration) very serviceable to us. We also began two enclosed works on the right of Pidgeon Hill—between that and the ravine above Mores Mill

From this time till the 6th of October nothing occurred of importance ; much deligence was used in debarking & transporting the stores cannon &[c], from Trebells landing (distant 6 miles) on James Riv[r] to camp; which for want of teams went on heavily—and in preparing Fascines, Gabions & C[n] for the seige, as also in reconnoitering the enemy's defenses, & their situation as perfectly as possible, to form our parallels & mode of attack

---

[1] From a copy of the original in the Library of the State Department, Washington. Printed in full in the *Magazine of American History*, February and August, 1881.

The teams which were sent round from the head of Elk, having arrived about this time, we were enabled to bring forward our heavy Artillery and Stores with more convenience and dispatch and everything being prepared for opening Trenches 1500 Fatigue men & 2800 to cover them were ordered for this service.

6th.—Before morning the Trenches were in such forwardness as to cover the men from the enemy's fire — The work was executed with so much secresy & dispatch that the enemy were, I believe, totally ignorant of our labor till the light of the morning discovered it to them ; our loss on this occasion was extremely inconsiderable not more than one officer (French) and about 20 men killed and wounded, the officer & 15 of which were on our left from the corps of the Marqs de St. Simon, who was betrayed by a deserter from the Huzzars that went in and gave notice of his approaching his parallel.

7th & 8th.—Was employed in completing our parallel, finishing the redoubts in them, and establishing Batteries

9th.—About 3 o'clock P.M. the French opened a battery on our extreme left, of 4 sixteen pounders, and six Mortars & Howitzers—and at five o'clock an American battery of six 18s & 24s four Mortars & 2 Howitzers began to play from the extremtiy of our right,—both with good effect as they compelled the enemy to withdraw from their Ambrazures the Pieces which had previously kept up a constant firing

10th.—The French opened two batteries on the left of our front parallel, one of 6 twenty-four pounders, and 2 sixteens with 6 Mortars & Howitzers, the other of 4 sixteen pounders. And the Americans two batteries between these last mentioned and the one on our extreme right the left of which containing 4 eighteen pounders, the other two Mortars,—

The whole of the batteries kept an incessant fire, the Cannon at the Ambrazures of the enemy, with a view to destroy them, the shells into the enemy's works where by the information of deserters they did much execution.

The French battery on the left, by red hot shot, set fire to (in the course of the night) the Charon frigate & 3 large Transports which were entirely consumed.

11th.—The French opened two other batteries on the left of the parallel each consisting of 3 twenty-four pounders—, these were also employed in demolishing the Ambrazures of the enemy's works & advance Redoubt.

Two Gentlemen, a Major Granchier & Capt. D Avilier being sent by Admiral de Grasse to reconnoiter the enemy's water defences, and state of the river at and near York, seemed favorably disposed to adopt the measure which had been strongly urged of bringing ships above the Town & made representations accordingly to the Count de Grasse.—

12th.—Began our second parallel within abt 300 yards (and in some places less) of the enemy's line, and got it so well advanced in the course of the night as to cover the men before morning. This business was conducted with the same secrecy as the former & undertaken so much sooner than the enemy expected (we should commence a second parallel) that they did not by their conduct & mode of firing, appear to have had any suspicion of our working parties till daylight discovered them to their Picket; nor did they much annoy the Trenches in the course of this day the parallel being opened last night from the ravine in front, and on the right flank of the enemy till it came near to the intersection of the line of fire from the American 4 Gun Battery to the enemy's advanced redoubt on their left, the French Batteries fired over the second parallel.

13th.—The fire of the enemy this night became brisk, both from their cannon and Royals, and more injurious to us than it had been; several men being killed and many wounded in the Trenches, but the works were not in the smallest degree retarded by it; our batteries were began in the course of the night and a good deal advanced.

14th.—The day was spent in completing our parallel and maturing the Batteries of the second parallel, the old batteries were principally directed against the abettis & salient angles of the enemy's advanced redoubt, on their extreme right and left to prepare them for the intended assault for which the necessary dispositions were made for attacking the two on the left—and, at half after six in the evening both were carried, that on their left (or the Bank of the river) by the Americans and the other by the French Troops. The Baron Viominel commanded the left attack, & the Marqs de la Fayette the right on which the light infantry were employed. In the left redoubt (assaulted by the Americans) there were abt 45 men under the command of a Major Campbell: of which the Major, a Capt., and Ensign, with 17 men were made Prisoners. But few were killed on the part of the enemy & the remainder of the Garrison escaped. The right redoubt attacked by the French consisted of abt 120 men commanded by a Lieutenant Colo— of these 18 were killed, & 42 taken Prisoners; among the Prisoners were a Capt. and two Lieutenants. The bravery exhibited by the attacking Troops was emulous and praiseworthy; few cases have exhibited stronger proofs of intrepidity coolness & firmness than were shown upon this occasion. The following is our loss in these attacks, and since the Investiture of York

PERIODS	AMERICAN																
	KILLED								WOUNDED								
	Corl.	Lt. Corl.	Maj.	Capta.	C. Lient.	Lient.	Sergt.	R. & F.	Corl.	Lt. Corl.	Majr.	Capt.	C. Lt.	Lient.	Sergt.	R. & F.	TOTAL.
From yᵉ Investt to opens 1st parall	1						1	4								8	14
To the opening of the 2nd par								2								6	8
To the Storm on the 14th				1				6				1				14	22
At the Storm								8		2	1	2	1	1	1	28	44
Total	1			1			1	20		2	1	3	1	1	1	56	88

The loss of the French from the Investiture to the assault of the Redoubts inclusive, is as follows, viz.—

APPENDIX.

Officers Killed... 2
     Wounded .... 7..........)
Soldiers Killed.. 50
     Wounded..127......177
     Total 186

15th.—Busily employed in getting the Batteries of the second parallel completed, and fixing on new ones contiguous to the Redoubts which were taken last
night,—placed two Howitzers in each of the captured redoubt wch were opened
upon the enemy about 5 o'clock in the afternoon.

16th.—About 4 o'clock this morning the enemy made a Sortie upon our second
parallel and spiked four French pieces of Artillery and two of ours, but the guards
of the Trenches advancing quickly upon them they retreated precipitately. The
Sally being made upon that part of the parallel which was guarded by the French
Troops; they lost an Officer & 12 men killed and ten Officers taken prisoners.
—The American loss was one Sergeant of Artillery (in the American battery)
wounded—The enemy, it is said, left 10 dead and lost 3 Prisoners. About 4
o'clock this afternoon the French opened two Batteries of 2 24s & four 16s each.
—3 pieces from the American grand battery were also opened, the others not
being ready.

17th.—The French opened another Battery of four 24s & two 16s and a Mortar
Battery of 10 Mortars and two Howitzers. The American grand Battery consisting of 12 twenty-four and eighteen prs 4 Mortars and two Howitzers. About ten
oclock the enemy beat a parley, and Lord Cornwallis proposed a cessation of hostilities for 24 hours, that commissioners might meet at the house of a Mr. Moore
(in the rear of our first parallel) to settle terms for the surrender of the Posts of
York and Gloucester. To this he was answered, that a desire to spare the further
effusion of Blood would readily incline me to treat of the surrender of the above
posts, but previous to the meeting of the commissioners, I wish to have his propo-
sal in writing and for this purpose would grant a cessation of hostilities two hours.
Within which time he sent out a letter with such proposals (tho. some of them
were inadmissible) as led me to believe that there would be no great difficulty in
fixing the terms; accordingly hostilities were suspended for the night & I proposed my own terms to which if he agreed, commissioners were to meet to digest
them into form.

18th.—The commissioners met accordingly, but the business was so procrasti-
nated by those on their side (a Colo Dundas & Majr Ross) that Colo Laurens & the
Viscount De Noailles who were appointed on our part could do no more than
make the rough draft of the articles which were to be submitted for Lord Cornwallis' consideration.

19th.—In the morning early I had them copied and sent word to Lord Cornwallis that I expected to have them signed at 11 o'clock, and that the Garrison
would march out at two o'clock—both of which were accordingly done; two re-

170 APPENDIX.

doubts on the enemy's left being possessed (the one by a detachment of French Grenadiers, & the other by American Infantry) with orders to prevent all intercourse between the Army & Country and the Town, while Officers in the several departments were employed in taking acct. of the public stores &c[a]—

20th.—Winchester and Fort Frederick in Maryland being the places destined for the reception of the prisoners they were to have commenced their march accordingly this day, but were prevented by the Commissary of Prisoners not having completed his accounts of them & taken the Paroles of the Officers.

III.—*Diary of the March from the Hudson to Yorktown, and Return, by Lieutenant Reuben Sanderson, Fifth Connecticut Continental Line, on Duty with Scammell's Light Infantry Corps.*[1]

18th July.—I joined Col[o] Scammell's Detachment near Dobb's ferry.

21st.—Marched to Morisseney—the night of the 23rd returned. The night of the 29th the Detachment marched to Philip's as a cover for the forraging Party from the main army.

Aug[t] 18th.—Marched from Dobb's Ferry—the night of the 19th crossed King's Ferry—Encamped at Kakeat.

25th.—Marched from Kakeat to Paramus.—26, March[d] to 2nd River.—27th March[d] to Springfield.—29th March[d] to Brunswick.—30th Marched to Princetown.—31st March[d] to Trenton.—1st Sep[tr] Crosed the Delaware, march[d] 17 miles, encamp[d] at Lower Doublan twelve miles from Philadelphia.—2nd Marched throw[h] Philadelphia about five miles, encamped near the Schoelkill.—3rd, March[d] 10 miles—encamp[d] three miles from Chester. Seven men Diserted from Capt Comstock's Company—4th, Marched through Chester, through Brandywine, through Wilmington—encamp[d] one mile from Wilmington, which was about twenty miles we marched the day.

5th, Marched 8 miles—marched one mile through Christeen where the Park of Artillery Landed the day before—Draw[d] one day's Provision and cooked the Same —Prime (?) Desert[d]. Marched 4 o'clock about five miles—encamped for the night. —6, Marched to the Head of Elk, 10 miles. Lay till the 9, then Marched to Chesipick Bay, 3 miles.—the tenth, embarked. The eleventh, waid anchor, sail[d] about ten Miles.—the 12, waid anchor, sailed about 70 miles which brought us to Annapilous.

We lay at Annapilous till the 15th. Then the whole fleet fell down about two miles.—the 16, we made sail with very little wind—sailed about thirty miles. Came to anchor off Pople point.—The 17, about the rising of the Sun, waid anchor, sailed about 35 (?) miles, came to Anchor off the Potomock.—the 18th came to Sayl about 12 o'clock with a strong wind.—the 19th, about 8 o'clock we made

---

[1] Original in the writer's possession.

York river which was about 80 miles—the wind died away—the fleet came to anchor till about 12 o'clock, then waid anchor, and a little before the setting of the Sun, made James river—Came to anchor before the mouth of the river. The 20th, about the rising of the Sun waid anchor—made up the river very little—came to anchor off Williamsburgh—Disembarked in the Evening—encamped near the Shore. The 24, March[d] about a mile through Williamsburg—encamped.

The 28, Marched within two miles of York—Encamped.—29, Marched about one mile—lay in fair view of the enemy. Rec[d] a few field piece shot—we returned same to them. At Evening encamp[d] within Cannon shot of the Enemies works—Rested unmolested, the night. The morning of the 30th we found the Enemy had avacquated their outlines. Col[o] Scammell was taken a reconnoitring the aband[d] works. About 10 o'clock we took possession of them and Continued there that day. At night broke ground within 700 yards of York. The enemy in the morning began firing Cannon shot and Continued the Day—kill[d] two men—kept up the fire, the night.

Oct[r] 2nd, fired more frequent than the day before—the evening, killed four of Gen[l] Muhlenberg's men—kept a Constant Cannonade the night. The 3rd kept up the Cannonade till night, then sceast a little, (fired very little the 4th. The night of the 4th fire[d] very brieff).—The 3rd, Tarlton made an axcurtion cross the river upon the D[ks] Leg[n] [Duke Lauzun's Legion]—the D. repuls[d] him with the loss of three men. Tarlton got wounded—had about 50 officers and soldiers killed and wounded, most the former.—The 5, Col[o] Scammell's Reg[t] went on fatigue—was called off about one o'clock. The enemy kept up their firing of Cannon—fired very brisk. The 6th, Col[o] Scammell Died.—The 6, was relieved and moved our encampment. The night of the 6th we hove up a Parallel line from right to left of the enemies works without any resistance from the Enemy—in the evening they gave us a few shot.—the night of the 7th we form[d] an Eight Gun battery for Eighteen lb[rs]. The 8th we were rel[d]—moved our encampment. The night of the 8th moved Cannon into the works—the 9th at 4 o'clock open[d] our batteries—kept up the firing the night. The morning of the 10, a most severe cannonade from our batteries and Continued all day. Gen[l] M.'s Division went on duty—the Cannonade was kept up—burnt two ships of the Enemies.—the 11, about one o'clock was rel[d].

The night of the 11th we hove up the 2nd Parallel Line—kept up a constant Cannonade and bombard—we had some men killed, and some wounded. The 12th, a constant Cannonade kept up on both sides which Continued the night. The 13th, went on duty at the lines—a very heavy Cannonade kept up—we had some men killed and a number wounded.—The 14th, we was rel[d]. The night of the 14th we stormed a Redoubt of the Enemies which was on their left—the French stormed another a little Distance of that with the loss of a very few men, and Continued the night in forwarding 2nd Line. The 15th continued in Camp—the 16th went on Duty at the Lines. The 17th was rel[d]—had a flag from the Enemy and Hostilities seast.—The 18th we prepared ourselves for the reception of Cornwalis.—the 19th, his Army marchd out, grounded their arms and marchd back.

The 20, I went into York, reconnoitrd the Town, and the Distruction made by our Shells and balls.—21, went on Duty in Town. The enemy marched out. Colecting Tents.—the 22nd, Colecting Nigars till 5 o'clock, then was Reld.—23d, Continued in Camp.—24, Continued in Camp.—25, Continued in Camp.—26, Continued in Camp.—27, Continued in Camp.—28, Attended divine Service in the forenoon; in the afternoon went into York. A fatigue party was sent from Colo Lawrens Battalion into York.—29th, Went on Guard in Town; had the left Redoubt Guard.—the 30th was Relieved.—the 31, Continued in Camp.—1 Novr went on Fatigue in York a loding Cannon and shells aboard shipping—4 o'clock two shells bust and kild two soldiers, wounded two or three others.—2nd, went in York, procured casks for water.—3, went in York for a walk.

4th.—Embarked on bord the Frigate Dilligante.—the evening of the 5, made Sail; about 3 o'clock ran a ground.—the 6, about 12 o'clock got off; about 5 waid anchor, ran out of York river, Came to anchor.—the 7th, about 7 o'clock waid anchor.—the 15th, Debarked at the mouth of the Patomac with Capt. Betts and a Detachment of one hundred men.—the 16, marched 10 miles in St. Maris County, put up for the night.—the 17, about 4 o'clock marched 7 miles. Continued till the 19th, then marched 12 miles to Mr. Ables; about 12 o'clock Ensn Foster was sent with a party of Sick to the water to go to Annapolous.—20, Crossed Patomack—marched 14 miles to Colo Sumerwills.—21st, Marched 16 miles to Huntington.—22nd, Marched 19 miles to Hering Creek Church in Anarandel County.—23, Marched 20 miles to Annapolous—put up 16 of our men in the hospital.—24, Ensn Foster Came up with his men; he had two died on his way. 3 o'clock we marched leaving Lieut. Jackson with 51 men; marched 10 miles.— 25, Marched 8 Miles, put up by reason of the rain (?).—26, Marched 8 miles, Crossed Patomac ferry, marched two miles to Baltomore, marched 6 miles from town.—27, marched 25 miles.—28, very rainy, remained in our Quarters.—29, marched 25 miles to the Head of Elk, found a number of our Soldiers sick with the small pox.—30, Continued in town.

1st Decr went a guning, killed 8 squirrals.—2, being Sunday Continued in Quarters.—3rd, went a guning, killed 10 squirles.—4th, Continued in town—the evening, Colo Olney arrived.—5, went a guning.—6, Continued in Quarters. Corpl Vose came up from Lt. Jackson, informed us that 6 of the men had died.— 7, Capt Betts marched up the men, left me.—8, I marched with the Rhode Island Regt 12 miles to Christian.—9, Marched 8 miles to Wmton.—10, Continued in town by reason of rain.—11, Marched 20 miles to Diarby.—12, Marched 7 miles to Philadelphia.—13, Marched 15 miles to Bucks County.—14, Marched 19 miles to Maidenhead.—15, Marched 23 miles to Sumersets County.—16, Marched through Brownswick to Baskingridge, which was 24 miles.—17, Marched 9 miles to Morristown. Capt Betts marched on with the party; left me with the Baggage to procure a waggon to transport it to King's ferry.—18, Continued in town.—19, Marched 6 miles to Pasipany.—20, Marched 16 miles to Pumpton.—21, Marched 26 miles to Haverstraw.—22, Marched 4 miles to Kings Ferry, cross^d, marched 16 miles to the Connecticut huts in the highlands.

IV.—*Letter from Lieut.-colonel William S. Smith, A.D.C., to Col. Samuel B. Webb, Third Connecticut Continental Line.*

Head Qrs, Head of Elk Sept 7th 1781.

DEAR COLO^r,—The long expected fleet from france is at last arrived, they made their appearance in the Cheasapeak the 26th ult with 28 ships of the Line and 5000 Land troops which have joined the Marquis and we hope effectually prevented Cornwallis's retreat to the Carolinas. He observes this and is fortifying himself with the greatest industry. We shall look as stern as the grave upon him about the 14th his position is at York & Gloster in Virginia on the South and North margin of York River—the fleet on their passage fell in with and captured a Packet from Charles Town bound to Europe on board of which was Lord Rawdon the plunderer of the South, returning to bask in the sunshine of Ministerial favours for butchering the patriotic Sons of America.

Inclosed I send you a Letter which I wish you to forward. Remember me to Mrs Webb and Miss Heth & believe me Dr Saml your friend &c

To COL. SAM^L B. WEBB.

W^M T. SMITH &c.

[*Webb MS.*]

V.—*Letter from Major William Popham, A.D.C., to Gov. Clinton, of New York.*

Head of Elk Sept 8th, 1781.

SIR,—After a very rapid march of near two weeks, attended with great fatigue, we at length are collected at this place, both french and Americans, amounting in the whole to near seven thousand, with an amazing train of ordnance and military stores—The light corps under Scammell, the advance of the french, and the detached Corps of our Army will embark with the stores &c to-morrow and proceed by water—the remainder of the Troops will move by Land, at least as far as Baltimore. The Count de Grass has arrived in the Bay with twenty-eight sail of the line, and landed a considerable Body of Troops who have joined the Marquis de la Fayette and taken post in the rear of Cornwallis, effectually cutting off his Retreat, as his whole Force does not consist of more than four thousand five hundred effective men, who are entrenched on the South side of York river at a Town of the same name—The Genl left camp this morning on his rout to Baltimore where a cutter is ready to receive him — Nothing can equal the Dispatch with which our opperations are carrying on, insomuch that by the 12th inst it is hoped we shall clear out from this Post,—and it is computed that five weeks from that date will compleat the grand Design.

This day will be famous in the annals of History for being the first in which the Troops of the United States received one month's Pay in Specie—all the civil and military staff are excluded—I cannot even obtain my pay as Captain in the Line. . . .

It is extraordinary that notwithstanding the Fatigue of such a long & rapid March, there is scarcely a sick man to be found—our Provisions are good in their kind, and our Supplies regular—and as far as my Judgment will enable me to determine, our Prospects are very flattering.

I have taken the Liberty to intrude thus far on your Exceˡˡˢ Patience without any apology, hoping it may not be disagreeable. I believe the Intelligence it contains may be depended on, as I have been particularly carefull in collecting it. . . .

Present my best respects to the Family & believe me to be, Sir,

Your Excellency's Most Obⁿ Servᵗ

W. POPHAM.

His Excˡʸ Govᴿ Clinton.

[*Vol. XIII., No.* 3977, *Clinton Papers, Albany State Library.*]

VI.—*Letter from Colonel John Lamb, Second Artillery, to Governor Clinton.*

Camp before York Town, 6ᵗʰ Octobʳ, 1781.

DEAR SIR,— . . . On the approach of our army Cornwallis abandoned some detached works in Front of the Town, and retired within his principal works.

This night the Troops (who are now paraded for that purpose) will begin the first Parallel which will be within 5 or 600 yards of the Enemy's works. So you may depend on its being a Night of Business.

As the greatest part of our ordnance and Stores are now here, we shall be ready to open our Batteries in a day or two—when I flatter myself, we shall soon be able to silence those of the Enemy who have been firing, every day, at the works they evacuated (and which we now possess) but with little effect, as they have not Killed more than 20 men since the army took its present position.

I am sorry to inform you, that the worthy Colonel Scammell was wounded and taken Prisoner on Monday last, by three of Tarleton's Horse, as he was reconnoitring the Enemy's works. He is Paroled and in a fair way to recover.

On Tuesday last Tarleton crossed the River with his Regiment and a Body of Infantry with a design to Forage. They were attacked by the Duke de Lauzun's Legion, and a few Militia, who defeated and pursued them to the Town of Gloucester. The Enemy had Fifty Men Killed and wounded. The Duke's Legion, three Killed and eleven wounded. As it is more than probable (from Circumstances) that I shall end my career, in the Course of this siege—should such an unlucky event take place, I must request the favor of you to interest yourself in behalf of my little Family, that they may have Justice done them by the Public with respect to what they are indebted to me. . . .

I am with Every Sentiment of Respect, Dear Sir,

Your Obedient Servant,

JOHN LAMB.

[Clinton Papers, Albany.]

VII.—*Letter from Lieut.-Colonel Henry Dearborn to Honorable Meshech Weare, of New Hampshire.*

Camp before York, Octob[r] 11th 1781.

SIR,—I am very unhappy that the fore part of my letter is on so disagreeable a subject, but so it is. our good friend Col° Scammell is no more. on the 1[t] Ins[t] as officer of the day he was visiting our advanced picquits & reconnoitering the Enemies works when a small party of the their horse made a sudden charge upon him & after making him prisoner one of them deliberately shot him, & after plundering him carried him into Town, next day he was sent out on parole for several days his simtoms appeered favorable, but the 6th Ins[t] very suddenly he altered for the wors, & at 5 oclock P.M. he expired, no officer of Col° Scammell's rank that has been killed or died in the Army has been more, if so *much*, lamented by all ranks as he is, the New Hampshire line is remarkably unfortunate in loosing our best officers.

Our Army is making regular approaches to the Enemies Works our works are within less than five hundred yards of their main works & I expect by to morrow morning we shall be much nearer, their resistence has not been great as yet ;— from what we can hear from them their principle dependence is on a superior Fleet, which I think they must fail in ; Count De Grasse s Fleet consists of 30 ships of the line exclusive of a considerable number of other ships of force ; if we should succeed in taking Corn Wallis, & Gen[l] Green continues successful in Carolina, it will. have a great tendency to put an end to this distressing war, & give liberty to us in the field once more to become peacible citizens.

I have the honor to be with the most sincere esteem Your honors

Obed[t] Hum[b] Serv[t]

HENRY DEARBORN.

HON[BLE] M. WEARE.

[MS., Mass. Hist. Soc.]

VIII.—*Letter from Peter Elting to Colonel Richard Varick.*

Kingston (N. Y.) 7th Nov. 1781.

DEAR BROTHER,— . . . I congratulate you on the Glorious News from all Quarters, & Inperticular on the Surender of Cornwallis, I am in Great hopes that the British Fleet had another Drobing. It was Currently Reported when I left Jersies that they Had Returned to the Hook much Sheterd, It would Be Needless to mention the Great News, Lumination, Rejoicings &c I had the satisfaction to partake of at Philadelphia as it has since all Transpired. . . .

        Remain your affectionate Brother & Humble Servt

To Col. Varick.
                                  Peter Elting.

[*From Tomlison MS., N. Y. Merc. Lib.*]

IX.—*Account of the Surrender by Lieutenant-colonel Harry Lee.*[1]

At two o'clock in the evening the British army, led by General O'Hara, marched out of its lines with colors cased, and drums beating a British march.

The author was present at this ceremony; and certainly no spectacle could be more impressive than the one now exhibited. Valiant troops yielding up their arms after fighting in defence of a cause dear to them (because the cause of their country), under a leader who, throughout the war, in every grade and in every situation to which he had been called, appeared the Hector of his host. Battle after battle had he fought; climate after climate had he endured; towns had yielded to his mandate, posts were abandoned at his approach; armies were conquered by his prowess; one nearly exterminated, another chased from the confines of South Carolina beyond the Dan into Virginia, and a third severely chastised in that State on the shores of James River. But here even he, in the midst of his splendid career, found his conqueror.

The road through which they marched was lined with spectators, French and American. On one side the commander-in-chief, surrounded by his suite and the American staff, took his station; on the other side, opposite to him, was the Count de Rochambeau, in like manner attended. The captive army approached, moving slowly in column with grace and precision. Universal silence was observed amid the vast concourse, and the utmost decency prevailed: exhibiting in demeanor an awful sense of the vicissitudes of human life, mingled with commiseration for the unhappy. The head of the column approached the commander-in-chief; O'Hara, mistaking the circle, turned to that on his left, for the purpose of paying his respects to the commander-in-chief, and requesting further orders; when, quickly discovering his error, with much embarrassment in his countenance he flew across the road, and, advancing up to Washington, asked pardon for his mistake, apologized for the absence of Lord Cornwallis, and begged to know his further pleasure. The General, feeling his embarrassment, relieved it by referring him with much politeness to General Lincoln for his government. Returning to the head of the column, it again moved under the guidance of Lincoln to the field selected for the conclusion of the ceremony.

[1] Lee's "Memoirs," vol. ii., pp. 360–62.

Every eye was turned, searching for the British commander-in-chief, anxious to look at that man, heretofore so much the object of their dread. All were disappointed. Cornwallis held himself back from the humiliating scene; obeying sensations which his great character ought to have stifled. He had been unfortunate, not from any false step or deficiency of exertion on his part, but from the infatuated policy of his superior, and the united power of his enemy, brought to bear upon him alone. There was nothing with which he could reproach himself; there was nothing with which he could reproach his brave and faithful army: why not, then, appear at its head in the day of misfortune, as he had always done in the day of triumph? The British general in this instance deviated from his usual line of conduct, dimming the splendor of his long and brilliant career.

The post of Gloucester, falling with that of York, was delivered up on the same day by Lieutenant-colonel Tarleton, who had succeeded to the command on the transfer of Lieutenant-colonel Dundas to the more important duties assigned to him in the defence of York. Previous to the surrender, Tarleton waited upon General Choisy, and communicated to that officer his apprehensions for his personal safety if put at the disposal of the American militia. This conference was sought for the purpose of inducing an arrangement which should shield him from the vengeance of the inhabitants. General Choisy did not hesitate a moment in gratifying the wishes of Tarleton. The Legion of Lauzun and the corps of Mercer were selected by the general to receive the submitting enemy, while the residue of the allied detachment was held back in camp. As soon as the ceremony of surrender was performed, Lieutenant-colonel Hugo, of the Legion of Mercer, with his militia and grenadiers, took possession of the redoubts, and protected the hostile garrison from those outrages so seriously, though unwarrantably, anticipated by the British commandant. It would have been very satisfactory to have been enabled to give the reasons which induced this communication from Lieutenant-colonel Tarleton, but Choisy did not go into the inquiry, and they remain unascertained.

X.—*Description of the Surrender by Colonel Fontaine, Virginia Militia.*

Richmond, Oct. 26th, 1781.

DEAR SIR,—Major Penn gives me an opportunity, the first I have met with since the glorious event, of congratulating you on the surrender of York, which I do with all imaginable cordiality. I had the happiness to see that British army which so lately spread dismay and desolation through all our country, march forth on the 20th inst. [19th] at 3 o'clock through our whole army, drawn up in two lines about 20 yards distance and return disrobed of all their terrors, so humbled and so struck at the appearance of our troops, that their knees seemed to tremble, and you could not see a platoon that marched in any order. Such a noble figure did

12

our army make, that I scarce know which drew my attention most. You coul
not have heard a whisper or seen the least motion throughout our whole line, bu
every countenance was erect, and expressed a serene cheerfulness. Cornwallis pre
tended to be ill, and imposed the mortifying duty of leading forth the captives o
Gen. O'Hara. Their own officers acknowledge them to be the flower of the Bri
ish troops, but I do not think they at all exceeded in appearance our own or th
French. The latter, you may be assured, are very different from the ideas former
inculcated in us of a people living on frogs and coarse vegetables. Finer troops
never saw. His Lordship's defence I think was rather feeble. His surrender wa
eight or ten days sooner than the most sanguine expected, though his force an
resources were much greater than we conceived.

[Va. Historical Register (1849), vol. ii., p. 34.]

XI. — Washington's Congratulatory Order to the Allied Army.[1]

"After Orders, 20th October, 1781.

The General congratulates the army upon the glorious event of yesterday. Th
generous proofs which his Most Christian Majesty has given of his attachment t
the cause of America must force conviction on the minds of the most deceive
among the enemy relative to the good consequences of the alliance, and inspii
every citizen of these States with sentiments of the most unalterable gratitud
His fleet, the most numerous and powerful that ever appeared in these seas, con
manded by an admiral whose fortune and talents insure great events—an army c
the most admirable composition, both in officers and men, are the pledges of h
friendship to the United States, and their co-operation has secured us the preser
signal success.

The General on this occasion entreats his Excellency Count de Rochambeau t
accept his most grateful acknowledgments for his counsels at all times; he pre
sents his warmest thanks to the Generals Baron de Viomenil, Chevalier Chastellu
Marquis de Saint Simon, and Count de Viomenil, and to Brigadier-general d
Choisy (who had a separate command), for the illustrious manner in which the
have advanced the interests of the common cause. He requests that Count d
Rochambeau will be pleased to communicate to the army under his immediate con
mand the high sense he entertains of the distinguished merits of the officers an
soldiers of every corps, and that he will present in his name to the regiments c
Agenois and Deuxponts the two pieces of brass ordnance captured by them (as
testimony of their gallantry) in storming the enemy's redoubt on the night of th
14th inst., when officers and men so universally vied with each other in the exerçis
of every soldierly virtue.

---

[1] Lieutenant Sanderson's MS. Diary. Yorktown Orderly Book.

The General's thanks to each individual of merit would comprehend the whole army, but he thinks himself bound by affection, duty, and gratitude, to express his obligations to Major-generals Lincoln, Lafayette, and Steuben for dispositions in the trenches, to General Du Portail and Colonel Carney [Querenet?] for the vigor and knowledge which were conspicuous in the conduct of the attacks, and to General Knox and Colonel d'Aboville for their great care, attention, and fatigue in bringing forward the artillery and stores, and for their judicious and spirited arrangement of them in the parallels. He requests the gentlemen above mentioned to communicate his thanks to the officers and soldiers of their respective commands. Ingratitude, which the General hopes never to be guilty of, would be conspicuous in him was he to omit thanking in the warmest terms his Excellency Governor Nelson for the aid he has received from him and from the militia under his command, to whose activity, emulation, and courage much applause is due. The greatness of the acquisition will be an ample compensation for the hardships and hazards which they encountered with so much patriotism and firmness.

In order to diffuse the general joy through every breast, the General orders that those men, belonging to the army, who may now be in confinement shall be pardoned, released, and join their respective corps. Divine service is to be performed to-morrow in the several brigades and divisions. The commander-in-chief recommends that the troops not on duty should universally attend with that seriousness of deportment and gratitude of heart which the recognition of such reiterated and astonishing interpositions of Providence demand of us.

XII.—*Extract from Wraxall's "Memoirs," Describing Reception of the News by the Home Cabinet.*

On Sunday, the 25th, about noon, official intelligence of the surrender of the British forces at Yorktown arrived from Falmouth at Lord George Germaine's house in Pall-mall. Lord Walsingham, who previous to his father Sir Wm de Grey's elevation to the Peerage, had been Under Secretary of State in that Department; and who was elected to second the Address in the House of Peers on the subsequent Tuesday; happened to be there when the messenger brought the news. Without communicating it to any other person, Lord George, for the purpose of despatch, immediately got with him into a hackney-coach and drove to Lord Stormont's residence in Portland Place. Having imparted to him the disastrous information and taken him into the carriage, they instantly proceeded to the Chancellor's house in Great Russel Street, Bloomsbury, whom they found at home. When, after a short consultation, they determined to lay it themselves in person before Lord North. He had not received any intimation of the event when they arrived at his door in Downing Street between one and two o'clock. The First Minister's firmness and even his presence of mind gave way for a time under this awful disaster. I asked Lord George afterward how he took the communication when made to him? "As he would have taken a ball in his breast," replied Lor George. For he opened his arms exclaiming wildly as he paced up and down th apartment, during a few minutes, "Oh God! it is all over!" Words which l repeated many times, under emotions of the deepest agitation and distress.

When the first agitation of their minds had subsided, the four Ministers di cussed the question whether or not it might be expedient to prorogue Parliame for a few days; but as scarcely an interval of forty-eight hours remained befo the appointed time of assembling; and as many members of both Houses we already either arrived in London, or on the road, that proposition was abandone It became however, indispensable to alter and almost model anew the King Speech, which had been already drawn up, and completely prepared for delive from the Throne. This alteration was, therefore, made without delay; and at tl same time Lord General Germain, as Secretary for the American Department, se off a despatch to His Majesty who was then at Kew, acquainting him with tl melancholy termination of Lord Cornwallis' expedition. Some hours havi elapsed, before these different but necessary acts of business could take place, t Ministers separated, and Lord George Germain repaired to his Office in Whiteha There he found a confirmation of the intelligence, which arrived about two hou after the first communication; having been transmitted from Dover, to which pla it was forwarded from Calais, with the French account of the same event.

I dined on that day at Lord George's. . . . Before the dinner was finished, o of his servants delivered him a letter, brought back by the messenger who h been despatched to the King. Lord George opened and perused it—then looki at Lord Walsingham, to whom he exclusively directed his observation, "The Ki writes," said he, "just as he always does, except that I observe he has omitted mark the hour and the minute of his writing, with his usual precision."

[By Germaine's permission Wraxall read the account of the surrender alou while the company listened in profound silence. We then discussed its conter as affecting the Ministry, the Country, and the War. It must be confessed tl they were calculated to diffuse a gloom over the most convivial society, and tl they opened a wide field for political speculation.

After perusing the account of Lord Cornwallis' surrender at York Town, was impossible for all present not to feel a lively curiosity to know how the Ki had received the intelligence; as well as how he had expressed himself in his n to Lord George Germain on the first communication of so painful an event.] gratified our wish by reading it to us, observing at the same time that it did t highest honor to His Majesty's fortitude, firmness, and consistency of charact The words made an impression on my memory, which the lapse of more th thirty years has not erased; and I shall here commemorate its tenor as serving show how that Prince felt and wrote, under one of the most afflicting, as well humiliating occurrences of his reign. The Billet ran nearly to this effect. have rec'd with sentiments of the deepest concern the communication which L eorge Germain has made me, of the unfortunate result of the operations in Virinia. I particularly lament it on account of the consequences connected with it nd the difficulties which it may produce in carrying on the public business, or in epairing such a misfortune. But I trust that neither Lord George Germain nor any Iember of the Cabinet will suppose that it makes the smallest alteration in those rinciples of my conduct, which have directed me in past time, and which will always ontinue to animate me under every event, in the prosecution of the present contest."

Not a sentiment of despondency or of despair was to be found in the letter; ie very handwriting of which indicated composure of mind. Whatever opinion e may entertain relative to the practicability of reducing America to obedience y force of arms at the end of 1781, we must admit that no Sovereign could ianifest more calmness, dignity, or self-command, than George the Third dislayed in this reply.

XIII.—*Cornwallis' Report of the Surrender.*

ARL CORNWALLIS TO SIR HENRY CLINTON, K.B., DATED YORK TOWN, VIRGINIA, OCT. 20TH, 1781.

SIR,—I have the mortification to inform your excellency that I have been orced to give up the posts of York and Gloucester, and to surrender the troops nder my command, by capitulation on the 19th instant, as prisoners of war to the ombined forces of America and France.

I never saw this post in a very favorable light; but when I found I was to be tacked in it, in so unprepared a state, by so powerful an army and artillery, othing but the hopes of relief would have induced me to attempt its defence; or I would either have endeavored to escape to New York by rapid marches from ie Gloucester side, immediately on the arrival of General Washington's troops at Villiamsburgh, or, I would, notwithstanding the disparity of numbers, have atcked them in the open field, where it might have been just possible that fortune ould have favored the gallantry of the handful of troops under my command. ut, being assured by your excellency's letters that every possible means would e tried by the navy and army to relieve us, I could not think myself at liberty venture upon either of those desperate attempts; therefore, after remaining for vo days in a strong position in front of this place, in hopes of being attacked, oon observing that the enemy were taking measure which could not fail of turng my left flank in a short time, and receiving on the second evening your letter the 24th of September, that the relief would fail about the 5th of October, I ithdrew within the works on the night of the 29th of September, hoping by the bor and firmness of the soldiers to protect the defence until you could arrive. verything was to be expected from the spirit of the troops; but every disadvange attended their labor, as the work was to be continued under the enemy's fire, d our stock of intrenching tools, which did not much exceed four hundred when e began to work in the latter end of August, was now much diminished.

The enemy broke ground on the night of the 30th, and constructed on that night, and the two following days and nights, two redoubts, which with some works that had belonged to our outward position occupied a gorge between two creeks or ravines, which come from the river on each side of the town. On the night of the 6th of October they made their first parallel, extending from its right on the river to a deep ravine on the left nearly opposite to the centre of this place, and embracing our whole left, at the distance of six hundred yards. Having perfected this parallel, their batteries opened on the evening of the 9th against our left; and other batteries fired at the same time against a redoubt over a creek upon our right, and defended by about one hundred and twenty men of the 23d regiment and marines who maintained that post with uncommon gallantry. The fire continued incessant from heavy cannon, and from mortars and howitzers, throwing shells from eight to sixteen inches, until all our guns on the left were silenced, our work much damaged, and our loss of men considerable. On the night of the 11th they began their second parallel, about three hundred yards nearer to us. The troops being much weakened by sickness, as well as by the fire of the besiegers, and observing that the enemy had not only secured their flanks, but proceeded in every respect with the utmost regularity and caution, I could not venture so large sorties as to hope from them any considerable effect; but otherwise, I did everything in my power to interrupt their work, by opening new embrasures for guns, and keeping up a constant fire with all the howitzers and small mortars we could man. On the evening of the 14th they assaulted and carried two redoubts that had been advanced about three hundred yards for the purpose of delaying their approaches and covering our left flank, and during the night included them in their second parallel, on which they continued to work with the utmost exertion. Being perfectly sensible that our works could not stand many hours after the opening of the batteries of that parallel, we not only continued a constant fire with all our mortars, and every gun that could be brought to bear on it, but a little before daybreak, on the morning of the 10th, I ordered a sortie of about three hundred and fifty men, under the direction of Lieutenant-colonel Abercrombie, to attack two batteries which appeared to be in the greatest forwardness, and to spike the guns.

A detachment of guards with the 80th company of grenadiers, under the command of Lieutenant-colonel Lake, attacked the one; and one of light infantry under the command of Major Armstrong, attacked the other; and both succeeded by forcing the redoubts that covered them, spiking eleven guns and killing or wounding about one hundred of the French troops who had the guard of that part of the trenches, and with little loss on our side. The action, though extremely honorable to the officers and soldiers who executed it, proved of little public advantage; for the cannon, having been spiked in a hurry, were soon rendered fit for service again; and before dark the whole parallel and batteries appeared to be nearly complete. At this time we knew that there was no part of the whole ront attacked on which we could throw a single gun, and our shells were nearly xpended; I had therefore only to choose between preparing to surrender next ay, or endeavoring to get off with the greatest part of the troops; and I deter- ined to attempt the latter, reflecting that, though it should prove unsuccessful n its immediate object, it might at least delay the enemy in the prosecution of urther enterprises. Sixteen large boats were prepared, and upon other pretexts ere ordered to be in readiness to receive troops precisely at ten o'clock: with hese I hoped to pass the infantry during the night; abandoning our baggage, and aving a detachment to capitulate for the towns-people, and the sick and wounded; n which subject a letter was ready to be delivered to General Washington. After aking my arrangements with the utmost secrecy, the light infantry, greatest part f the guards, and part of the 23d regiment landed at Gloucester; but at this ritical moment, the weather, from being moderate and calm, changed to a violent torm of wind and rain, and drove all the boats, some of which had troops on oard, down the river. It was soon evident that the intended passage was im- racticable; and the absence of the boats rendered it equally impossible to bring ack the troops that had passed, which I had ordered about two in the morning. n this situation, with my little force divided, the enemy's batteries opened at day- reak: The passage between this place and Gloucester was much exposed, but the oats having now returned, they were ordered to bring back the troops that had assed during the night, and they joined in the forenoon without much loss. Our orks in the mean time were going to ruin; and not having been able to strengthen em by abattis, nor in any other manner than by a light fraizing, which the ene- y's artillery were demolishing wherever they fired, my opinion entirely coincided ith that of the engineer and principal officers of the army, that they were in any places assailable in the forenoon, and that by the continuance of the same re for a few hours longer, they would be in such a state as to render it desperate, ith our numbers, to attempt to maintain them. We at that time could not fire single gun; only one eight-inch and little more than a hundred cohorn shells emained; a diversion by the French ships of war that lay at the mouth of the ork River was to be expected. Our numbers had been diminished by the enemy's re, but particularly by sickness; and the strength and spirit of those in the works ere much exhausted by the fatigue of constant watching and unremitting duty. nder all these circumstances, I thought it would have been wanton and inhuman the last degree to sacrifice the lives of this small body of gallant soldiers, who ad ever behaved with so much fidelity and courage, by exposing them to an ssault which, from the numbers and precautions of the enemy, could not fail to cceed. I therefore proposed to capitulate, and I have the honor to enclose to our excellency the copy of the correspondence between General Washington and e on that subject, and the terms of the capitulation agreed upon. I sincerely ment that better could not be obtained; but I have neglected nothing in my ower to alleviate the misfortune and distress of both officers and soldiers. The men are well clothed and provided with necessaries, and I trust will be regularly supplied by the means of the officers that are permitted to remain with them. The treatment in general that we have received from the enemy since our surrender has been perfectly good and proper; but the kindness and attention that has been showed to us by the French officers in particular, their delicate sensibility of our situation, their generous and pressing offer of money, both public and private, to any amount, has really gone beyond what I can possibly describe, and will, I hope, make an impression on the breast of every officer, whenever the fortune of war should put any of them into our power.

Although the event has been so unfortunate, the patience of the soldiers in bearing the greatest fatigues, and their firmness and intrepidity under a persevering fire of shot and shells, that I believe has not often been exceeded, deserved the highest admiration and praise. A successful defence, however, in our situation was perhaps impossible; for the place could only be reckoned an intrenched camp subject in most places to ensilade, and the ground in general so disadvantageous that nothing but the necessity of fortifying it as a post to protect the navy could have induced any person to erect works upon it. Our force diminished daily by sickness and other losses, and was reduced, when we offered to capitulate on this side, to little more than three thousand two hundred rank and file fit for duty including officers' servants and artificers; and at Gloucester about six hundred including cavalry. The enemy's army consisted of upward of six thousand French nearly as many Continentals, and five thousand militia. They brought an immense train of heavy artillery, most amply furnished with ammunition, and perfectly well manned.

The constant and universal cheerfulness and spirit of the officers in all hardships and dangers deserve my warmest acknowledgment; and I have been particularly indebted to Brigadier-General O'Hara and Lieutenant-colonel Abercrombie the former commanding on the right, and the latter on the left, for their attention and exertion on every occasion. The detachment of the 23d regiment, commanded by Captain Apthorpe, and the subsequent detachments, commanded by Lieutenant-colonel Johnson, deserve particular commendation. Captain Rochfort who commanded the artillery, and indeed every officer and soldier of that distinguished corps, and Lieutenant Sutherland, the commanding engineer, have merited in every respect my highest approbation: and I cannot sufficiently acknowledge my obligations to Captain Symonds, who commanded his Majesty's ships and to the other officers and seamen of the navy, for their active and zealous cooperation.

I transmit returns of our killed and wounded; the loss of seamen and towns people was likewise considerable. I trust your excellency will please to hasten the return of the *Bonetta*, after landing her passengers, in compliance with the article of capitulation.

Lieutenant-Colonel Abercrombie will have the honor to explain this despatch and is well qualified to explain to your excellency every particular relating to our past and present situation.   I have the honor to be, &c.

[Correspondence of Cornwallis. Ross.]   CORNWALLIS.

XIV.—*Correspondence on, and the Articles of, the Capitulation.*

COPY OF EARL CORNWALLIS'S LETTER TO GENERAL WASHINGTON, DATED YORK, IN VIRGINIA, OCTOBER 17TH, 1781.

SIR,—I propose a cessation of hostilities for twenty-four hours, and that two officers may be appointed by each side, to meet at Mr. Moore's house, to settle terms for the surrender of the posts of York and Glocester.

I have the honor to be, &c.

CORNWALLIS.

COPY OF GENERAL WASHINGTON'S LETTER TO EARL CORNWALLIS, DATED CAMP BEFORE YORK, 17TH OCTOBER, 1781.

MY LORD,—I have the honor of receiving your lordship's letter of this date.

An ardent desire to save the effusion of human blood will readily incline me to listen to such terms for the surrender of your posts and garrisons at York and Glocester as are admissible.

I wish, previous to the meeting of the commissioners, that your lordship's proposals, in writing, may be sent to the American lines; for which purpose a suspension of hostilities during two hours from the delivery of this letter will be granted.   I have the honor to be, &c.

G. WASHINGTON.

COPY OF EARL CORNWALLIS'S LETTER TO GENERAL WASHINGTON, DATED YORK, IN VIRGINIA, 17TH DAY OF OCTOBER, 1781, HALF-PAST 4 P.M.

SIR,—I have this moment been honored with your Excellency's letter, dated this day.

The time limited for sending my answer will not admit of entering into the detail of articles; but the basis of my proposals will be, that the garrisons of York and Glocester shall be prisoners of war, with the customary honors; and for the convenience of the individuals which I have the honor to command, that the British shall be sent to Britain and the Germans to Germany, under engagement not to serve against France, America, or their allies, until released or regularly exchanged: That all arms and public stores shall be delivered up to you; but that the usual indulgence of side-arms to officers, and of retaining private property, shall be granted to officers and soldiers: And that the interest of several individuals, in civil capacities and connected with us, shall be attended to.

If your excellency thinks that a continuance of the suspension of hostilities will be necessary to transmit your answer, I shall have no objection to the hour that you may propose.   I have the honor to be, &c.

CORNWALLIS.

APPENDIX.

MY LORD,—To avoid unnecessary discussions and delays, I shall at once, in answer to your lordship's letter of yesterday, declare the general basis upon which a definitive treaty of capitulation may take place.

The garrisons of York and Gloucester, including the seamen as you propose, shall be received prisoners of war. The condition annexed, of sending the British and German troops to the parts of Europe to which they respectively belong is inadmissible : Instead of this, they will be marched to such parts of the country as can most conveniently provide for their subsistence ; and the benevolent treatment of the prisoners, which is invariably observed by the Americans, will be extended to them. The same honors will be granted to the surrendering army as were granted to the garrison of Charlestown.

The shipping and boats in the two harbors, with all their guns, stores, tackling, furniture, and apparel, shall be delivered in their present state to an officer of the navy appointed to take possession of them.

The artillery arms, accoutrements, military chest, and public stores of every denomination shall be delivered, unimpaired, to the heads of the departments to which they respectively belong.

The officers shall be indulged in retaining their side-arms ; and the officers and soldiers may preserve their baggage and effects, with this reserve, that property taken in the country will be reclaimed.

With regard to the individuals in civil capacities, whose interest your lordship wishes may be attended to, until they are more particularly described, nothing definitive can be settled.

I have to add, that I expect the sick and wounded will be supplied with their own hospital stores, and be attended by British surgeons, particularly charged with the care of them.

Your lordship will be pleased to signify your determination, either to accept or reject the proposals now offered, in the course of two hours from the delivery of this letter, that commissioners may be appointed to digest the articles of capitulation, or a renewal of hostilities may take place.

I have the honor to be, &c.

G. WASHINGTON.

SIR,—I agree to open a treaty of capitulation upon the basis of the garrisons of York and Gloucester, including seamen, being prisoners of war, without annexing the condition of their being sent to Europe ; but I expect to receive a compensation in the articles of capitulation for the surrender of Gloucester in its present state of defence.

I shall in particular desire that the sloop of war *Bonetta* may be left entirely at my disposal from the hour that the capitulation is signed, to receive an aide-de-camp to carry my despatches to Sir Henry Clinton. Such soldiers as I may think proper to send as passengers in her, to be manned with fifty of her own crew, and to be permitted to sail, without examination, when my despatches are ready; engaging, on my part, that the ship shall be brought back and delivered to you if she escapes the dangers of the sea; that the crew and soldiers shall be accounted for in future exchanges; that she shall carry off no officer without your consent, nor public property of any kind; and I shall likewise desire, that the traders and inhabitants may preserve their property, and that no person may be punished or molested for having joined the British troops.

If you choose to proceed to negotiations on these grounds, I shall appoint two field officers of my army to meet two officers from you, at any time or place that you may think proper, to digest the articles of capitulation.

I have the honor to be, &c.

CORNWALLIS.

COPY OF THE ARTICLES OF CAPITULATION SETTLED BETWEEN HIS EXCELLENCY GENERAL WASHINGTON, COMMANDER IN CHIEF OF THE COMBINED FORCES OF AMERICA AND FRANCE; HIS EXCELLENCY THE COUNT DE ROCHAMBEAU, LIEUTENANT GENERAL OF THE ARMIES OF THE KING OF FRANCE, GREAT CROSS OF THE ROYAL AND MILITARY ORDER OF ST. LOUIS, COMMANDING THE AUXILIARY TROOPS OF HIS MOST CHRISTIAN MAJESTY IN AMERICA; AND HIS EXCELLENCY THE COUNT DE GRASSE, LIEUTENANT GENERAL OF THE NAVAL ARMIES OF HIS MOST CHRISTIAN MAJESTY, COMMANDER IN CHIEF OF THE NAVAL ARMY OF FRANCE IN THE CHESAPEAKE ON THE ONE PART: AND THE RIGHT HONORABLE EARL CORNWALLIS, LIEUTENANT GENERAL OF HIS BRITANNIC MAJESTY'S FORCES, COMMANDING THE GARRISONS OF YORK AND GLOUCESTER; AND THOMAS SYMONDS, ESQUIRE, COMMANDING HIS BRITANNIC MAJESTY'S NAVAL FORCES IN YORK RIVER, IN VIRGINIA, ON THE OTHER PART.

ART. I. The garrisons of York & Gloucester, including the officers and seamen of his Britannic Majesty's ships, as well as other mariners to surrender themselves prisoners of war to the combined forces of America and France. The land troops to remain prisoners to the United States; the navy to the naval army of his most Christian Majesty.

Granted.

ART. II. The artillery, guns, accoutrements, military chest, and public stores of every denomination, shall be delivered unimpaired, to the heads of departments appointed to receive them.

Granted.

ART. III. At twelve o'clock this day the two redoubts on the left bank of York to be delivered; the one to a detachmant of American infantry; the other to a detachment of French grenadiers.

Granted.

The garrison of York will march out to a place to be appointed in front of the posts, at two o'clock precisely, with shouldered arms, colors cased, and drums beating a British or German march. They are then to ground their arms, and return to their encampments, where they will remain until they are dispatched to the places of their destination. Two works on the Gloucester side will be delivered at one o'clock to a detachment of French and American troops appointed to possess them. The garrison will march out at three o'clock in the afternoon; the cavalry with their swords drawn, trumpets sounding; and the infantry in the manner prescribed for the garrison of York. They are likewise to return to their encampments until they can be finally marched off.

ART. IV. Officers are to retain their side-arms. Both officers and soldiers to keep their private property of every kind and no part of their baggage or papers to be at any time subject to search or inspection. The baggage and papers of officers & soldiers taken during the siege to be likewise preserved for them.

Granted.

It is understood that any property obviously belonging to the inhabitants of these States, in the possession of the garrison, shall be subject to be reclaimed.

ART. V. The soldiers to be kept in Virginia, Maryland, or Pennsylvania, and as much by regiments as possible, and supplied with the same rations or provisions as are allowed to soldiers in the service of America. A field officer from each nation, to wit, British, Anspach, and Hessian, and other officers on parole in the proportion of one to fifty men, to be allowed to reside near their respective regiments and be witnesses of their treatment; and that their officers may receive and deliver clothing and other necessaries for them; for which passports are to be granted when applied for.

Granted.

ART. VI. The general, staff & other officers, not employed as mentioned in the articles, and who choose it, to be permitted to go on parole to Europe, to New York, or any other American posts at present in possession of the British forces, at their own option and proper vessels to be granted by the Count de Grasse to carry them under flags of truce to New York within ten days from this date, if possible, and they to reside in a district to be agreed upon hereafter until they embark.

The officers of the civil department of the army and navy to be included in this article. Passports to go by land to those to whom vessels cannot be furnished.

Granted.

ART. VII. Officers to be allowed to keep soldiers as servants according to the common practice of the service. Servants, not soldiers, are not to be considered as prisoners and are to be allowed to attend to their masters.

Granted.

ART. VIII. The *Bonetta* sloop of war to be equipped and navigated by its present captain and crew and left entirely at the disposal of Lord Cornwallis from the hour that the capitulation is signed, to receive an aid-de-camp to carry dispatches to Sir Henry Clinton; and such soldiers as he may think proper to send to New York, to be permitted to sail without examination, when his dispatches are ready. His lordship engages on his part that the ship shall be delivered to the order of the Count de Grasse, if she escapes the dangers of the sea; that she shall not carry off any public stores. Any part of the crew that may be deficient on her return, and the soldiers passengers, to be accounted for on her delivery.

ART. IX. The traders are to preserve their property, and to be allowed three months to dispose of or remove them; and those traders are not to be considered as prisoners of war.

The traders will be allowed to dispose of their effects, the allied army having the right of preemption. The traders to be considered as prisoners of war upon parole.

ART. X. Natives or inhabitants of different parts of this country, at present in York or Gloucester are not to be punished on account of having joined the British Army.

This article can not be assented to, being altogether of civil resort.

ART. XI. Proper hospitals to be furnished for the sick & wounded. They are to be attended by their own surgeons on parole; and they are to be furnished with medicines & stores from the American hospitals.

The hospital stores now in York and Gloucester shall be delivered for the use of the British sick & wounded. Passports will be granted for procuring further supplies from New York as occasion may require; and proper hospitals will be furnished for the reception of the sick & wounded of the two garrisons.

ART. XII. Wagons to be furnished to carry the baggage of the officers attending on the soldiers, and to surgeons when travelling on account of the sick, attending the hospitals at public expense.

They are to be furnished if possible.

ART. XIII. The shipping and boats in the two harbors, with all their stores, guns, tackling, and apparel, shall be delivered up in their present state to an officer of the navy appointed to take possession of them, previously unloading the private property part of which had been on board for security during the siege.

Granted.

ART. XIV. No article of capitulation to be infringed on pretence of reprisals; and if there be any doubtful expressions in it, they are to be interpreted according to the common meaning and acceptation of the words.

Granted.

Done at York Town in Virginia Oct 19 1781.

CORNWALLIS
THOMAS SYMONDS.

Done in the trenches before York Town in Virginia Oct 19 1781.

G. WASHINGTON
LE COMTE DE ROCHAMBEAU
LE COMTE DE BARRAS, en mon nom
& celui de Comte de Grasse.

[*Sparks' " Washington," vol. viii., appendix.*]

XV.—*American Loss in the Skirmish with Simcoe at Spencer's Ordinary.*

RETURN OF THE KILLED, WOUNDED, AND MISSING OF THE LIGHT CORPS UNDER COLONEL BUTLER, IN THE ACTION OF THE 26TH OF JUNE, 1781.

Cavalry under Major Macpherson, of the First Regiment of Dragoons: 1 captain wounded; 5 privates killed; 1 private taken (since returned).

Of Armand's horse: 2 lieutenants killed, 1 private ditto; 1 sergeant prisoner.

Infantry and riflemen under Major Macpherson: 1 lieutenant killed.

Captain Long's company of riflemen: 1 private wounded; 5 ditto missing.

Horses lost, 11.

Loss of Major Willis' corps of riflemen: 1 captain wounded, 6 privates ditto; 1 lieutenant missing, 7 privates ditto.

Total: Wounded, 2 captains, 2 lieutenants, 10 privates; killed, 2 lieutenants, 1 sergeant, 6 privates; missing, 1 lieutenant, 12 privates; prisoners, 1 sergeant, 1 private (returned since).

RICHARD BUTLER,
Colonel Commanding advanced Light Corps.

[*Penn. Gazette, July,* 1781.]

XVI.—*American Loss in the Action of Green Spring.*

RETURN OF THE KILLED, WOUNDED, AND MISSING, OF THE DETACHMENT COMMANDED BY GENERAL WAYNE, IN A SKIRMISH WITH THE BRITISH ARMY NEAR THE GREEN SPRINGS, IN VIRGINIA, JULY 6, 1781.

Major Galvan's advanced guard: 4 rank and file killed; 1 sergeant, 7 rank and file, wounded.

Colonel Stewart's detachment of Pennsylvanians: 11 rank and file killed; 2 captains, 3 lieutenants, 4 sergeants, 30 rank and file, wounded.

Colonel Butler's detachment of Pennsylvanians: 2 sergeants, 4 rank and file, killed; 15 rank and file wounded; 9 rank and file missing.

Colonel Humpton's detachment of Pennsylvanians: 1 sergeant, 4 rank and file, killed; 3 captains, 1 lieutenant, 1 sergeant, 19 rank and file, wounded.

Major Willis' [Wyllys] detachment of light infantry: 1 sergeant, 1 rank and file, killed; 7 rank and file wounded.

Captain Ogden's company of Macpherson's Legion: 2 rank and file wounded.

Captains Savage and Duffy's artillery: 1 captain-lieutenant, 1 sergeant, 2 rank and file, wounded.

Total: 4 sergeants, 24 rank and file, killed; 5 captains, 1 captain-lieutenant, 4 lieutenants, 7 sergeants, 82 rank and file, wounded: 12 rank and file missing.

Names of the officers wounded:

Captains Vanlear (division inspector), Doyle, Finney, Montgomery, Stoke, and McClellan.

Lieutenants Piercy, Feltman, White, Herbert (taken prisoner), Captain-lieutenant Crosby [Crossley], of artillery.

N.B.—A few riflemen were wounded ; number not ascertained.

WILLIAM BARBER,
Major and D.A.G.

[*New Jersey Gazette, July*, 1781.]

XVII.—*Loss of the Allies at Yorktown.*

RETURN OF THE KILLED AND WOUNDED OF THE FRENCH TROOPS SINCE THE BEGINNING OF THE SIEGE OF YORK.

From the 6th to the 7th October.

	Killed.	Wounded.
In making the first parallel—main attack	0	1
Attack up the river at the left	0	7
One officer of the Artillery wounded.		

From the 7th to the 8th.

| In making the batteries upon the first parallel—main attack | 0 | 6 |

From the 8th to the 9th.

| Continuation of the batteries—main attack | 1 | 1 |

From the 9th to the 10th.

| Continuation of the batteries | 0 | 2 |
| Attack up the river | 0 | 0 |

From the 10th to the 11th.

| The batteries firing—main attack | 1 | 1 |

From the 11th to the 12th.

| Opening the second parallel—main attack | 0 | 4 |
| Attack up the river | 0 | 3 |

From the 12th to the 13th.

| Commencing of the batteries on the second parallel | 6 | 11 |
| Two officers wounded. | | |

From the 13th to the 14th.

| Continuation of the batteries | 1 | 28 |
| Attack up the river | 0 | 3 |

From the 14th to the 15th.

Attack of two redoubts of the enemy down the river	41	57
Six officers wounded.		
Total	50	127

Nine officers wounded, two of them since dead.

RETURN OF THE KILLED AND WOUNDED OF THE AMERICAN ARMY, FROM THE 28TH OF SEPTEMBER, 1781, THE DAY OF THE INVESTITURE OF YORK, TO THE STORM OF THE ENEMY'S REDOUBTS, ON THE NIGHT OF THE 14TH OF OCTOBER FOLLOWING, INCLUSIVE.

From the investiture of York to the opening of the first parallel, on the evening of the 6th October, exclusive.

Continentals: killed, 1 sergeant, 3 rank and file; wounded, 1 colonel,[1] 2 rank and file. Militia: killed, 1 rank and file; wounded, 6 rank and file.

From the opening of the first parallel to that of the second, on the evening of the 11th October, exclusive.

Continentals: killed, 2 rank and file ; wounded, 3 rank and file.

From the opening of the second parallel to the 14th October, inclusive.

Continentals: killed, 1 captain, 3 rank and file; wounded, 1 captain, 7 rank and file. Militia: killed, 3 rank and file; wounded, 7 rank and file.

At the storm, on the evening of the 14th October.

Continentals: killed, 8 rank and file; wounded, 2 lieutenant-colonels, 1 major, 2 captains, 1 captain-lieutenant, 1 lieutenant, 1 sergeant, 28 rank and file.

Total—Continentals killed: 1 captain, 1 sergeant, 16 rank and file ; wounded: 1 colonel, 2 lieutenant-colonels, 1 major, 3 captains, 1 captain-lieutenant, 1 lieutenant, 1 sergeant, 40 rank and file.

Total—Militia: killed, 4 rank and file ; wounded, 16 rank and file.

Officers killed at the opening of the second parallel.

Captain White, of Colonel Vose's battalion, infantry.

Officers wounded at the opening of the second parallel.

Captain Gosselen, of General Hazen's regiment.

Officers wounded at the storm.

Lieutenant-colonels Barber and Gimat; Major Barber, inspector to Light Infantry division; Captains Olney and Hunt, of Colonel Gimat's battalion, infantry ; Captain-lieutenant Kirkpatrick, Corps of Sappers and Miners; Lieutenant Mansfield, of Colonel Gimat's battalion, infantry.

EDWARD HAND, A. G.

[These returns were published in the Philadelphia and other papers of the day—November, 1781.]

---

[1] Colonel Scammell, since dead.

XVIII.—*American Loss at the Storming of Redoubt No. 10.*

RETURN OF THE KILLED AND WOUNDED IN THE ADVANCED CORPS, COMMANDED BY LIEUTENANT-COLONEL HAMILTON, IN AN ATTACK ON THE ENEMY'S LEFT REDOUBT, ON THE NIGHT OF THE 14TH OF OCTOBER, 1781.

	LIEUT.-COLS.		MAJORS.		CAPTAINS.		SUBALTERNS.		SERGEANTS.		RANK AND FILE.	
	Killed.	Wounded.	Killed.	Wounded.	Killed.	Wounded.	Killed.	Wounded.	Killed.	Wounded.	Killed.	Wounded.
Lt.-Col.Hamilton's battalion	...	...	...	...	...	...	...	...	...	...	...	4
Lieut.-Col. Gimat's battalion	...	1	...	...	...	2	...	...	1	1	7	15
Lt. - Col. Laurens' detachment	...	...	...	...	...	1	...	...	...	...	1	5
Corps of Sappers and Miners	...	...	...	...	...	1	...	...	...	...	...	1
Total	...	1	...	...	...	4	...	...	1	1	8	25

[*Hamilton's Works*, vol. i., pp. 270–72.]

XIX.—*British Loss at the Siege of Yorktown.*

RETURN OF THE KILLED, WOUNDED, AND MISSING IN THE ARMY UNDER LORD CORNWALLIS, FROM THE 28TH OF SEPTEMBER TO THE 19TH OF OCTOBER, 1781.

Royal Artillery: 24 rank and file, killed; 21 ditto, wounded; 3 ditto, missing.

Guards: 1 sergeant, 3 rank and file, killed; 1 sergeant, 21 rank and file, wounded.

Light Infantry: 1 lieutenant, 3 sergeants, 24 rank and file, killed; 3 lieutenants, 2 sergeants, 1 drummer, 51 rank and file, wounded.

Seventeenth Regiment: 1 drummer, killed; 1 sergeant, 6 rank and file, wounded.

Twenty-third Regiment: 2 lieutenants, 1 sergeant, 8 rank and file, killed; 3 sergeants, 2 drummers, 15 rank and file, wounded.

Thirty-third Regiment: 1 captain, 7 rank and file, killed; 1 lieutenant, 1 sergeant, 10 rank and file, wounded; 1 subaltern, 7 rank and file, missing.

Forty-third Regiment: 1 sergeant, 9 rank and file, killed; 1 sergeant, 1 drummer, 16 rank and file, wounded; 1 captain, 11 rank and file, missing.

Seventy-first Regiment: 1 lieutenant, 9 rank and file, killed; 3 drummers, 19 rank and file, wounded; 1 major, 10 rank and file, missing.

Seventy-sixth Regiment: 1 drummer, 5 rank and file, killed; 1 lieutenant, 4 rank and file, wounded.

Eightieth Regiment: 1 rank and file, killed; 11 ditto, wounded; 1 captain, 9 rank and file, missing.

Two battalions Anspach: 1 sergeant, 11 rank and file, killed; 4 sergeants, 30 rank and file, wounded.

Prince Hereditaire: 2 sergeants, 2 drummers, 19 rank and file, killed; 7 sergeants, 1 drummer, 49 rank and file, wounded; 2 sergeants, 14 rank and file, missing.

Regiment de Bose: 1 captain, 4 sergeants, 13 rank and file, killed; 1 ensign, 4 sergeants, 3 drummers, 32 rank and file, wounded; 1 sergeant, 10 rank and file, missing.

Total: 2 captains, 4 lieutenants, 13 sergeants, 4 drummers, 133 rank and file, killed; 5 lieutenants, 1 ensign, 24 sergeants, 11 drummers, 285 rank and file, wounded; 1 major, 2 captains, 1 subaltern, 3 sergeants, 63 rank and file, missing.

RANK AND NAMES OF OFFICERS IN THE ABOVE RETURN.

Hon. Major Cochrane, acting aide-de-camp to Earl Cornwallis, killed.

Light Infantry: Lieutenant Campbell, 74th company, killed; Lieutenant Lyster, 63d ditto, wounded, since dead; Lieutenant Dunn, 63d ditto, wounded, since dead; Lieutenant Lightburne, 37th ditto, wounded.

Twenty-third Regiment: Lieutenants Ware and Guyon, killed.

Thirty-third Regiment: Captain Kerr, killed; Lieutenant Carson, wounded.

Seventy-first Regiment: Lieutenant Fraser, killed.

Seventy-sixth Regiment: Lieutenant Robertson, wounded.

Captain Rall, killed; Ensign Sprangenberg, wounded.

Commissary Perkins, killed.   J. DESHARD,
                                                      Dep. Adj. Gen.
[*Tarleton's "Campaigns."*]

STATE OF THE ENEMY'S LOSS DURING THE SIEGE OF YORK.

	Majors.	Captains.	Lieuts.	Ensigns.	Sergts.	Rank and File.	Total.
Taken in the redoubts	1	2	2	1	1	66	73
Taken at the sortie	......	......	......	......	......	......	6
Deserted during the siege	......	......	......	......	......	......	44
Killed	......	......	......	......	......	......	309[1]
Wounded	......	......	......	......	......	......	120
Total	......	......	......	......	......	......	552

N.B.—The total number is taken from the British Adjutant-general's Report, the number of wounded from the hospital books, the prisoners from the Commissary's return, and the deserters from the Adjutant-general's Register.

                                                      EDWD. HAND, A.G.
[*From Archives, State Department, Washington, D.C.*]

[1] General Hand's figures of the enemy's killed and wounded are based on inference, as he implies in his note. The correct figures are given in the preceding British returns.

XX.—*Strength of the Armies at Yorktown.*

A search among the papers of Adjutant-general Hand, in the possession of the Government, might bring to light one or more of the official returns showing the exact strength of the French and American armies before Yorktown. In their absence there are data which enable us to form a close estimate. For instance, Colonel Harry Lee states in his " Memoirs " that the official returns made the American wing 9000 strong — 5500 Continentals, 3500 militia; the French wing, 7000. These are the figures it is proposed to inscribe on the National Monument, and, as *round* numbers, they are to be accepted as nearly correct. The French wing was probably somewhat stronger. In President Stiles' " Diary," Yale College, the following entry is found under date of December, 1781, in reference to Washington's force. The regiments were : " 1 R. I., full; 1 Hazen, 2 or 300; 2 N. Y., full; 2 N. J.; 3 Penn.; 2 Md., full, 1100; 1 Va. Continental; 1 Va. State reg^t; 1 Batt. of Col. Hamilton's, being four companies; 1 Detatch Infantry, Col. Scammel, being eight companies; 3 Reg^{ts} Light Inf. Amer., ' being all the Light Inf. of the Am. Army, except those with G. Green in So. Ca^{ro}.' Besides these perhaps—3000 Va. militia, equal 18 *regts* besides militia. 8000 Am., 7000 French (4000 from R. I., 3000 landed from French fleet)." As Dr. Stiles had just spent an evening with Lieutenant-colonel Humphreys, Washington's aide, who gave him " an acc° of the Siege & Capture of Ld. Cornwallis," the latter probably furnished him with the above figures. One official item is preserved in the New Jersey archives, extracted from General Hand's " Weekly Report of the Continental Army for October 13th, 1781," which gives Dayton's brigade 54 commissioned officers, 101 noncommissioned officers, and 1173 rank and file, for that date.

As to the British army, copies of Major Despard's returns for the 19th of October, 1781, in the State Department, give a total of 5886 officers and men in Yorktown on that date, of whom 1882 are entered as sick or wounded. At Gloucester, on the same date, 900 officers and men, of whom 153 were sick. Grand total, 6786, with 4751 fit for duty on the day of the surrender. This total is 461 less than the American return of prisoners (7247); but as Major Despard does not include the camp followers and about 100 persons connected with the several departments, the discrepancy is reduced to about 250 between the final British and American return of prisoners surrendered at York and Gloucester.

XXI.—*List of Original Authorities on the Campaign.*

BLANCHARD, Claude.—" Journal, 1780–'83." Translated from the French manuscript by William Duane, and edited by Thomas Balch. Albany, 1876.

BUTLER, Colonel Richard.—" Journal of the Siege of Yorktown." *Historical Magazine*, vol. viii., p. 102.

CHASTELLUX, Marquis de.—"Travels in North America in 1780–'82."   London, 1787.

CLINTON, Sir Henry.—"Narrative of the Campaign."   London, 1783.

"Observations on some parts of the Answer of Earl Cornwallis."   1783.

" Observations on Mr. Stedman's History of the American War."   1794.

Clinton's "Explanation," in "Washington's Contemplated Attack on New York."   Page 177 of *New York City During the American Revolution.*   Mercantile Library Association, N. Y.   1860.

CORNWALLIS, Earl.—"Answer to Clinton's Narrative."   London, 1783.

"Correspondence."   Edited, with notes, by Charles Ross.   London, 1859.

DENNY, Lieutenant.—"Journal."   Pub. Pennsylvania Historical Society.

DEUXPONTS, Count William.—"My Campaigns in America."   Translated, with introduction and notes, by Samuel A. Green, M.D., Librarian, Massachusetts Historical Society, Boston.

" DIPLOMATIC Correspondence of the American Revolution," Sparks.   Boston, 1829.

EVANS, Chaplain.—"Journal of the Siege of York in Virginia."   Collections Massachusetts Historical Society, vol. ix., First Series, p. 102.

[The Chaplain's name is not given in connection with the Journal, but it appears, from a reference in Thacher's "Military Journal," that the writer was Chaplain Evans, of Colonel Scammell's corps.]

FELTMAN, Lieutenant William.—"Journal of the Campaign."   Pub. Pennsylvania Historical Society.

FERSEN, Count.—"Letters and Journal of Operations, 1780–'81."   *Magazine of American History,* 1879.   Also, in same Magazine, May and June, 1880, "Diary of a French Officer," with Engineer's journal added.

GRAHAM, General Samuel.—"Memoirs."   Edinburgh.

GRAVES, Rear-admiral. — "Two Letters Respecting the Conduct of Rear- admiral Graves on the Coast of the United States, July to November, 1781."   By William Graves, Esq., of the Inner Temple.   Morrisania, N. Y., 1865.   H. B. Dawson.

"JOURNAL of the Siege of Yorktown."   By an Officer.   Martin's "Gazetteer of Virginia," title, Yorktown.

LAFAYETTE, Marquis de.—"Memoirs, Correspondence, and Manuscripts of."   American edition, N. Y., 1837.   [See, also, a few letters in Graham's "Life of General Daniel Morgan."]

LAUZUN, Duc de.—"Memoires."   Paris, 1832.

Lee, Lieutenant-colonel Harry.—" Memoirs of the War in the Southern Department of the United States." Philadelphia, 1812.

Muhlenberg, General Peter.—" Life of." By Henry N. Muhlenberg. Philadelphia, 1849.

Nelson, Governor Thomas.—" Letters." Pub. Virginia Historical Society. New Series. No. I. 1874.

" Operations of the French Fleet under De Grasse." Bradford Club, N. Y. 1864.

" Orderly Book of the Siege of Yorktown from September 26th, 1781, to November 2d, 1781." Philadelphia, 1865.

" Parliamentary Register for 1781–'83."

Pickering, Colonel Timothy.—" Life of." Boston.

Rochambeau, Count.—" Memoir Relative to the War of the Independence of the United States." Translation of M. W. E. Wright. Paris, 1838.

Rochefoucault-Liancourt, Duc de.—" Travels Through the United States . . . in 1795–'97." London, 1800.

Simcoe, Lieutenant-colonel J. G.—" Military Journal of the Campaigns in American Revolution." New York, 1844.

Steuben, Baron.—" Life of." By Friedrich Kapp. New York, 1859.

Tarleton, Lieutenant-Colonel Banastre.—" History of Campaigns of 1780–'81 in the Southern Provinces of North America." London, 1787.

Thacher, Surgeon James.—" Military Journal During the American Revolutionary War from 1775 to 1783." Hartford, 1854.

Tilghman, Lieutenant-colonel Tench.—" Memoir of, with Revolutionary Journals and Letters." Albany, 1876.

Washington, General. —" Writings of." By Jared Sparks. New York, 1847. [Also Sparks' " Correspondence of the Revolution."]

Wayne, General Anthony.—" Life and Letters of." By his Son. Philadelphia Casket. 1829.

Weld, Isaac.—" Travels in the Northern States and Canada, 1795–'97." London, 1799.

[In addition to these special Journals and Narratives, the documents printed in this Appendix, and the contemporary histories of Gordon, Stedman, Marshall, and others, the writer has been favored with access to the ample manuscript collections of the New York and Massachusetts Historical Societies, and those at Albany, Hartford, and elsewhere. For other references on the campaign the " Handbook of the American Revolution," by Mr. Justin Winsor, Librarian of Harvard College, is to be consulted.]

MAPS AND PLANS OF THE SIEGE.

1. The earliest plan or "draft" was doubtless the one Washington states, October 26th, 1781, that he transmitted to Congress with the returns of prisoners and the captured standards. It is not known to be in existence.

2. Map of the Investment of York and Gloucester, in Virginia. Surveyed October 22–28th, 1781, by Major Sebastian Bauman, Second Continental Artillery. Philadelphia, 1782. Dedicated to Washington.—[Copies in libraries of the New York and Pennsylvania Historical Societies. Published, on reduced scale, in Gordon's History, and in *Magazine of American History*, January, 1881.]

3. Plan of the Siege and adjacent Country. Drawn by J. F. Renault "with a crowpen, and presented to the Marquis de Lafayette." Engraved by B. Tanner, Philadelphia. 1825 (?)—[This appears to be a copy of Bauman's, with the legend differently executed and ornamented.]

4. A Plan of York and Gloucester, showing the British and American Works in 1781. By Captain Edward Fage, Royal Artillery. London, 1782.—[Elaborate.]

5. Plan of the same from "an actual survey in possession of Jno. Hills, late Lieut. in the 23rd Regt. and Asst. Eng."—[This is known as the Faden map, London, 1785, and was probably compiled from the survey by Fage.]

6. Plan of the Siege of Yorktown in Virginia. London, March 1st, 1787.

7. A Plan of the Entrance of Chesapeake Bay, with James and York Rivers; wherein are shown the respective positions (in the beginning of October):

   1st, Of the British Army commanded by Lord Cornwallis, at Gloucester and York, in Virginia.

   2d, Of the American and French Forces under General Washington.

   3d, Of the French Fleet under Count de Grasse. By "an Officer." Published by Wm. Faden, Charing Cross, November 26th, 1781, London.—[This and the preceding map, No. 6, are on file at the office of the Chief of Engineers, U.S.A., Washington, D. C.]

8. Plan D'York en Virginie avec les attaques et les Campemens de l'Armée combinée de France et d'Amérique.—[This plan, by a French engineer, appears in the fourth volume of Soulé's "Histoire Des Troubles de l'Amérique Anglaise," Paris, 1787; also in *Magazine of American History*, June, 1880. In Soulé's work, also, is a clear and accurate map showing the march of the French from Newport, R. I., to Yorktown, and return. The camp before Yorktown is marked as their "40th."]

   N. B.—Bauman's, Fage's, Hill's, and the French map are the best authorities, the first-named covering the entire field, including the allied camps, with great accuracy.

XXII. — *Washington's Orders at Williamsburg.*[1]

Head-quarters, Williamsburg, September 15th, 1781.

The Commander-in-chief takes the earliest opportunity of testifying the satisfaction he feels on joining the army under the command of Major-general the Marquis de Lafayette, with prospects which, under the smiles of Heaven, he doubts not, will crown their toils with the most brilliant success. A conviction that the officers and soldiers of this army will still be actuated by that true martial spirit and thirst of glory which they have already exhibited on so many trying occasions, and under circumstances far less promising than the present, affords him the most pleasing sensations.

The arrival of a powerful fleet and army, under the command of his Excellency Count de Grasse and the Marquis de St. Simon, displays a new and striking instance of the generous attention of his Most Christian Majesty to the interests of these United States.

A very respectable body of troops, both French and Americans, are on their march from the eastward, and may soon be expected to aid our operations in this quarter.

The zeal and celerity with which Major-general de St. Simon debarked his troops and joined the army under the command of the Marquis de Lafayette, at so critical a juncture, demands his most grateful acknowledgments, which he entreats the marquis to accept. He also prays him to have the complaisance to signify to the officers and soldiers under his command the high sense the General entertains of the *spirit* and *ardor* they have shown on that occasion. He particularly admires the patience with which they supported the scarcity of provisions that unfortunately existed at the time of their junction, owing to particular circumstances—circumstances which he exceedingly regrets, but hopes they are already remedied, and that the like misfortune will not be again experienced.

Accurate returns of the two different corps, as well Continental as militia now serving here, to be given in at head-quarters to-morrow, at ten o'clock, specifying the number of militia that are unarmed. Commanding officers of the corps must be answerable for the correctness of their returns, and that the men returned on duty must be particularly and satisfactorily accounted for.

---

[1] These orders, issued by Washington from the 15th to the 25th of September, 1781, do not appear in the "Yorktown Orderly Book," which begins with September 26th. They complete the series issued by the commander-in-chief after his arrival in Virginia to conduct operations against Cornwallis. The author is indebted for them to Mr. F. D. Stone, Librarian of the Pennsylvania Historical Society, who will also publish them in the third number of the *Pennsylvania Historical Magazine*, 1881. The original orders appear in the diary of Captain Davis, of the Pennsylvania Line, which was first printed in the Westchester, Pa., *Village Record*, in 1821.

Head-quarters, Williamsburg, September 16th, 1781.

During the present scarcity of provisions the Quartermaster will take care that a sufficient number of corn-fields are procured for the use of the troops. The Commander-in-chief in the most pointed manner forbids the soldiers entering or taking corn from any field but those pointed out by the Quartermasters, and hopes that every officer will see this order attended to.

Head-quarters, Williamsburg, September 17th, 1781.

The Quartermasters of brigades and separate corps are to make returns of camp equipage and all other articles in the Quartermaster's department to the Quartermaster-general to-morrow at orderly time. The President and members of the General Court-martial will return to their duties in their respective lines until the pleasure of the Commander-in-chief be known with respect to their proceedings.

Head-quarters, Williamsburg, September 19th, 1781.

The Inspector-general will review the Maryland troops Friday morning, at eight o'clock. At the same hour he desires to see all the Continental field-officers on the grand parade. The grand parade for the present is assigned on the field in the rear of the College.

Head-quarters, Williamsburg, September 24th, 1781.

An accurate inspection of arms, accoutrements, and ammunition to be made immediately, and the deficiencies completed.

The Continental troops composing the troops in Virginia are to be brigaded as follows:

Colonel Vose's, Lieutenant-colonel Barber's, and Lieutenant-colonel Gimat's battalions of infantry will form a brigade, to be commanded by Brigadier-general Muhlenberg.

Colonel Scammell's regiment, and Lieutenant-colonel Hamilton's battalion of infantry, and Hazen's regiment — the brigade to be commanded by Brigadier-general Hazen.

Colonel Gaskins' Virginia Regiment, and the two battalions of Pennsylvania —brigade to be commanded by Brigadier-general Wayne.

The two Jersey battalions, and the Rhode Island battalion — a brigade to be commanded by Colonel Dayton.

The Third and Fourth Maryland Regiments—a brigade to be commanded by Brigadier-general Gist.

The First and Second New York Regiments—a brigade to be commanded by General Clinton.

The Inspector-general desires the commanding officers of regiments and corps may have them inspected without delay, agreeably to the General Orders of this day, and report to him the state of their arms, ammunition, and accoutrements.

Head-quarters, Williamsburg, September 25th, 1781.

All deserters and persons coming from the enemy's lines are to be sent in the first instance to head-quarters. No horses, arms, or accoutrements are to be purchased from them, except for the public service, unless it is specified to the contrary in the written papers which will be granted them by the Adjutant-general. Any person of the above description found without proper passes with the army, or within the environs of the encampment, to be apprehended and sent to the provost guard.

The Deputy Commissary-general of prisoners will report to head-quarters all prisoners of war immediately after their capture.

The several issuing Commissaries will be particularly careful, reserving all the sheepskins for the use of the artillery — they will be delivered to Mr. Thomas Jones, D.C.M.S., on his application.

At a general court-martial assembled at Williamsburg, by order of Major-general the Marquis Lafayette, Colonel Vose president, Captain Wilkin, of Colonel Stewart's battalion of the Pennsylvania line, charged by Colonel Stewart with riotous behavior, in his tent, in an unreasonable hour of the night, with disobedience in not desisting when ordered to do so by the field-officer of the day, through the Adjutant, Capt. Vanhorne, and for using language and conduct subversive of good order and discipline, was tried and acquitted.[1]

The following interesting letter is from the "Irvine Papers," as published in the *Pennsylvania Magazine of History*, No. 3, 1781:

COLONEL BUTLER TO GENERAL IRVINE.

Camp at York, October 22^d, 1781.

DEAR GENERAL,—As time presses, I know you'll be so good as to excuse me from giving you a journal of the minutia of the siege of Yorktown. Let it suffice to say, that on the 6th ultimo, we open^d our first paralell, on the 9th, at 3 o'clock P. M., our batteries. On the 11th I began the second paralell within 200 paces of the enemy's works, & on the 14th two of their advanced redoubts were taken by storm by a detachment under the Marquis Lafayette, who attacked the one with his Americans, & Baron Viominel with the French, which put it in our power to complete the second Paralell that night. 16th form^d Batteries & fir^d seventy, did great damage to their works. 17th, Ld Cornwallis sent a flag requesting a cessation of arms for 24 hours, & 2 commissioners from each army to be appointed to form a capitulation for the army, and the surrender of the shiping and posts of York &

---

[1] The absence of Washington on a visit to Count de Grasse, to arrange for the close investment of Yorktown by sea and land, accounts for the gap in the orders between the 19th and 24th.

Gloster. The General sent no answer to the first message which came about 10 o'clock A. M., he rec[d] a second about 4 P. M., & hostilities were ordered to cease & a capitulation agreed to—the general purposed thus, The garisons prisoners of war till exchang[d], the whole to march out with Colors cased, and not to beat a French or an American march. The whole to keep their private baggage. All public stores to be delivered to American Commissary, &c. &c. &c. On the 19th, at 11 o'clock.

Their Flag was struck, and Major Hamilton, with 100 men (Americans) took possession of one work and planted our flag, and a French major, with 100 men (French) another. Then the Allied Army and the American Army was drawn up opposite to each other, and, I assure you Sir, they made a most elegant appearance. About 3 o'clock P. M., the British & Foreigners march[d] out to a place assgn[d], & was ordered by General Lincoln to ground their Arms. The same was done on the side of Gloster, and the whole march[d] off this day for the places asign[d] for their residence during Captivity. The Earl & a number of his favourites are allow[d] to go to Britain on Parole, & (I am told) Col. Laurens is to be sent out in his Room on Parole, or else the earl to return to America or France. Their stores are immense, there are about 70 pieces of Brass ordinance, beside ship-guns, with a great quantity of ammunition, & arms almost innumerable.

Their force will amount to better than 7000 total, officers included, in the two posts, their loss considerable, in killed and wounded, ours really trifling for so great an affair.

Thus has the Earl been brought to anchor in the height of his career. Col. Craig & his detach[t] just arrived in time for some of his officers to see the surrender, what the effect may be, God knows, but I hope it will bring a speedy peace. I expect we shall immediately press for Carolina, but this is a surmise. My next shall be more particular, in the meantime be assur[d] of the sincerity of my wishes, and believe me to be your real friend and Obd[t] Humble Serv[t]

RICHD. BUTLER.

P. S.—Not a principal officer wounded or killed, and but very few men, & I think I may with propriety now congratulate you, my friend, and country in general, with certain Independence, and the pleasing approach of Peace.

To GENERAL IRVINE, at Carlise or Pittsburg.

INDEX.

THE END.